UNBROKEN

Celebrating
30 Years of Publishing
in India

UNBROKEN

THE UNTOLD STORY

INDRANI MUKERJEA

HarperCollins *Publishers* India

First published in India by HarperCollins *Publishers* 2023
4th Floor, Tower A, Building No. 10, DLF Cyber City,
DLF Phase II, Gurugram, Haryana – 122002
www.harpercollins.co.in

2 4 6 8 10 9 7 5 3 1

Typeset in 11.5/15.5 Adobe Garamond at
Manipal Technologies Limited, Manipal

Printed and bound at
Thomson Press (India) Ltd

To the women who shake up society's confines: may this book ignite the fire within and remind you that your worth knows no boundaries. Shatter the shackles of prejudice and disdain, embrace your power and reclaim your voice.

CAST OF CHARACTERS
(IN ORDER OF APPEARANCE)

(The names that have been changed in the book are marked as bold)

Indrani Mukerjea, author

Sana Raees Khan, bail lawyer

Edith Dey, friend and divorce lawyer

Vidhie Mukerjea, Indrani's younger daughter

Peter Mukerjea, Indrani's ex-husband

Mekhail Bora, Indrani's son

Sheena Bora, Indrani's elder daughter

Rupa Dalal, neighbour

Isha, Vidhie's best friend

Shruti, Indrani's yoga instructor

Prashant, family driver

Dhyaneshwar Ganoria, cop

Maya, family cook

Ranjeet Panchnanda, family friend and IPS officer

Manoj Malviya, family friend and IPS officer

Deven Bharti, former ATS chief and family friend of the Mukerjeas

Mahesh Jethmalani, Indrani's lawyer

Ranbir Singh, one of Peter's lawyers and a family friend

Sanjeev Khanna, Indrani's ex-husband and Vidhie's biological father

Shyamvar Rai, former family driver

Gunjan Mangla, Indrani's lawyer from Jethmalani's chamber

Shangon Dasgupta, Peter Mukerjea's sister

Rakesh Maria, former police commissioner of Mumbai

Rahul Mukerjea, Peter's younger son and Sheena's ex-boyfriend

Upendra Kumar Bora, Indrani's father

Durga Rani Bora, Indrani's mother

Vish Chaudhuri, Indrani's boyfriend

Nanny, Boras' help and Indrani's nanny

Priya Chaudhuri, Vish's sister

Uncle and Aunt Chaudhuri, Vish's parents

Moses, family cook

Siddharth Das, Indrani's ex-partner and Mekhail Bora's father

Dr Mason, gynaecologist

Shantu and Baby, Siddharth's siblings

Wasima, prison constable at Byculla Undertrial Jail

Savitri, kaamwali at Byculla Undertrial Jail

Chandramani Indulkar, prison superintendent

Javed Ahmed, former police commissioner, Mumbai

Dr Khan and Dr Nivedita, doctors at prison infirmary

Daisy and Nawaz, officials from the UK Embassy

Rabin Mukerjea, Peter's older son from his first marriage

Dr Wiqar Sheikh, the head of medicine at J.J. Hospital

Dr Rana, senior doctor at J.J. Hospital

Shabnam Anand Singh, Peter's ex-wife

Vir Sanghvi, journalist and former head of NewsX

Neena, Upendra Bora's sister

Leena Seth, Durga Rani Bora's cousin

Rajesh Seth, Leena's husband

Raj and Reena, Leena's kids

Mrs Mandal, YWCA Hostel Warden

Vidya, Indrani's friend from YWCA

Pratibha, Indrani's friend from YWCA

Shrikant, Indrani's boss at Diners Club

Astra, **D.P., Taran** and Philo, Vidya's friends

Vivek Khanna, Sanjeev's brother

Hormez, Vidya's boyfriend

Sudha Khanna, Sanjeev's mother

Gour Mohan Kapur, Sanjeev's uncle

Mukul Agarwal, Sanjeev's friend

Nikhil, Sanjeev's cousin

Nikita, Nikhil's baby sister

Badi Maa, Sanjeev's grandmother

Aunt Uma, Sanjeev's aunt

Mitra, Vivek's partner

Sanjana, Indrani's colleague

Alyque Padamsee, ad guru

Sarla, Peter's friend

Sumantra, COO of Radio City

Gautam Mukerjea, Peter's brother

Aarti, Gautam's wife

Madhukar Kilje, Marlow building manager

Saveena Bedi, advocate and Indrani's friend

Sudeep Pasbola, Indrani's lawyer

K.K. Singh, the CBI officer on the case

Raveena Raj Kohli, former president of Star News

Shobhaa Dé, author and columnist

Queenie Dhody, former model, socialite and jewellery designer

Raj Nayak, Peter's colleague

Bhola, the Mukerjeas' house help

Maya, the Mukerjeas' house help

Sushant, the Mukerjeas' house help

Shikha, the Mukerjeas' house help

Sanjoy Dasgupta, Shangon's husband

Ajay Sharma, legal head, Star

Ghazala and Mahua, Indrani's friends

Aveek Sarkar, family friend of the Mukerjeas

Suhail Buddha, security chief of Star

Vivek Mittal, Indrani's colleague

Sameer Nair, Peter's colleague at Star

Steve Askew, regional programming head, Star

Uday Kotak, head of Kotak Mahindra Finances

Vynsley Fernandes, head of operations, INX

Vikas Varma, head, 9XM

Avirook Sen, INX News

Radhika Radia, Indrani's colleague and Sheena's landlady

Vibhuti, Sheena's roommate

Sarah, Rahul's ex-girlfriend

Pritul Sanghvi, HR head, INX

Rajeev Bhaduria, HR head, ADA Reliance

Karti Chidambaram, businessman and alleged conspirator in the INX media case

P. Chidambaram, former finance minister

R. Parthasarathy, CBI officer on the INX Media case

Arun Jaitley, former finance minister

Alok Verma, the CBI director

Rakesh Asthana, special CBI director

Manjula Shetty, fellow prisoner at Byculla Undertrial Jail

Maryam, fellow inmate

Manisha Pokharkar, jailer at Byculla Undertrial Jail

Advocate Bhavesh, Advocate Sudeep Pasbola's junior

Dr Upadhyay, DG of prisons

Shriparna Mukerjea, Gautam and Aarti Mukerjea's daughter; Peter's niece

Nid, Vidhie's boyfriend

Dr Zeba Khan, assistant professor of the anatomy department, J.J. Hospital

Kajal Sharma, Peter's secretary

Mukul Rohatgi, Indrani's bail lawyer in Supreme Court

Justice Nagashwar Rao, Supreme Court judge

बस कर्म तुम्हारा कल होगा।

और कर्म में अगर सचाई है तो,कर्म कहा निष्फल होगा।

हर एक संकट का हल होगा।वो आज नहीं तो कल होगा।

लोहा जितना तपता है, उतनी ही ताकत भरता है,

सोने को जितनी आग लगे, वो उतना प्रखर निखरता है,

हीरे पर जितनी धार लगे, वो उतना खूब चमकता है,

मिट्टी का बरतन पकता है, तब धून पर खूब खनकता है,

सूरज जैसा बनना है तो, सूरज जितना जलना होगा।

नदियों सा आदर पाना है, तो परबत छोड़ निकलना होगा।

और हम आदम के बेटे हैं, क्यों सोचे राह सरल होगा।

कुछ ज्यादा वक़्त लगेगा पर, संघर्ष जरूर सफल होगा।

हर एक संकट का हल होगा,वो आज नहीं तो कल होगा

PROLOGUE

Have you ever looked up at the sky and marvelled at the twinkling stars? Or looked at a perfectly crescent moon as it shines upon the sea, recalling all the songs and poems that praise the night?

For six years and eight months, I didn't see any stars, the moon, or the night sky. All I saw were the grey walls of prison. For, Byculla District Jail Circle-1 was my home for these 2460 days.

But now, as I stand on my terrace of Flat No. 19 Marlow Apartments, I see the sky above, the sea beyond and the swarm of reporters downstairs. I am free at last! Marlow is the same building I had once called home, a home I had been immensely happy in, a home that I had been married in. The walls of this house have been witness to so many stories and memories—some precious family time, warm get-togethers and glorious parties.

But the journey to this moment has been a long one.

20 MAY 2022

As I drove back home today, I felt a sense of triumph take over me. A long arduous battle had been won. Though my lawyers and I had anticipated the bail coming our way, we couldn't be certain as we had filed for bail five times before. My family court lawyer, now a friend and confidante, Edith Dey had asked me during our last meeting in prison a week earlier if I wanted anything specific for today. Of all the things in the world, I had requested for my favourite Starbucks coffee—a plain black—that she brought to my advocate Sana Khan's car that had come to pick me up from Byculla Jail.

I have been standing for a long time on the terrace after I have got back. Prior to my exit from prison, this apartment was given a facelift—my favourite paintings that I had bought during a vacation in Bali now grace the walls, my four-poster bed has been placed in the bedroom, and other little touches have been added that has made it the safe haven I need at this time.

Prison can be extremely humbling. I had always led a life of comfort, even luxury I would say. I have been privileged to be blessed with all the creature comforts any person can ask for. I never had to worry about how food got cooked, or how my tap got water. In prison, I met women who would have to walk miles from their houses to fetch water. I met guards who told me tales of how when they were young their parents would just have enough money to purchase one bar of washing soap that would be used to wash their school uniforms only, whereas the regular clothes of the family would be washed with just water. The daily despair of other people's existence was eye-opening for me.

In the last six years and eight months, I overcame my rage at the unfairness life meted out to me—the trauma of what happened to me in Guwahati as a teenager, or after I was arrested, no longer makes me weak. I have somehow always had to bear the shame for things that weren't in my control. But now I refuse to let life pull me down. My experiences in prison have helped me evolve into a stronger person.

The one thing in prison that you have in plenty is time. You almost never run out of it. So I allowed time to help me gain perspective and heal me. I let myself be enraged, shocked, disillusioned, heartbroken, even devastated, by all the bad things that have happened to me in life. And then, I started reflecting on the things I have had the good fortune of experiencing.

Prison puts you in an emotional cubbyhole as well—where you feel your life's control is in someone else's hands. I didn't have the liberty to go out of my cell after 5.30 p.m. I was bereft of the luxury of spontaneously making plans and saying, 'Hey, let's go to Worli Sea Face for a walk.' When you do time, you start attaching value to things in life you had previously taken for granted. Over time, as this feeling deepens, you start moving towards peace.

In prison, I have often mulled over the concept of happiness. Today, as I am standing on the terrace looking at the majestic sea in front of me, I ask myself again—what is happiness? I can't find an answer amidst the rush of overwhelming emotions. As I write this, I realize that happiness is when you can look at your own life from a detached point of view. In the last six years and eight months, I have overcome the loss of every comfort I had known in my life. I lost my family, all my friends—everyone I had known and loved. I was all alone. What I initially experienced as loneliness, after much introspection, I was able to convert to solitude. It happened naturally, with meditation, and I eventually journeyed to a place where I was at peace with my own solitude. The rage within me turned into empathy, even for people who had wronged me. I knew that I needed to move on and, for that, I needed to forgive. If I continued to let anger consume me from within, I wouldn't have found my way out. The three men in my life—my father Upendra Kumar Bora, my son Mekhail, my ex-husband Peter—the people I thought I could bank upon, put me through turmoil I don't feel I deserved. My empathy led me to the calm which eventually offered clarity.

A year into my time in prison, I knew I had to survive on my own. I had to claw my way back into the world. I am not someone whose spirit can so easily be broken. I had to break ties and cut the umbilical cord from relationships that mattered the most. I remember my daughter Vidhie, not very long ago, came to meet me in prison. She was in tears then. She stood there telling me, 'If you don't do this for me, I will never speak to you or have anything to do with you ever again.'

I remember replying, 'Vidhie, what I will tell you now might be very painful to hear. I have lived without any of you having anything to do with me for a long time. I have learnt to live alone! I have learnt to be detached! I love you very very much but I am not attached to you anymore. I love you unconditionally and will even take a bullet for you. But I am detached from you …' There had been a snap, an irreparable one. I have evolved into a person who can now love without attachment.

I have stayed away from everyone I loved for six years and eight months. My love never changed but my way of looking at things did. It is a really odd thing to say, but prison gave me peace. Like Lord Buddha said, attachment is the root cause of all suffering. Detachment leads to happiness, and all circumstances outside of this are superficial.

Today, I can sleep on the floor as comfortably as I can on a memory foam mattress. After I walked out of prison, everyone told me, 'You don't look like someone who has weathered the harshness of prison …' Upon my release, a couple of TV anchors barked out how I was fully made-up, with jet-black hair. Everyone seemed really disappointed, even upset with the fact that I wasn't crying. People complained about how I was 'shamelessly' laughing while talking to the reporters who had assembled outside Byculla Jail to speak with me after my release.

I am not apologetic about beaming today, much like I am not apologetic about any part of my life, or how I decided to live it. I am not apologetic about being an ambitious woman, a point that made its way into my chargesheet. Ambition for a woman is a cardinal sin. I am not apologetic about my chiffon sarees that I apparently wore to lure powerful men. I am definitely not apologetic about being the attractive woman I am. Over the years, after my arrest, I have had muck thrown at me from all sides. I was stripped naked to the world, called everything from a hooker to a man-eater to a social climber to the most bizarre claim of them all—a veritable monster who killed her own daughter.

But the fact remains that for six years and eight months a woman was kept behind bars, without the charges and accusations being proved till date. Today, I have decided to shut the noise and start my journey to fight for the truth ...

So, what is the truth?

PART 1

❦

2015

1

I had spent most of August in Puerto Banus Marina, Marbella, Spain. I had, in fact, spent the previous six months there in our lovely home—it was simply idyllic.

On 19 August, I flew down from Spain to Delhi. I was selling a property in Gurgaon. Peter and Vidhie also flew back to India, to Mumbai, before Peter joined me in Delhi to complete the final paperwork for the property transfer. By the 23rd, we were in Mumbai, hosting a get-together for Vidhie's friends ahead of her eighteenth birthday on 26 August.

That day, Peter and I went to meet our friends, the Desais, at their Breach Candy home, leaving Vidhie to party with her friends at our home. When we returned, our home was bustling with young energy. We had a drink with the kids, before retiring to bed.

The next day, Vidhie went out with her friends, while Peter and I had dinner with the Dalals who live on the ground floor of our building. That evening, I asked Rupa Dalal if she knew of any orphanages in the city. I wanted to do some charity work on Vidhie's birthday. She recommended Anand Ashram to me, not very far away from where we lived—I had driven past the grey building many times having lived for over a decade in the city. A little later that night, we picked up Vidhie from her friend's house on Peddar Road.

On 26 August, for Vidhie's birthday, we planned to book a table for four at the Zodiac. We wanted to keep it a small affair—just Vidhie, her best friend Isha, Peter and I.

A day before Vidhie's birthday, I walked into her bedroom at about seven in the morning. Her room was dark, with the blackout blinds still down.

'Hon, wakey wakey,' I said, 'Time to wake up!'

She was tucked snugly under her duvet. I didn't get a response but the duvet moved.

'I am checking out this orphanage. It will be wonderful if you can spend a couple of hours with the children there and cut your cake with them tomorrow,' I said.

As I did not get a response, no 'hmms', I continued, 'A cake, some balloons, and toys will cheer them up. What do you think?'

Still no response. I realized that it was time to add a sweetener.

'Sweetheart, only a couple of hours in Anand Ashram. By the way, dinner is booked at the Zodiac, 7 p.m., tomorrow,' I said.

The mention of Zodiac did the trick. It was amongst the most expensive and exclusive restaurants in town: fine dining, personalized serviettes, the best champagnes and wines, and a menu to tempt even the most jaded palate. I had never been an indulgent mother, but it was Vidhie's big eighteenth after all.

'Okay, Mum. Will I be given a serviette with my name on it?' she asked, one eye peeping out of the duvet.

I knew that the answer to visiting Anand Ashram depended on a 'yes' to this request from her.

'Sure, Hon,' I said and left her room after rolling up one of the window blinds.

I returned to our bedroom where I found Peter sitting up on the bed, spectacles on his nose, reading the day's newspaper sprawled atop his beer belly and watching snippets of news on the television at the same time.

Peter, the man I fell in love with fourteen years ago, was my husband of thirteen years. I changed into my track pants. Shruti, my yoga instructor, was due in the next ten minutes.

'Mumu, lunch at 12. I will head out in a bit to the club gym, do a few lengths in the pool and be ready by 11. Meet me at the club by then. We can have a quick drink and meet Aditya and Anu at noon for lunch,' said Peter looking at me, his reading glasses now perched over his cleanly shaved head.

'Mumu, that works for me. I am visiting Anand Ashram at 10. It is just round the corner,' I said.

'Mumu' is what Peter and I would call each other. I don't remember how and when we became 'Mumu' to each other. But he knew that I called him Peter only when I was upset because he had done something that he was not supposed to, or not done something that he was supposed to!

He and I had our moments like most couples. But I loved him, warts and all, and could never imagine a life without him.

As I adoringly looked at my Mumu, the doorbell rang. I rushed out to the guest room which I used as my yoga room when we had no guests.

Shruti was a fabulous yoga teacher and could do all the twists and turns like she had no bones. Lessons with her thrice a week and a gym workout on three other days kept me fit despite my daily glass of wine and a sumptuous meal most evenings with Peter's family or friends, or at times by ourselves.

He and I were both foodies, so, for me, sweating it out five to six days a week to continue indulging our palates with less guilt was a no-brainer. After all, neither of us was getting any younger. I was forty-three and Peter was almost sixty, though he still behaved like a boy of sixteen—men rarely ever grow up!

While I was perfecting a new asana that Shruti showed me, Peter popped his head in and said, 'Mumu, I am leaving.'

I knew that he was waiting for our ritual when either of us stepped out of home or returned home.

We hugged and kissed. He said, 'See you at 11, Mumu.'

I said, 'Love you, Mumu.'

I didn't know that this was going to be the last time that I would kiss Mumu, ever again.

After an hour-long session with Shruti, a quick shower and a change of clothes—cream slacks, a checked bottle-green shirt, Bally pumps, kohl on my eyes, pink gloss on my lips, and a generous spray of 24 Faubourg—later, I was all set and ready for the day.

Vidhie yelled a bye before leaving while I was in the shower. She would be returning home by lunchtime.

As I was walking out of the house, I told Maya, our cook, that Peter and I would eat out, and asked her to toss up something for Vidhie once she got back. Maya was an old hand and almost like a second mum to Vidhie.

Our chauffeur and man Friday, Prashant aka Pronto, had the car ready in the driveway in front of the lobby. I got into the car, a black Honda Amaze, and Pronto drove me to Anand Ashram. We reached in a few minutes and I soon found myself in the drab reception area with yellow paint peeling off the walls, two cane chairs, a metal table with a chest of drawers, and a noisy ceiling fan.

I waited for the caretaker to arrive. A middle-aged woman, maybe in her early fifties, clad in a yellow sari walked in and introduced herself as the manager of the ashram. With no smile on her face, she was anything but joy.

'Hello,' I said, 'I am Indrani. I have an appointment with you. My secretary, Kajal, spoke to you yesterday.'

She gave me a blank look.

I continued, 'It is my daughter's birthday tomorrow. She will be eighteen. We would be delighted if we can bring a few toys for your children, cut a cake and spend a couple of hours with them.'

She shot me another blank stare even though I thought I gave her the most winsome smile. She clumsily pulled out a dusty tattered register from one of the drawers and placed it on the even dustier table top.

'Write down your name, address and mobile number. Come tomorrow at 11.30 with your daughter and bring ten thousand rupees in cash. We have twenty-seven children, two nurses, a cleaner, and myself. You may bring savoury and sweet snacks and a cake. The children will be ready,' she said in a monotone, her face still joyless.

I jotted down my details in the register as commanded.

'How old are the children?' I asked, smiling at her.

'Youngest is two months. Oldest is seven years,' she said looking into space.

'We will be here by 11.15 tomorrow. Thank you for your kindness,' I said once again putting on my best smile, trying to elicit even a hint of emotion or expression from the robotic creature in front of me.

My smiles did nothing.

'Okay,' she said, still expressionless.

I nodded at her and walked out of the reception area.

I headed towards the front yard to where Pronto had parked the car, and was now sitting in the driver's seat, fast asleep, mouth wide open. I reached the car and opened the door to get in. Pronto woke up with a start.

A woman, maybe in her thirties, modestly dressed in salwar kameez, approached me and said, 'Indrani Mukerjea?'

'Yes,' I responded.

Before I could utter another word, I was surrounded by perhaps twenty people. They all looked like goons to me.

'Get into the car,' one of them growled.

'Who are you? What's going on?' I asked, putting up a brave front even though I was terrified.

Too many scenarios started running through my head. I thought I was being kidnapped and that Peter would receive a call in the next couple of hours and be asked to pay a huge ransom or I'd be dead meat.

Pronto, otherwise a meek fellow, resisted, 'You can't do this. We will call the police.'

'Shut up!' bellowed another goon.

I was asked to get into the back seat of my car. As I got in, I was asked to sit in the middle, which I obediently did, fearing a physical assault if I didn't. Two women climbed into the car and sat on either side of me. One of them snatched my handbag and pulled out both my mobile phones and my wallet.

The man, who was barking instructions before, sat on the passenger seat. Suddenly, the car was surrounded by goons on motorbikes.

Growler instructed Pronto, 'Start the car. Follow the motorcycle in front of us.'

Pronto started the car and drove out of the gates of the ashram. I could see Pronto's hands trembling on the wheel.

I felt a chill running down my spine as I had visions of being gagged and tied up in some dark and dingy room till Peter showed up with a bag full of cash.

Little did I know what was in store for me.

2

I was convinced that this was a kidnapping.

I asked the people again, 'Who are you?'

There was pin-drop silence in the car. No words were exchanged. The growler shot a look at me again before telling Pronto, 'Drive home.'

What kind of kidnappers take you back home? I was even more puzzled now.

A few minutes passed by and the growler introduced himself as a Mumbai Police official, Dhyaneshwar Ganoria. He flashed his ID at me. Honestly, knowing his identity made me a little relaxed. I was worried but at least now I knew that I wasn't being held for ransom.

He told me, 'We are from the Mumbai Police. We are investigating an accident. We need you to come home with us so we could ask you a few questions.'

My instant thought was that Pronto had perhaps hit a car or somebody, and didn't tell us. I snapped at Pronto immediately.

'You had an accident and didn't tell me?' I said.

Pronto replied, 'No, Madam, I haven't been in an accident.'

I retorted saying, 'Don't lie. If something has happened, now is the time to come clean.'

Pronto vehemently denied being in an accident.

9

Exasperated, I asked the lady next to me for my phone back. She, very matter-of-factly, said, 'You will get the phone back at the right time. We can't allow you to make calls.'

I began to process the information I could gather and it was still making no sense. If Prashant had an accident, why was I not allowed to use my phone? In the drive between the ashram and my home, I had considered all possibilities there could be. I have never driven in Mumbai so this can't be directed at me, I thought. I assumed that because the cars were in my name the cops wanted to question me.

When we reached Marlow, the car was let in. I pressed the lift button that took us to Flat 18, where we lived. I had the house keys with me so I opened the door and led them to the living room. Maya looked at me, perplexed, after noticing the two women and the group of men accompanying me. In a few minutes, Pronto was escorted up as well. Behind them, yet another bunch of cops in civil clothes walked in.

I sat on the large green leather sofa in the living room and the two female constables positioned themselves on either side. Every time I got up, the cops got up as well. When I went to my bedroom to use the washroom, they came after me and said, 'Don't close the door.'

I closed the door anyway. By now, I had a nagging feeling that something was very wrong.

Pronto had been made to sit at the dining table. Maya wore a rattled look on her face. The cops took away her cell phone as well.

I tried to remain composed despite the confusion in my mind. I asked them if they wished for some tea. I asked Maya to make tea for everyone, so we could get on with the conversation.

Then, I addressed the elephant in the room. 'What is going on, officer?' I asked Ganoria.

By then his team was all over the house, opening my wardrobes, looking in Peter's study, asking for my laptop, passport, etc. My passport used to be kept in Peter's safe in the bedroom. I asked to speak with Peter. I was not allowed to use my mobile or the house phone. Ganoria said that the cops will call Peter. As it appeared, the cops tried Peter's number multiple times, but he didn't pick up any of the calls. A few hours had passed, and around 1 p.m. Vidhie returned home. She walked in angry, hopping mad at both Peter and me, as both of us had not taken her calls; even Pronto or the house helps had not answered her calls.

I could hear her shouting from the lobby, 'What is the matter with all of you? Why isn't anyone answering my calls?'

Maya said, almost in a whisper, 'There are cops all over the house!'

She barged into the room I was in. We looked at each other. She sensed the trouble in the air.

Vidhie looked around and started asking questions about the search, 'Do you have a search warrant? You can't do this at our place!'

I realized that till now there had been no mention of a warrant. At this point, they confiscated Vidhie's phone too. 'Stay quiet and don't interfere with the investigation,' Ganoria told her.

I gestured at Vidhie to calm down. She quieted down, but being defiant by nature she tucked a cordless phone inside her dress that she had picked up from her bedroom and went to the bathroom, without the cops getting any wind of it. She called Peter multiple times from the bathroom and he didn't answer. She called her friend Isha, who lived in the next building, and asked her to keep trying Peter's number. 'There are cops in the house and I don't know what's going on.'

She hid the phone in the bathroom and kept going back to call Peter and Isha. Finally, after many unsuccessful attempts, she finally got through to Peter. 'Papa, there are cops at home! They are ripping your study apart and pulling down things,' she told him.

Peter apparently reacted to her call with absolute shock and horror.

Up until then, we were told that the cops were investigating an accident and that's what Vidhie told Peter as well.

After a couple of hours, Peter walked in. My instant reaction was to run up to him and hug him. As we hugged, I knew something was not right. It didn't strike me then but later, when in prison, the more I thought about that moment the more I realized that I should have known something was gravely amiss in that moment itself. It wasn't a reassuring hug, it was the kind of hug I received from him when he lied to me, or hid something from me or when we were fighting. I know Peter inside-out and I am very sensitive to 'touch' when it comes to Peter. But this realization came to me three months into my time in prison at Byculla when I first got the sense that something was amiss.

Peter was taken away to the terrace by Ganoria. I stood away from sight in a corner and tried to read his expressions. I saw no look of shock on his face.

I walked up to them and asked, 'What is going on?'

That's when Peter told me there were charges of Section 302 and Section 364 of the Indian Penal Code (IPC) that the team was investigating. I had no idea what the charges meant.

Peter offered, 'Murder and kidnapping.'

I looked at him, horrified, not able to fully comprehend what all this implied. The cop reiterated, '*Murder aur kidnapping ka charge hai …*'

I asked the obvious next question, 'On whom and for what?'

Peter looked at me and, in a voice dripping with sarcasm, said, 'On me. I must've done something. Right?'

'Peter, what nonsense are you talking about?'

That's when Ganoria intervened, saying, 'Madam, there is a 302 charge on you.'

By then, Vidhie was there, too. She and I were the only two people reacting to this, while Peter seemed calm. We were both freaking out in front of him.

The officer said, 'You'll need to come to the station with us for questioning.'

Peter told me, 'You need to get a lawyer!'

By then, I understood the severity of the situation. It was evident. I needed to get a lawyer. But, I still hadn't been told who had been kidnapped and murdered.

The officer kept saying they needed to question Peter and me—we were asked to go with the team of policemen to the station.

I asked Peter to call my cop friends. Ranjeet Panchnanda and Manoj Malviya were both IPS officers stationed in Delhi and Kolkata respectively. We had stayed with Ranjeet just a few days ago when we were in Delhi. I also told Peter to call Deven Bharti, a senior police officer from Mumbai whom I had known for several years, ever since he was posted at the Foreign Regional Registration Offices (FRRO). Manoj didn't answer the call but Ranjeet picked up immediately. I told Ranjeet what had happened.

He asked me, 'Are they saying it's you?'

'Yes. And the guy said I need to get myself a lawyer. So it appears it's me.'

I asked him about the intricacies of the sections quoted to me. Ranjeet sounded worried. He was a dear friend and an upright cop. He asked me again, 'What's going on?'

His parting advice was, 'Get a good lawyer.'

I then asked Peter to call Deven Bharti. He answered Peter's call but when I came on the line, he went silent. He was at that time the head of the crime branch in Mumbai, and I am sure he was well aware of what was going on.

I told Peter to call our family friend Tony, aka Mahesh Jethmalani, who is a renowned lawyer. Though Peter advised we call another lawyer, Ranbir, who was a childhood friend's son, I insisted on Tony, as by now I knew this was something pretty serious and I needed Tony to represent me.

On the phone, Tony sounded distressed. 'It is a mistake. Right? It must be a case of mistaken identity. I will organize for someone to come see you straight away.'

I handed the phone back to Peter. Peter and Tony then spoke for a few minutes after which Peter told me that the cops might want to detain me at the station for the night.

I was shocked. I was someone who had never been given a parking ticket in my life. And here I was, being accused and framed for a heinous crime.

I pleaded to Peter, 'Make sure I am home by night. It's Vidhie's birthday tomorrow. Get me out of this bloody thing. I haven't done anything!'

After this, I started to get paranoid.

I kept begging Peter, 'Don't let them keep me for the night!'

I was getting visions of the lock-ups shown in movies and how the accused get bashed up in stations! I was a law-abiding citizen and never in my wildest dream could I have imagined a day like this in my life.

Peter then handed over my passport to the cops. It was time to go to the station. I went to grab my handbag.

Peter told me, 'Don't carry your purse, you won't need it.'

I left the purse behind and I never saw either the purse or its contents—my credit cards, driving license, everything it had—ever again.

The cops then returned Vidhie's phone to her. And all the while they kept mumbling, 'We need you and Peter to come in for questioning ...' All of this came back to me when I started recollecting the chain of events of that day. There was something odd in what was going on. It was almost as if Peter knew exactly what was going to happen to me. While I sat there thinking of him as the love of my life, who will save me, his actions seemed to suggest otherwise.

As I was leaving home, I saw the look on Vidhie's face. The word 'murder' was being thrown around a lot, and it scared her—she realized this was all much more serious than we had first imagined. Right before I left, I hugged her tight.

'Don't worry, Hon,' I told her.

With tears in her eyes, she asked me, 'Mamma, you are coming back in the evening. Right?'

I was confident, I was. So I said, 'I will be back in a few hours. It is all a big mistake. Everything will be all right.'

She then asked, 'You promise me?'

'I promise,' I swore to her, giving her a peck and another hug.

Peter pressed the elevator button and went down to the lobby. We sat in the police jeep together; the cop instructed Prashant to follow the police jeep in our car.

Suddenly, Peter asked me, 'Tell me something, do you have Sheena's mobile number on your phone?'

I was stumped by this question—it was completely a bolt from the blue. 'No. She contacted you last. How can I have her number?'

This was the first mention of Sheena that day. Sheena Bora is my daughter. In fact, we hadn't mentioned her in the last few months.

I was almost clinging to Peter in fear when we reached the Khar police station. Right before we got down, I looked at Peter and said, 'Everything will be all right. Right?'

He didn't respond. And then, we entered the police station.

3

I had never been in a police station before. The Khar police station was the unkempt, dingy place that I had imagined it to be till I was taken into a separate room in the station which was an air-conditioned cabin. After that, I didn't see Peter. I assumed he was being questioned separately.

I was seated across the table from a police officer. He wasn't in a uniform, either. I was nervous.

He asked me point-blank, 'Where is Sheena?'

'I don't know. Look, I haven't been in touch with her. I think she is either in the UK or in the US. But I haven't met her or spoken to her in several years.'

It suddenly dawned on me—was Sheena okay? I asked him, panicking, 'What happened to Sheena?'

He looked at me intently, 'You have murdered Sheena. Haven't you?'

There was a coldness in his voice. He was straightforward, didn't beat around the bush, and said it in a rather calculated way. It was almost as if he was certain my daughter was no more.

I glared at him and bellowed, 'What the hell are you talking about?'

I was trying to make sense of his words. As I looked at him, multiple thoughts ran through my mind: Where is Sheena? Is Sheena dead? Why would they think I would kill my *own* daughter?

16

'*Chai piyenge, aap?* (Do you want some tea?)'

This sudden switch baffled me. This was my first time dealing with a cop, so I hadn't known that this is how cops interrogate.

'I don't want tea. I don't want anything. I just want to know what is going on here!' I snapped at him.

He didn't react, but calmly said, 'We have information that you have got together with your husband and driver and murdered Sheena.'

'Are you out of your mind?' I said, infuriated. 'I have not met Sheena in three and a half years. How can I kill her ...'

He said my driver has admitted to the crime. I asked him to get Prashant in front of me. I knew he couldn't have said that. Prashant was with me till five minutes ago.

'It's complete bullshit!' I yelled.

It took me a bit of time to settle down.

I then looked at him and asked, 'Has something happened to Sheena?'

No response.

He then went on to level accusations against my husband.

I again said, 'Both my husband and I haven't met Sheena since 2012.'

'We will pick up your husband from Kolkata!' he said, almost like a threat.

I was confused. 'My husband is in the station right now. He is not in Kolkata. I came here with him!'

'*Aapka pehla pati* (Your first husband),' he clarified. '*Aapka pehla pati Sanjeev Khanna hai na* (Your first husband is Sanjeev Khanna)?' he asked.

I responded with a yes.

'*Aapne apne pehle pati, Sanjeev, ke saath mil ke Sheena ko mara hai* (You and your first husband killed Sheena).'

'I haven't met Sanjeev in a long time. The last time I saw him was when I met him in Kolkata many years ago.'

He replied with a chilling smile, '*Tabhi toh maara tha aapne* (That is when you killed her).'

Slowly, the picture started getting clearer. My voice's decibel levels kept rising as the blasphemy and idiocy of the situation were getting the better of me. Sanjeev had never met Sheena in his life. I hadn't met Sheena or Sanjeev in a long time. Prashant is the sort of meek man who would never hurt a fly. This fictional tale of my daughter's death was beginning to sound incredibly outrageous!

'*Aap chillao mat* (Do not raise your voice),' he warned me. '*Main aapse shanti se baat kar raha hoon. Aap shanti se baat karo* (I am talking to you peacefully. You talk to me peacefully).'

I defiantly shot back, '*Main bilkul shanti se baat nahi karungi. Aap kuch bhi bakwas kar rahe hai* (I will not talk peacefully. You are talking rubbish). You are wasting my time. Tomorrow is my daughter's birthday, I have to go back home.'

But I calmed myself down. I asked him yet again. 'What is it? Is Sheena all right?'

'*Kaise all right ho sakti hai? Aapne toh maar daala usey* (How can she be all right? You have killed her)!'

He noticed my face go white. He softened a bit. '*Humari aapse koi personal dushmani hai nahi* (I do not have any personal grudge against you). This is the information that has come to us. You confess to whatever you have done. Everything will be easy for you after that.'

'I have nothing to confess because I have done nothing!' Tears rolled down my face as these words came out of my mouth.

'Madam, can I get you some water or tea?' the cop asked me again.

I nodded, 'Some water, please.'

Cops deal with hardened criminals daily. Their gut feelings are supposedly so sharp they very often instinctively know after talking to a person how they ought to conduct their interviews with the accused sitting across them.

As he handed me a bottle of water, I could see his eyes almost softening and then he said to me, 'Please cooperate with us. *Humko upar se bohot dabav hai. I am only doing my duty. Humko aapse koi dushmani nahin hai* (There is a lot of pressure from the top. I am only doing my duty. I have no personal vendetta against you).'

I took some minutes to cool off.

When we resumed, the cop asked me, 'Did a guy called Shyamvar Rai work for you?'

I answered, 'Yes.'

He asked, 'What did he do for you?'

I said, 'He was our driver. But he hasn't worked with us for several years now!'

'We have arrested him and he has informed us that in 2012, Sanjeev and you killed Sheena.'

I once again told him, 'Officer, there is a mistake. It is not possible! Sheena is alive. I am very certain she is alive.'

I didn't believe my child was gone. I, till date, don't believe she isn't around.

He asked me, 'Can you give me Sheena's number then?'

But I wasn't in touch with Sheena for nearly three years. 'I don't have her number. She hasn't been in contact,' I said. It probably sounded stupid to him.

He mockingly said, '*Woh hai hi nahi, kahan se contact karegi aapko* (How will she contact you when she is not alive)?'

I exasperatedly replied to him, 'No, she did get in touch with Peter. I know.'

He sighed and left the room. I sat there alone for an hour. I kept asking for my lawyer and Peter. The officers stationed there told me that Peter was being questioned in another room. I insisted on speaking to my lawyer. Since my phone wasn't with me, one of the officers said that he would get it for me so that I could speak to my lawyer and then left the room. He never returned.

I was dressed up for a normal day. So when, a little while later, they asked me to take off my jewellery, I was confused. I was wearing my watch, a bracelet, my wedding ring, earrings, etc. I didn't know police protocols or procedures.

I asked them, 'Why am I taking off my wedding ring?'

I took off every piece of jewellery I was wearing, standing there in the station in my green shirt, trousers and loafers. I then asked for my eye drops that I needed to use regularly every four to five hours as I had left the bottle behind in my purse. I sat there quietly, waiting for the eye drops to come from the chemist shop.

I was informed that I was being taken to the Bandra magistrate court then. The mere mention of court began to worry me all over again.

As I entered the court, a young girl came running to me. She was perhaps in her late twenties. She introduced herself, 'My name is Gunjan Mangla. I have come from the office of Mahesh Jethmalani. I am going to represent you. Please sign this vakalatnama.'

I signed on the paper in front of me and was led into a crowded courtroom.

In the courtroom, my eyes kept looking for Peter, but I could not find him. My heart was racing. I was feeling a mix of fear and doom. I was made to stand in the witness box and listen as the allegations against me were rattled off. The words 'Sheena Bora', 'murder' and 'kidnapping' kept being used frequently. The public prosecutor spoke in Marathi, most of which I didn't understand.

Gunjan pleaded to the judge saying that I come from a respectable family and custodial interrogation wasn't required. I suppose the fear was that influential people can abscond.

The Ld Magistrate's words were loud and clear and he passed the order: 'Khar police station is granted custody of Mrs Indrani Pratim Mukerjea for three days for the purpose of interrogation.'

No sooner did I hear this, I felt all the energy sucked out of my system. Everything became a blur and I passed out in court.

When I woke up a few minutes later, a cop was holding me and another one was sprinkling water on my face. My bleary eyes kept looking for Peter, still.

I was driven back to the station and then taken to the ladies' guard room. The female guards were polite to me.

I kept mumbling, 'I want to go home, I want to go home!'

One of them said to me kindly, 'You know that won't be happening today. Please cooperate with us.'

I felt helpless. I had promised Vidhie I'd be back.

The guard assured me, 'Nothing will happen to you. We are here. Ask us if you need anything. Just say if there is any truth to what's being said.'

'There is no truth to it!' I blurted out and I started weeping,

I was then taken to another room—there were six cops in the room. They pulled out my laptop (that they had seized from my house), asked me for my Facebook password and email passwords. I gave them everything they asked for. And they kept looking for any titbit of detail they could find in my accounts.

Then, the questions started again: 'When was the last time you met Sheena?'

I gave them a minute-by-minute account of the last time Sheena and I had met. They asked me for a written statement, and I gave it to them gleaning whatever I could from my memories of that day.

4

Hours had passed, and it was late evening now; the cops kept asking me what I wanted for dinner.

All I could say, weeping, was, 'I want to go home.'

Vidhie was turning eighteen. I had promised her I would be home. I kept replaying our hug in my head and wailed helplessly at the situation. Peter was right, I was obviously not going home that night.

The cops made a nice bed for me in the ladies' guard room, but I couldn't sleep. I kept tossing and turning, passing out for a few minutes every now and then, and waking up suddenly.

When I woke up the next morning, I was in a bad shape. I requested a call to Vidhie and Peter, but the police declined. I sat and cried for a long time, feeling utterly helpless. After some time, I had to get up and get ready. There was a small bathroom and an attached toilet. I kept looking for shower knobs and was told that there was only a bucket with a mug. I stared at it for a second. Fresh clothes had come for me from home. I wanted to shampoo, but the cops obviously couldn't arrange for it so early in the day. Once I was ready, they coaxed me to have some tea and breakfast. I declined politely, asking them to get either Peter or my lawyer.

Eventually, Ganoria called me into his office. There was a set of blank papers resting on his desk.

By then, it was evident to me that someone wanted to frame me. I kept wondering about possible enemies. Surely there were people I had rubbed the wrong way and who would love getting back at me. But I couldn't think of anyone who would have something against me to push me to this extent.

As a rule, those in custody have to go for a medical check-up every day. Every time I went out of the station, they covered my face with a black cloth or dupatta, to protect my identity from the media. It was evident the cops didn't want me to talk to the press. When I reached the hospital for the check-up, the attendant checked my vitals and asked me if the cops had raised their hands at me. I truthfully told them no, they had treated me well.

At the medical examination centre, I saw Shyamvar Rai and Sanjeev in another jeep for the first time. This was also the first time I was seeing Sanju, as I called him, after many years. I stood there looking at him helplessly, asking the cops if I could talk to him. They didn't allow it.

When I was brought back to the station, I sat around doing absolutely nothing all day. Sometimes I was in someone's cabin, sometimes in the room I was kept in, but I wasn't questioned anymore. They kept asking me what I wanted to eat but I knew the turbulence inside me wouldn't allow me to stomach any food. Along with the next change of clothes that came from home, they'd sent me some fruits which I ate. I was never really kept in the lock-up.

The next day when I was taken to court, I was overjoyed to see Vidhie and Peter's sister, Shangon Dasgupta, there. I knew that they were all there to support me. 'This is my family and they are all here for me,' I thought to myself and I breathed easy.

Earlier that day, I was visited by officials from the UK embassy at the police station. I am a British citizen and they wanted to meet me. My lawyer Gunjan had also applied to meet me; she had visited me a day earlier.

Standing in the witness box that day, I was dead sure I was going to go home. Till that point, I didn't know that from police custody one went to jail—even if one is exonerated—it is protocol that while an investigation is going on, the accused has to be in an undertrial prison. So, when I heard the words that my custody was extended, the realization dawned on me—I won't be going home. I passed out in the court again. It was obviously because I wasn't eating. I was physically weak, mentally drained out and emotionally distraught, and my body just shut down when the stress took its toll.

When I came to consciousness, I saw Vidhie standing in front of me. She was crying, kissing me on my forehead, and holding me in her arms. Vidhie told the cop who was escorting me away, 'Mumma is very fragile. *Please inka dhyan rakhna* ... take care of her ...'

Outside the court that day, Vidhie was cornered by a few journalists to give a byte.

She told them, 'My mother is a loving mom. She would never do something like this!'

As my daughter stood out there announcing this, I was taken back to the station. It was late evening by the time I got back and I had to brace myself for another three days of doing nothing. As I walked back into the Khar police station that evening, I felt I had hit rock bottom. Because I had fainted in court yet again, I was coaxed by the constable to eat something. Finally, on the third day, I ate a sandwich. I had no appetite. My whole system had gone into a state of shock.

When I was back at the station, I was again asked about Sheena: When was the last time I had spoken to her? When was the last time I met her? After the last time we had met, I hadn't spoken to her—I told them so. Peter had told me that he had spoken to Sheena after that.

Then came stories from them about how I was allegedly trying to kill my son Mekhail as well. It was laughable because, apparently, I had bought an 'additional suitcase' to put his body in. But, all the while these stories were created, they saw texts and emails from 2012 to 2014 exchanged between Mekhail and me that said, 'I love you, Mom.'

My informed guess is that a lot of these 'stories' came from Rakesh Maria and his team. This would have been the last celebrity case from his kitty before he retired, and his last moment in the sun before calling it a day. He was due for retirement in thirty-three days. When I met him, he was sitting with his coterie. About fifteen officers were sitting with him, several of them senior IPS officers.

Everyone at the police station, before my meeting with him, kept urging me, 'Why don't you confess?'

Maria reiterated the same, 'Why don't you just confess?'

I was told if I confess, I would be made an approver in the case.

He snarled, 'Don't give me attitude …'

I was threatened that I would rot in Arthur Road Jail for many years. 'You will be hung to death,' he told me.

At that point, I didn't even know who Rakesh Maria was; I had not lived in India for quite a while, and we didn't know each other socially.

The alleged story of how I killed my daughter kept changing from version to version. The first story that I read much later in Maria's book, *Let Me Say It Now*, too, alleges that Sanjeev sat on the back seat while I sat in front. The Khar cops stuck to the story that Shyamvar was driving, I was sitting in the front and Sanjeev was sitting in the back. Perhaps it is best to quote from Maria's book itself:

> On the day of the murder, Sanjeev Khanna flew down to Mumbai and stayed at Hotel Hill Top in Worli near the Mukerjeas' flat. Indrani lured Sheena to meet her in Bandra. Rahul dropped her at the given spot where the car was waiting with Shyamwar Rai at the wheel, Indrani in the front seat and Sanjeev Khanna on the back seat.

And this is not even half of what was said about my case in Maria's book.

But at that time, I put my foot down.

I told Maria, 'Please do what you have to do but I am not going to admit to something that's not true.'

I kept telling the cops, '*Aap Peter se poocho. Sheena aur Peter ka baat hua hai* (Ask Peter. He had spoken to Sheena).'

Peter wasn't there to say any of this, of course. He, instead, went around town painting a picture of what a poor gullible guy he was.

I was twenty-nine when I met Peter who was forty-six at that time, and the CEO of Star India. I can't blame the media for the trial of the case. As I write this, in hindsight, I kind of think the stories were laughable. The allegations levelled at me included that I was ambitious and I stayed on amicable terms with my ex-husband. They couldn't stomach the fact that a woman can have beauty, brains, money and power, all at once. It was all made to look like I had sinned by being true to myself.

Amidst all this, now and then, I would close my eyes and replay my last few moments with Sheena. The news that Sheena could have been killed was the most traumatic thing for me in those days. How could it be that she was no more? My heart still doesn't believe it. Till the day of my arrest, I thought of her as my angry daughter who doesn't wish to speak to me anymore. I was slightly mad at her too because she had lied to me. Sheena had gone cold on me before as well and had stopped talking to me for a few years when she started dating Rahul. It wasn't unusual for her. She'd even stopped talking to my parents, save a stray call a month, if at all. I didn't even care that I was accused of murdering her. I had no idea how the judicial system worked in India. I was telling the truth. I would tell them exactly what happened and I'd be let off, I thought.

But that didn't happen. They took the truth from me and built a story around it. Over the years, the story fell through because they went by the approximate time I gave them and used that to create the 'window' in which the alleged murder could've happened. When the Call Detail Record (CDR) was later procured, the time was off by a good margin and the cops' theory did not add up. But more on this later.

I was at the Khar police station for fourteen days. In those two weeks, they must've interrogated me for a maximum of ten hours in total. I sat in the police station waiting for it to get better. But the remand kept getting extended. My lawyer Gunjan came to meet me twice during this period but at no point did she tell me I would go to jail. I kept believing I would go back home once the interrogation was over.

A day before I was remanded to judicial custody, Gunjan came over and said, 'You'll have to spend some time in jail …' She explained, 'It is a procedure. It is a non-bailable offence. Nothing can be done until the chargesheet is ready.'

These fourteen days changed my life.

It was on 7 September 2015 that the court decided to send me into judicial custody. It felt as if the cops at Khar knew my impending fate. A day or two before the day I was remanded to judicial custody, I was taken for a round across Worli in the police jeep. I was taken back home. I have come to understand that this is a common tactic used by the police to try and leverage the accused person's emotional state by giving them a glimpse of their familiar life. By then Vidhie had left for England to join college. Peter and his family were living at 18, Marlow at that time—the whole family had parked themselves there.

As soon as I entered home, my eyes only kept looking for Peter. He was in our bedroom and came out a few minutes after I arrived, while I sat in the living room of my own home like a guest. My instant reaction when I saw him was to ask for a hug. He didn't hug me, and just said, 'Later.'

It suddenly dawned on me that he was no longer my Mumu. I could feel that the love was lost between us. The warmth was absent suddenly. Nothing had changed from my end, but Peter felt different. My heart sank. I think I knew at that point that this would be my battle to fight alone. Up until then I was in denial. I believed that Peter was going to leave no stone unturned to save me from the nightmare that I was in. But when I met Peter that day, I knew that something was not right.

While I sat in the living room in a state of confusion, Maya made me tea. She hugged me, and said, '*Aap tension mat lo, sab thik ho jayega* (You don't worry, everything will be fine) …'

After tea, just as I was leaving Marlow, I gave Shangon a hug. Her hug lacked any warmth too. All she said was, 'Please confess to the crime and free us so that we can carry on with our lives as we had earlier.'

I remember how standing in the living room of the place that I once called home, I felt alienated, ostracized and abandoned. At that moment, prison, cops, lock-up, none of it mattered. That feeling of being left alone by the man I loved so deeply, even at a time of adversity, was the lowest of the lows. How would I ever recover from this?

PART 2

1970s and 1980s

5

I was born in Guwahati in north-east India. Nuclear families were supposedly in vogue. It was the time of 'burn the bra' and '*Dum Maro Dum*'. In keeping up with the times my parents decided not to live with my grandparents, uncles, aunts or cousins. We lived in a big house with my nanny, the cook, the chauffeur, the cleaner and the dog—the perfect nuclear family!

Everyone tells me that I have an elephant's memory. I probably do. Often, I am just unsure whether it is a boon or a curse.

I remember when I was two, I thought our dog was a horse.

I remember when I was three, I wanted to sit with an open umbrella inside the car.

I remember when I was four, the pots and pans of the house were my favourite toys. I would spread out my toy cups and saucers, dishes, and other utensils, and prepare meals for my teddies and dolls and Nanny.

I remember a time when I was four, of hearing angry voices coming from upstairs.

I looked at Nanny, who was the kindest soul on earth.

'Angel, I am hungry. Is dinner ready?' Nanny asked, motioning towards the pots and pans in my hands.

'Pari' was what everyone called me in my hometown. To my parents, when I was born, I looked like an angel—a pari—don't all babies look like angels when they are born? I thought of this often when I was young. Anyway, Pari, I was, and remained as long as I lived in Guwahati.

The voices grew louder and angrier.

'Nanny, is Papu angry with Mom?' I asked. I used to call my father 'Papu'.

Nanny looked at me with her soft eyes. 'No Pari, Papu is not angry with Mom!'

'Is Mom angry with Papu?' I asked again.

'No Pari, Mom and Dad are just talking,' Nanny said.

'But, Nanny, they are fighting.' I needed to know why Mom and Dad sounded so angry.

I ran up the stairs with Nanny following me, trying to stop me. I opened the door to my parents' room. I saw Mom sitting on the bed and Papu towering over her. They were both still shouting. I do not remember what they said to each other.

But I do remember what my father said to Nanny. 'Take the bastard down!' pointing at me. At four, I did not understand why my father called me a 'basket' instead of Pari.

From then on my parents always seemed to be angry with each other. Everyone would walk on eggshells at home. I would not understand why ever so often I used to get shouted at by Mom or Papu when I would go for a cuddle.

And so, school became my retreat. Ms Lobo, the first teacher I have memories of, was ever so kind. In between Ms Lobo and Nanny, I got all the cuddles that I did not get from my parents.

I often wondered if most children my age were happier being at school than having to deal with the constantly bickering adults at home.

I remember when I was nine, Granny, Nanny and Mom started giving me lessons on, what I call, 'becoming a woman soon'. At the age of nine, to hear about becoming a woman is pretty daunting. I was introduced to the sanitary napkin and made to carry one every day to school in case I 'became a woman' while at school.

Junior school was an all-girls day convent with conservative ideologies. At ten, I finally became a 'woman', as warned by everyone. I was further cautioned by the nuns in grey habits at school: 'When you bleed, you are ready to breed.'

Having hit puberty at such an early age was awkward for me. I became the gawky adolescent sprouting at all the wrong places well before I was a teenager. But by the time I was fourteen, I blossomed. While most girls my age were still gawky and ugly ducklings on their way to becoming beautiful swans, I was already ahead and there—doe-eyed with honeydew skin, rounded hips, long brown hair, and even longer legs.

At home, things had become quieter with time. Mom and Dad were at work during the day, running the family construction and hospitality business. Their fights were almost non-existent, which was a relief. But I could always sense their cold vibes between them at dinner, and I conditioned myself to believe that they were both just exhausted after a long day's work. Mom and Dad no longer shared a bed, or even a bedroom. Their conversations at dinner were limited to, 'Can you please pass the salt?'

Mom spoke very little most of the time. She often carried heaps of paperwork from the office and immersed herself in work in the evenings while sipping a glass of scotch. Dad would sip on his scotch, too, and watch the television unless he had his friends over for a game of bridge or he was out socializing.

My parents entertained very often on the weekends. In one of the garden parties that Mom had organized at home, Dad's friend, Uncle Chaudhuri, said, 'Buddy, your Pari looks as if she just descended from heaven. She is gorgeous.'

Uncle and Aunt Chaudhuri were a cheerful and elegant couple who had seen me almost from the day I was born. Their son Vish was twenty-three, and I thought he was the most handsome and coolest dude in the world. Vish, who often ignored me or never noticed me, was giving me side glances that evening. I was in seventh heaven. And then Vish walked up to me with his swagger and said, 'Hello, Pari! You've grown up.' I was tongue-tied and weak in the knees as I looked into Vish's sea-green eyes. He was much taller than me with an athlete's physique and chiselled features.

That night I lay awake and thought of handsome Vish. I was fourteen, and the coolest dude in town had said, 'You've grown up.' I had arrived—I was in love! I couldn't wait to go to school the next day and tell my friends that I had fallen in love! And I was sure Vish loved me too. He had, after all, said, 'You've grown up.'

At school, I told my friends about the love of my life—some of them congratulated me; some sighed, saying how lucky I was to have Vish compliment me; some were envious. I was daydreaming about him throughout all my lessons. I was going to call Vish that Sunday and tell him how much I loved him.

I felt a joy I had never known before. Even the usual grim atmosphere at home couldn't dampen my spirit. And then the telephone rang. Nanny called out, 'Pari, Vish is on the line. He wants to speak to you.'

When I picked up the receiver, my hand was shaking and my 'Hello' was squeaky.

Vish said, 'Hey Pari, how was school?'

'Good,' I said, barely hearing my own voice.

'I was spring cleaning. Before I get rid of my high school notes, I thought I would check with you if you needed any,' said Vish.

'Yes, please,' I squeaked. My heart was beating ever so loudly. I was sure that Vish could hear it over the phone.

'Great, Pari! Why don't you pop by on Sunday and take whatever you need? I'll get rid of the rest, after that,' said handsome Vish.

'Thank you, Vish,' my voice was a bare whisper by then.

Vish said goodbye. But I was tongue-tied. I said nothing.

I was right. Vish was in love with me as I was with him. Why would he give me his notes otherwise? I knew that this was going to be a fairy-tale where handsome Vish and I would get married one day and live happily ever after. I smiled to myself.

That evening, Mom was at work. When Dad came home from office, I still had that silly grin on my face.

Dad looked at me and said, 'You have grown up, Pari. Haven't you now?'

Dad smiled at me. I couldn't remember the last time Dad had smiled at me. This was turning out to be the best day of my life. Dad went up to his room while I was still walking around the living room with butterflies in my stomach, with thoughts of groovy Vish. Mom was still not back from work. It was almost time for dinner.

Despite the stoic silence at the dinner table, I liked and looked forward to having Mom and Dad with me when I ate supper in the evenings. Mom always smelt good, very often floral. She was svelte and smart. Dad was stockily built and mostly smelt of cheroot. Sometimes, they asked me about my day at school. I often grabbed those precious moments to interact and lessen the icy vibe in the room; not that I ever succeeded. I longed to be held and cuddled and feel loved.

That day however was different. I had Vish in my heart and mind. My heart was smiling and having Mom at dinner would have been perfect even minus the cuddles. Dinner was served for Dad and me. Dad somehow seemed more approachable that evening. He did not ask me about school but started talking about his own university days and how, as a lad, he was accustomed to having young girls swooning over him. It was awkward as I had never imagined my parents with anyone else except each other. Nevertheless I was delighted that Dad treated me like an adult that evening and was confiding in me. While having dessert, Dad even asked me if I wanted to sit and watch the telly with him afterwards.

I said, 'Yes, Papu. I'd love to!'

My eyes were moist, but I held back my tears. My heart was going pit-a-pat, what with Vish falling in love with me and my father being so affectionate—all in one day. I thought that the heavens had opened up and showered me with all the happiness in the world.

It was half past eight, and Mom was still not back from work. I sat down with Dad to watch *Dynasty*, which was playing on the television then. But, I was miles away with Vish planning my own dynasty.

Dad even called me to sit next to him and when I did, he put his arm around me. Life was perfect. I thanked God for listening to my prayers and making everything all right for me and my family. I was overwhelmed and overjoyed with the events of the day.

'May I be excused if it is all right, Papu?' I asked. Even though I was cherishing every moment of my time with Dad that evening, I could barely keep my eyes open. It was almost 10 p.m., well past my bedtime.

'Of course, Pari,' said Dad, planting a kiss on my forehead. 'Goodnight, sweetheart.'

I hugged Dad for the first time in many years. I had a spring in my step when I headed back to my bedroom. I let the tears of joy roll down my cheeks.

Mom was still not home. I wanted to call her but was too tired to go back to the living room to ring her. Back then, there were no mobile phones. We were dependent on landlines, and I still did not have an extension in my bedroom.

I was tired and I needed to think of my Vish before I fell asleep. I tucked myself under my duvet and lay down thinking of my future with Vish. Sunday was only a few days away. Was Vish going to kiss me? Was Vish going to hold my hand? What was I going to wear on Sunday? Should I write a love note for Vish and leave it on his desk on Sunday? With all these thoughts, I dozed off feeling lightheaded, happy and exhausted.

Vish was so handsome—he took my breath away. Vish was at home with me. Vish was caressing me. Vish was touching my breasts. Vish had his lips on mine. And then I smelt the cheroot. Oh my God! My father was in my room; he was going to see Vish in my bed. My father was going to be furious. Why was Vish still pressing his lips on mine and pushing his tongue into my mouth? Was he not afraid of my father? Could he not smell the cheroot?

Vish's hand went to my knickers and my eyes opened wide.

'No, Papu!' I screamed.

'It is all right. You will like it, baby,' said my father.

'Papu, please don't!' I begged.

I was stripped. I had no nightgown, no knickers.

'This is going to be our little secret. My gorgeous Pari is now mine,' whispered my father into my ears.

I was numb with shock and pain. Dad left my room while I lay in bed naked, bleeding, shattered.

With my body throbbing with pain, I dragged myself to the bathroom and sat down in the tub with the shower on over my head. I scrubbed myself till my skin was red and sore. I sobbed and sobbed, and scrubbed and scrubbed even though I felt I was never going to be clean again. My heart felt like lead, my mind was numb, my body was dirty and my soul was dead.

I did not sleep that night. I could not sleep that night. I got out of bed and went to Mom's bedroom. It was locked, which meant she was back. I knocked but there was no answer. I sat down outside the door of her bedroom. What was I going to tell my mother when she opened the door?

I went back to my room. All kinds of thoughts crossed my mind while I lay in bed, tears streaming down my face. I was not just shocked and shattered, I was ashamed and guilty. I just wanted to die.

The 6 o'clock alarm rang on my bedside table. I turned it off and looked up at the ceiling. Daylight was filtering in through the curtains on the windows in my room, but my life was in darkness.

I got out of bed. I could barely walk. Nanny came to my room and looked at me, concerned with a frown on her brow.

'You are ill, Angel. You look pale,' she said.

She touched my forehead to check if I had a fever. I must have looked terrible. I burst into sobs in Nanny's arms.

'What's the matter, Pari?' Nanny asked. She looked really worried. I was speechless and couldn't stop my tears and sobs.

What was I going to tell Nanny? Should I tell her what happened last night? Should I tell Mom first? I was devastated. I just wanted to hide somewhere and never have to face anybody I knew ever in my life again. Why did Papu hurt me? Why?

Nanny was confused. She held me in her arms as I sobbed. She took me to the bathroom to brush my teeth and tucked me back in bed again.

'Take the day off, Pari. I will inform Madam that you are unwell. I am getting you a cup of hot chocolate. There's nothing that a cup of hot chocolate can't fix,' said Nanny and left.

Mom walked into my bedroom in her sashed robe bringing in a waft of floral scent that I can smell even today whenever I think of her.

'Good morning, Pari. Nanny says you are feeling under the weather,' she said and sat down on the bed next to me.

I knew that everything was going to be all right now. I was going to tell Mom everything and she would confront Dad for what he did to me. I took Mom's hand in mine and before I could utter a word, tears rolled down my cheeks.

Just then Nanny walked into my room with a cup of hot chocolate for me and a coffee for Mom. I told Mom that I needed to tell her about something really bad that had happened to me and if Nanny could stay while I spoke to her. Mom dismissed Nanny and told me that I should speak to her first and, if needed, she would tell Nanny later.

In between sobs and stutters, I told Mom about the previous night. When I finally looked at Mom, I could see that she had an unfathomable expression—it was impossible to understand what she was thinking or feeling. She did not give me a hug, nor did she show any grief, she merely sat there staring outside the window.

Then she squeezed my hand and said, 'I will take you to Dr Mason today. Get changed, and don't talk about this to anyone. We don't want tongues wagging.'

She stood up and as she was heading out of the door, she looked back at me and said, 'We will sort this out.'

Sort this out? How? Could she not see what I was going through? Did I not deserve even a hug? Was she not going to confront Dad? How was she planning to undo this?

Nanny came back to my room and started making my bed while I was getting changed. When she lifted the duvet, she saw the stained sheets. I could see how relieved she was.

She smiled at me and said, 'Ah! So that's it. You've got your periods. You can't be bunking school for that now, can you?'

I wished it was just as simple. I longed to pour out my grief to Nanny and tell her everything. But I was cautioned not to breathe a word to anyone, not even to Nanny.

I did not go down for breakfast. My stomach was churning, I had lost my appetite for food and life and, most of all, I was petrified of bumping into Dad. I stepped out of my room only when I heard Dad's car leave.

I went with Mom to see Dr Mason. She had been our family gynaecologist for years. She was with Mom when I was born. On the way, Mom told me that she will explain everything to Dr Mason and that I need not tell her anything more than the physical problems that I had down there at that moment.

When we reached Dr Mason's clinic, I was made to wait in the reception area while Mom went into Dr Mason's chamber to have a chat with her first. I guessed that Mom wanted to save me the embarrassment of repeating the gory details about the previous night.

I was called in a little later into Dr Mason's chamber. Both Mom and Dr Mason had serious faces when I walked in.

Dr Mason asked the nurse to help me undress and put on the green gown that was neatly folded and kept on the bed in her chamber.

She then asked me to lie down on the bed and instructed the nurse to draw the curtain near the bed.

The doctor looked at me and smiled. 'This will just take a couple of minutes. Tell me if it hurts.'

I wondered what she meant and I blurted out, 'It is hurting and really bad.'

Dr Mason asked me to part my legs and before I knew it, I could feel something cold going in, ripping me apart. I couldn't tell what was worse, the previous night or what I was going through in the doctor's chamber at that moment. I could not figure out why I was being poked and prodded to cause me more excruciating pain, after what I had gone through last night. I think I passed out.

And then I heard Dr Mason's voice over my head, 'It's all done, Pari. You can get dressed now.'

I sat down on the chair next to Mom in front of the doctor's desk.

'Did you guys use a condom? What's with the young generation today? Pari, you are barely fourteen! Would it have been so difficult for you to wait for a few more years?' Dr Mason reprimanded me, frowning, and sounded disappointed with my conduct.

I was confused. Was Dr Mason actually saying that she would have approved had I waited for a few more years to have sex with my father? Was she serious when she asked me if I told my father to use a condom while he raped me?

She asked me again when I did not respond, 'How old is he?'

Before I could respond, Mom said, 'Fifteen. One of the boys from her tennis group.'

And that was when the penny dropped. Mom had lied to Dr Mason. That was her grand idea of sorting it out. She blamed it all on me and told Dr Mason that I had landed up in her clinic because I partied with one of my mates who was fifteen.

My stomach was churning, and I could feel the bile rising up my throat. I ran to the sink in the chamber and threw up.

I was in a trance after that. I could hear Mom saying on our way back home, 'Pari, we are not going to talk about this anymore. If anyone gets to know what happened last night, you will have to live with the stigma and shame for the rest of your life. We will leave for Granny's tonight and then decide on what to do next.'

Her voice sounded distant, as though it came from somewhere far, far away. I wanted to hear no more.

I was alone from that moment. My childhood was brutally torn by the man who was supposed to be my protector. And all Mom could say was that I would have to live with the shame of it all if anyone knew about it!

Somewhere at the back of my mind, I felt this was all a bad dream. I was going to wake up and the clocks would have turned back twenty-four hours. But I was awake and the clocks would never turn back.

Nanny was given instructions by Mom to pack my bags. My wardrobe was emptied out, and my books and toys were packed in boxes.

I do not know what Mom told Nanny, or if she told Nanny anything at all. But I could see Nanny holding back her tears. She said nothing; nothing at all.

Nanny came to the driveway to see us off. Before I could get into the car, Nanny gave me her warm bear hug and whispered into my ear, 'I will miss you, Pari. Stay out of trouble. I will come and see you soon if Madam allows. Remember to pray and thank God every night before you go to bed. May the good Lord be with you and protect you always.'

Granny and Gramps lived a few hours away from us in another town. Before we drove out of the gate, I looked back and saw Nanny standing there till we were out of sight. We both knew that we were not going to see each other for a long time. I wanted to cry but there were no tears left.

Mom and I did not speak till we were a few minutes away from Granny's home. The sun was setting on the horizon like every other day, unaffected by the physical agony and emotional upheaval that I was experiencing.

Mom held my hand and said, 'We are not going to talk about the accident last night to anyone at Granny's. When you are older, you will understand and appreciate the need for and importance of silence in such matters.'

I nodded in submission.

'Mom, when are we returning home? What if Papu does this again?' I asked with apprehension as I knew the answers even though I was only thirteen. But I needed to hear it.

'We are going to look for another school for you, Pari, and perhaps you should stay away from home for a while. We should give it some time before you come home. What happened last night was an accident. Your father had too much to drink. It will not happen again, I promise you,' answered Mom.

We drove into the avenue leading to the home of my maternal grandparents. My grandparents were lovable and good people. Anybody who knocked on their door was helped without demur. One could succumb quite naturally to their charming grace and the gentleness of their hearts.

Granny and Gramps were delighted to see us. I wasn't sure whether they thought it was odd for us to have arrived with so many bags and boxes amidst school term and Mom's work. If they did, they said nothing. They were just happy to have us home.

I used to always walk into Granny's home like I owned the place. But that night, I felt like a stranger—I had become a stranger to myself.

My bags and boxes were taken to the guest room and Mom's to her own childhood room. I could not bear the thought of spending the night alone and being haunted by the terrible memories of the previous night.

I asked Granny if I could sleep in her room, to which Granny most lovingly and readily agreed.

Climbing onto Granny's bed made with nice-smelling fresh sheets was comforting. I lay down and shut my eyes trying hard to obliterate the events of the last twenty-four hours.

Granny came to bed almost an hour after I turned in. I lay restlessly tossing and turning, sleep eluding me.

She said, 'Is everything all right at school, dear?'

I nodded, unsure of what she had been told.

'Why then do you want to move to a new school in the middle of the term?' she asked.

'I don't. Mom wants me to,' I said. I knew that I had given her a leading answer despite being sworn to secrecy by Mom. If only at that vulnerable moment Granny had asked 'Why?' I would have disclosed the reason with a detailed account.

But the 'why' from Granny never came. She probably didn't want to interfere or probe into Mom's decision or cause me any distress by asking me too many questions about school, oblivious to the jarring reality.

I soon drifted off to sleep as Granny stroked my head. Fatigue overpowered my physical and emotional pain.

I woke up the next morning feeling as if there was a huge boulder tied to my heart. In just one day I had lost so much—my friends at school, Vish, Nanny who I loved so dearly, my home, my virginity, my self-esteem and, above all, faith in the human race.

I had a past that I wanted to forget, a present that was shrouded by long shadows, and a future that was uncertain. Little did I know that I would forever have shadows of my past chasing me.

Granny had woken up earlier and left the room, letting me sleep in. I could tell that she knew I was troubled about something. I got out of bed and looked at myself in the mirror. Pari stared back at me—only that I was not an angel anymore. That Pari was dead. I decided I would not be called Pari anymore. I was now just Indrani.

I went into Granny's bathroom and took a long hot shower cleaning myself, ready to face the world. I changed into a pair of denims and a blouse, slipped on my sandals and walked out of the house to the beautiful garden that Gramps spent hours tending to every day. I saw Mom standing there lost in her own thoughts. I was no longer angry with her. Even though I was just fourteen, the last twenty-four hours of my life had pushed me to a different space. She was in pain, and I could feel it, sense it and see it.

I walked up to her and stood next to her, saying nothing—nothing at all. I didn't know what to say. Mom was a very pretty woman and she looked even prettier when she smiled. But that day when she smiled at me, she looked sad and helpless, and lost.

She said, 'Pari, I am going back to see a new school today. It will be nightfall by the time I return.'

'Mom,' I said, 'I don't want to be called Pari anymore. Indrani—that sounds better.'

'Mom,' I continued, 'Can I go with you to see my new school?'

Mom was probably taken aback by the sudden show of enthusiasm. She frowned and asked, 'Are you sure? I haven't decided on it being your new school yet.'

'Yes, Mom, I am dead sure,' I said.

That was my moment of awakening. I was not going to heal unless I moved away and as soon as possible. If the school was a dump, so be it, I was going to like it and make good of it. I had to move on.

The school was not a dump. It had British colonial architecture, almost out of the pages of the Harry Potter series—classrooms, dorms, dining room, and cathedral, all in separate buildings, large playing grounds, and green fields.

I was a good student despite the lack of any adult supervision at home. I very often topped my class even though I was the youngest of the lot in my previous school. The Mother Superior in the new school interviewed me for a few minutes and told Mom that I was fit to join their tenth grade but then it was mid-term so it would be more practical for me to actually move once I had finished my boards. Mom decided that it was perhaps a much better idea for me to finish my tenth and then move to a boarding school.

Mom, however, made up her mind that I still needed to move schools, just in case I decided to speak with any of my friends at the old school who were more my family in the real sense than my real family ever was. I moved schools in Guwahati itself and was also shifted to my aunt's house till the board exams were over, so that I didn't see my father and was not disturbed by his presence.

I settled into my new school much faster than most children of my age would have done. I was, after all, no longer a child while others my age were still children.

I did well in academics, drama and debates. I was diligent and determined to do well. I enjoyed my time there and made new friends. Slowly and steadily the nightmares were replaced by new dreams and aspirations.

Granny and Gramps visited me as often as they could. Mom and Nanny came to see me almost every day. School holidays meant staying at Granny's cottage and being pampered and spoiled silly. Gradually, I returned to being a normal fourteen-year-old and the unpleasant incident became a blip in the radar. I was, finally, at peace with myself and happy once again.

During one of Mom's visits, she told me that Dad felt a lot of remorse about what had happened and that I must forgive him and let go of any bitterness that I had for him. Talking about Dad after almost a year was difficult. But I thought that Mom had a point. Maybe he was really drunk, and he had lost his mind that night. People say that children are really forgiving. And the fact that I could forgive my father at the age of fourteen after what he had done to me just a few months ago was a testimony to the fact that the child in me was still not dead. Despite all that happened to me, I was still a child at heart and just a fourteen-year-old. Time at school flew by, each day healing me, eventually enabling me to love life again and slowly restoring my faith in the goodness of mankind.

The class ten board exams were over and to everybody's joy, I passed them with flying colours. Without any difficulty, I got enrolled into pre-university at Cotton College in Guwahati.

I was still living with my aunt when Mom told me that I would return home and live with her and Dad. I had not been home for over a year and despite all that had happened—which I had tried to push back somewhere into the innermost recesses of my mind—I was looking forward to going back home and sleeping in my own bed.

Mom and Dad had both come to take me back home. I was not expecting Dad and seeing him wreaked havoc with my emotions. I hugged Mom but somehow could not bring myself to walk into the outstretched arms of my Dad.

Instead, I just said, 'Hello, Papu. You have gained some weight.'

If my aunt noticed the awkwardness, she said nothing to show it.

It was odd to have Dad at such close proximity in the car when we drove back home. Mom and I sat behind; Dad sat in the passenger's seat in the front. There was tension in the air and we barely spoke.

Nanny and the other house help were genuinely happy to see me. In turn, I hugged and greeted them.

I had bought tiny presents for each of them, that I promised to give the next day when we unpacked. I ran up to my room which was freshly painted in pink, my favourite colour. I could not help noticing that the furniture in my room was new, including the bed. I suppose it was thoughtful of Mom to have done that. A new beginning was good and much needed.

After showering and freshening up, I went downstairs to dinner, which was a lavish spread that evening, with all my favourite dishes on the table. Mom and Dad asked me if there was anything in particular I wanted to do the next day. I was tempted to say, 'I want to go and see Vish.' But I could only manage to say, 'Not really.'

Dad's next phrase froze me.

'Pari, I am sorry,' he said. His apology sounded sincere, but I could not bring myself to look him in the eye and say 'Accepted' or 'It's all right'.

'Can you please not call me Pari anymore? I am Indrani. That's what everyone calls me. I am no Pari. I am just Indrani,' I said instead, sounding defiant.

'Papu,' I continued, 'can you please not smoke your cigars when I am around. It's passive smoking for me, you know. And the smell gives me nausea.'

'Sure,' he said and asked for the box of cigars and the cut cigar, that was waiting to be lit and smoked with coffee after dinner, to be removed from the table.

'Thank you,' I said, relieved at not having to smell the cheroot which had unpleasant memories attached to it.

The grandfather's clock chimed at eight, bringing my attention back to my dinner plate just as my thoughts were drifting back to the past.

6

Once dinner was over, I excused myself and went upstairs to my room. I dialled Vish's number, which was etched in my memory. Vish's mother answered the call and when I greeted her, she said, 'Oh Pari, how are you, my darling? When did you come? Why have you not been coming home during school vacations? We have missed you.'

So many questions. I didn't know which to answer. But I liked the sound of 'We missed you', which in my head meant Vish missed me, too.

'I came yesterday. How are you, Aunty? I missed you all too,' I said.

'Why don't you come and have lunch with us tomorrow, Pari? Vish and Priya would be happy to see you,' said Aunt Chaudhuri.

'Yes, Aunty, I'd love to. I will just check with Mom and let you know. Shall I call you back?' I asked.

I ran across to Mom's room and told her about the invitation. Mom readily agreed.

I ran back to tell Aunt Chaudhuri that I was granted permission to come by. Then, I asked her if I could speak with Vish. Vish came on the call after a couple of minutes.

'Hello,' he said.

My heart missed a beat. I was tongue-tied once again.

'Hello,' Vish said again.

I whispered, 'Hello, Vish, how are you?'

'I am good. And you?' he asked.

'Good,' I said, choking.

And what Vish said next, stayed with me for the rest of my life, 'Pari, I waited for you on Sunday. I waited the whole day. When I called your house, you had left. You were gone. Have you been so busy that you could not even call me once in all this time?'

I could not speak. And haltingly said, 'Vish, I am sorry. I should have called. We had to leave very suddenly and when we spoke last time, I did not know that I was going to move the next day. Vish, you are the first person I have called after I have come back. I will explain when I see you at lunch tomorrow,' I said, tears streaming down my cheeks.

'Cool. Make sure you show up tomorrow and not a year later,' answered Vish, his words laced with sarcasm.

'Bye, Vish. See you tomorrow,' I said.

Vish hung up. It was obvious that Vish was cross with me for being stood up a year ago. I wasn't sure if he was hurt, but that it didn't go down very well for his ego was apparent. I told myself that I was going to win Vish's love once again now that I was back.

I woke up the next morning with butterflies in my stomach knowing that I was going to see Vish in a couple of hours.

My clothes were still in the bags waiting to be unpacked. 'They must be all crumpled and creased,' I thought. I needed to be in my Sunday best to see Vish—it was important for me to look stunning when I met him that day. I needed to look at least eighteen; maybe a dash of make-up would have helped, but I had none with me.

I went to Mom's bedroom. Mom was getting ready to leave for work. Mom had the best collection of trendy-to-chic outfits for any and all occasions.

'Mom,' I said, 'can I please wear one of your dresses today?'

'Sure, you can,' said Mom, putting make-up on her face as she spoke to me.

I gave Mom a hug and walked back to my room to get ready.

Aunt Chaudhuri was delighted to see me. She could not stop complimenting me and yelled out for Priya and Vish to come down.

And then I saw Vish. He looked ever so handsome. My palms were sweaty, I was feeling weak in my knees, and I could feel my heart clench. Vish walked up to me and hugged me. I must have fainted because I couldn't remember later what I did when he hugged me.

Vish spoke very little. Aunt Chaudhuri and Priya asked me about the time I was away. I could barely eat lunch. I just kept looking at Vish.

And then he said the magic words, 'Pari, would you like to come with me to the District Library? I will be leaving in a bit.'

'Yes, Vish, I'd love to,' I said. And then I realized how stupid I must have sounded when I said that I'd love to go to the District Library. What I really meant to say was: 'I'd love to go and be with you wherever you take me, Vish.'

Vish and I left for the library in his car.

'You look beautiful, Pari. I missed you,' said Vish, without looking at me, his eyes on the road.

'Vish,' I said, 'I swear I had no idea when we spoke the last time that I'd leave the next day. I was really looking forward to picking up the notes from you.'

'Pari, do you like me? Are you seeing anyone?' he asked.

I chose my words carefully and said, 'Vish, I've always liked you … a lot. And no, I do not have a boyfriend. But there are things that have happened that we need to talk about.'

Vish remained quiet.

Once we reached the library, Vish walked around his car to open the door for me. We sat on the bench in the courtyard of the library. Vish had no intention of searching for books in the library. He just wanted to be with me.

'We should spend more time together. In fact, we should meet every day! How about that?' he asked.

I smiled at him and said, 'Yes, Vish, we could.'

That moment was magical. Vish held my hand and asked, 'What is it that you wanted to tell me, Pari?'

I did not want to spoil this precious moment, and said, 'Nothing really, Vish. Nothing important.'

Vish was a lovable and charming young man. We spent a lot of days together and we were a couple now. Everyone in my family, including Gramps, Granny, my cousins, Mom and Nanny, warmed up to the idea of us seeing each other. Dad did not exactly express similar emotions towards Vish, but he was always courteous when he met Vish. Vish was no stranger to our family. They had seen him as a youngster, who had grown up to become an accomplished and dignified man, in other words, a suitable bachelor.

I, too, became almost a part of Vish's family effortlessly. Uncle and Aunt Chaudhuri treated me as though I was their own. Priya and I bonded as sisters, and Vish loved me.

The next two years of my life were peaceful. My father stayed away from me as did I from him. I never came out of my room when he was at home. I buried myself in my books, studying more than I needed to, preparing for exams that were months away. But I loved every minute that I spent with Vish. Life was good. As expected, I passed my pre-university exams with flying colours, which made everyone at home and in college proud of me.

I often remembered the lovely boarding school in the hills that I had visited a few years ago but never attended. I was now all of sixteen and told my Mom that I would love to pursue my higher education in the hills as a boarder. I was pleasantly surprised to note that Vish too did not create a fuss about it and, on the contrary, encouraged me to go and be a boarder for a few years and complete my graduation. His sister Priya had studied in Shillong while at university and had been very happy there. So, before I knew it, much to my delight, I became a full boarder at Lady Keane College in Shillong for my graduation.

I met Siddharth in Shillong. He was a day scholar at St Anthony's College. Siddharth was a lanky eighteen-year-old with glassy eyes and longish hair. He was neither as suave nor as affluent as Vish. He hailed from a modest middle-class family. His mother was the sole bread earner, as his father had left them to live with another woman in a bigger city when Siddharth was barely ten. He was an average student and was without that fire in the belly to achieve anything outstanding in life.

But Siddharth was a good human being. His non-imposing persona, laid-back attitude and pleasant demeanour were attributes that I liked about him. I enjoyed hanging out with him during the weekends when we were allowed trips to the local square. It was an easy friendship between us. We started writing to each other and, before I realized it, Siddharth became my best friend with whom I could talk to about anything and everything. I knew that Siddharth would never rat on me, no matter what.

The first term of college was almost over with most assignments handed in and exams completed. It was the end of term and we got busy with farewell parties for the seniors and secret midnight feasts.

The last night of boarding for that term was teary-eyed for all of us. We had our personal diaries filled with addresses and phone numbers of the seniors who were leaving college, and we all promised each other to remain friends for the rest of our lives.

The next morning our college was a madhouse. We waited with our hold-alls and packed bags for our families to collect us. Granny and Gramps arrived later in the morning and amidst teary goodbyes to friends and professors, I left for home after finishing the first term at Lady Keane College. Siddharth was standing outside the college gates waiting to say goodbye.

I asked Gramps if he could stop the car. When we stopped, I got out of the car and pressed a note with my house address as well as Granny's along with the phone numbers into Siddharth's palm. I told him that we would stay in touch till I returned for the next term.

I was happy to go to Guwahati. Returning home meant spending ample time with Nanny, meeting friends in my neighbourhood whom I grew up with and, most importantly, being with Vish.

As I looked out of the window at the streams and the mountains listening to my Walkman as we drove through the countryside, I was almost humming, 'Country road, take me home, to the place I belong; country road take me home …'

I must have dozed off while looking at the serene countryside, and opened my eyes to see city lights twinkling against the dark sky. I was home at last.

I could not wait to meet Vish the next morning. While I loved my new life at college in Shillong, I did miss Vish very much. I was glad to be back home because Vish was just a call and a drive away.

It so happened that one day during my holidays, Vish and I did not meet because he had gone to a football match. Mom was at work, and Nanny and the other house help had retired to their quarters for their afternoon siesta.

I had the headphones of the Walkman on while I lay in bed slowly dozing off to a blissful afternoon nap. I did not hear the car in the driveway. Maybe there was a knock on the door, but I did not hear it.

I woke up to see Dad sitting on my bed. He had a weird look on his face. His expression was unfathomable.

'Pari, what is it that you see in Vish? You need a man, a real man,' he said, his eyes now filled with lust as he undressed me.

I tried to escape and run out. But it was too late. His strength overpowered me, my screams for help were muffled, and it happened again.

I was left alone after that to deal with my wounds, physical and emotional. I dialled Vish's number, sobbing uncontrollably, but he wasn't there.

I realized that day that my father loathed me for some reason, otherwise, why would he do what he did to me? I was filled with anger and hatred for him. I was not going to let him go unpunished for what he had done to me, I decided. He was going to pay for it.

I rang Mom at her office and asked her to send me the car. I told her nothing about what had happened except that I needed to go and meet Vish. I showered and changed, and waited for the car to arrive.

On my way to Vish's, I thought that I could never bring myself to ever forgive Dad. Fear gripped me at the thought of having to face him again. The sky was overcast with grey clouds, and as I walked up the garden to Vish's house, I felt a few tiny raindrops on my skin. When I left home, Dad was still there, probably in his bedroom, as I saw his car outside in the driveway. I wondered if he knew that Vish was at a football match, and that I was home by myself that day, with Mom at work and the house help in their staff quarters as always in the afternoons after lunch. It surely wasn't a coincidence; I was convinced about that.

Heavy rains lashed on the window panes of Vish's house while I sat in his room waiting for him to return. Vish was surprised to see me when he walked in.

'What a pleasant surprise,' he said, planting a kiss on my lips, making himself comfortable next to me on the settee.

And then he looked at me, into my eyes, and knew instantly that something was not right.

'What's it, Pari? Are you upset that we didn't plan to meet today?' he asked, searching my eyes for a clue.

I wished it was that simple. I began sobbing and revealed to him all the traumatic upheaval I had experienced more than once, at my own home.

Vish was astonished and horrified. I could see the fury in his eyes. He cradled me in his arms and said, 'Pari, we are going to deal with this together. We need to talk with Mom and Dad. You are not alone. I am with you.'

I believed Vish. I knew that he loved me and had the gumption to face my father and, once and for all, put an end to this. Vish slowly lifted me from the settee, laid me down on his bed, and took off my shoes, while I sobbed, unable to stop the constant flow of my tears.

Then he left to talk to his parents. I looked at the grey sky outside, which felt like an extension of the gloom within me. I sat on Vish's bed looking out of the window, sipping a cup of tea, trying to clear my head while thinking of what to do next.

Vish was probably right. While I was filled with shame for what had happened to me, I owed it to the Chaudhuris to be outright and honest with them. Aunt and Uncle Chaudhuri were good people. They would understand my plight and would never look down on or undermine me for what happened.

Vish returned after almost an hour. He sat down next to me, planted a kiss on my forehead, and nestling me in his arms tenderly, said, 'Baby, I have spoken to Mum and Dad. Mum has called your mother. She will reach home around the same time as us.'

I was terrified by the thought of going home and having to see my father. I looked at Vish with pleading eyes, 'Can I please stay back at your place tonight? I am not going home.'

'Have faith in me, Pari. You will not run away from this. It is not your fault. Your father needs to give some answers. He is sick!' said Vish with a firmness in his voice, while gently holding my hand.

I stood up, wore my shoes and told Vish that I was ready to meet Aunt and Uncle Chaudhuri. The moment Vish's mother saw me, she rushed to me and embraced me with a long warm hug. Uncle Chaudhuri was in a contemplative mood and just about managed a smile as he said, 'Little one, the grief that you feel right now cannot be measured. No child ought to go through what you have. But you are our family, and almost a Chaudhuri. You are strong and you will no longer be browbeaten into accepting such morbid treatment by anyone. I shall see to it. Let's go.'

Getting up on his feet, Uncle Chaudhuri led us to his car.

None of us spoke a word in the car. Mom and Dad were both at home when we reached. There was tension in the air when we walked into the living room where they were waiting for us to arrive. Seeing my father on the chesterfield with the backdrop of thick silk brown curtains, sent a shiver down my spine.

Mom came to me and hugged me with Vish still not letting go of my hand. I could not hold back my tears. As one of the house help walked in with a jug of water and glasses on a tray, Mom asked if anyone would like tea or coffee. Everyone declined and said that the water was just fine.

Uncle Chaudhuri looked at my dad finally and said, 'What have you done? Have you lost your mind?'

There was pin-drop silence. I could see Vish's fists clenching, rage in Aunt Chaudhuri's eyes, disgust in Uncle Chaudhuri's face and sadness in Mom's eyes. The only person who was devoid of any expressions was my father. There was no remorse or apology from him. Even though the damage was done, and no apology could have made me feel any better, that was the least he could do.

Uncle Chaudhuri continued, 'You need to leave.'

That evoked a response from Dad, 'What do you mean?'

Uncle Chaudhuri repeated, 'You need to leave; move out of the house and stay away from the child.'

'Are you asking me to leave my own home? And who has given you the authority to ask me out of my home?' asked my father defiantly.

'I could help you pack, or we could call a few friends to help you pack, the more the merrier. The choice is yours,' said Uncle Chaudhuri.

As though Uncle Chaudhuri could not stop himself anymore, he said, 'For today I am merely asking you to leave instead of clobbering you to death. But don't try me. You will never ever come anywhere near this child again—is that clear?'

Mom was quiet throughout that entire showdown. Her gaze followed me as I got up and left with Vish. All the while my mind had questions: Why could Mom not shout at Dad like the way Uncle Chaudhuri did? How could she detach herself so easily from what was going on right under her nose, causing such grief to her daughter and only child?

When we were in my room, Vish hugged me. I could hear Vish's heartbeat as I put my head on his chest. I loved Vish, and I knew he did too, but I felt that he deserved better. I did not know at that moment what life had in store for me, how long it would take for me to heal or if I would ever heal.

I had no clue what transpired in the living room that evening after Vish and I left. But Dad was gone. I did not go down for dinner that night. Mom came to my room after the Chaudhuris had left. She came and lay down next to me on my bed.

She sobbed saying, 'I am sorry, love. I asked Papu to leave. I should have done this a long time ago.'

'Mom,' I said, 'you did not ask Papu to leave. Uncle Chaudhuri did.'

I knew I was being rude, and I was hurting Mom on purpose. But I felt she was spineless and incapable of either protecting or standing up for me when she had to. She had no business taking credit for what Uncle and Aunt Chaudhuri had done for me. Had she asked my father to leave three years ago, I would not have been hurt so cruelly … again. But all she did was send me away and brush everything else under the carpet.

Another thing that played on my mind was that I was no longer the Pari that Vish had fallen in love with. I had to let him go.

7

The next few days were a downward spiral for me. Vish tried hard, really hard, to reach out to me but I was unable to respond. I did not leave my room for days. My meals were brought up to my room, most of which went back untouched.

Nanny and Mom often coaxed me to go out for some fresh air in the garden or to have a meal in the dining room with Mom. But getting out of bed was a struggle—I had lost the appetite for food, happiness, love and life—I was incapable of emoting in any manner to anyone or anything.

I lost weight and fell ill. My menstruation cycle went for a toss. When friends rang, including my besties, Rose and Siddharth, I did not take or return their calls. Gradually, the calls became fewer, as did Vish's visits.

Three months had gone by since the end of my first term and it was finally time for the big day: the results were announced. Gramps and Granny had gone to my college to get my report card. They rang Mom and me to say that I cleared my exams with flying colours, with a distinction and topped the college in several subjects. They said that they would come down with my report card and spend the weekend with us.

Mom pleaded with me that day to get out of my jammies and my room, as it was a day of celebration for my efforts and hard work, that too despite all the disruptions in my life and the emotional havoc that I had gone through.

Mom said to me, 'You have done it before, and you can do it now. It's a new day, a new beginning. You have a bright future ahead of you. Don't let the past drag you down, Pari. Let go of the pain. I love you, my darling, and will hold your hand along the way. Just let me. That's all I ask for.'

I nodded and could feel tears pushing their way through my eyes. I felt a lump in my throat. I felt something after many many days. Finally, I could emote, and cry at the joy of my success and the assurance that I felt listening to Mom's words.

Mom drew the curtains, tied them back and opened the windows allowing the golden sunlight and the fragrant morning breeze into my room. She gave me a long warm hug as I got out of bed. I dragged myself to the bathroom and looked at myself in the mirror. I had lost so much weight, my eyes had sunk in and looked hollow, my hair had not been washed for days and had lost its sheen, and my skin no longer looked radiant as it used to. I looked like a zombie.

I stayed under the shower for a long time washing my hair and body with my favourite shampoo and soap that smelt nice. The warm shower was invigorating and prompted me to take the next baby steps to seem normal, which was to look for something decent in my wardrobe to wear that day instead of slipping back into another pair of pyjamas like I did the last few days.

I dressed in a cream lacy top and a pair of black jeans, sat in front of my dresser, and brushed my long hair. Despite all the effort, I felt bitter and thought that a ghost stared back at me in the mirror.

I wore my flip-flops and walked down the stairs into the dining hall after a month and a half. I could hear the phone ringing throughout the morning. Everyone was calling to congratulate me. Nanny and Mom kept all the messages for me and thanked everyone on my behalf, promising that I would return their calls once I was better. The house help and Nanny were hustling and bustling around me—relieved and delighted to finally see me sitting at the dining table.

When Vish visited, he was pleasantly surprised to see me downstairs and not in my bedroom. I noticed after several days how handsome Vish was even though he looked tired, as if he had not slept for days. I melted when he flashed his killer smile and opened his arms to me.

Just as I thought that I would snatch a few minutes with Vish, Gramps and Granny arrived. I was so glad to see them. Gramps was over the moon and waved the report card in glee even before he could get out of the car. After all the greetings and hugs, I excused myself, and asked Vish to come upstairs with me.

I was tired and my head was swooning. I needed to sit down for a while without having to continue with polite conversations and my room was the best retreat. Vish followed me as I walked up. The moment we were in my room, Vish lifted me up in his arms and kissed me. I was not ready for it yet. I froze. I loved Vish and wanted the comfort of his presence, but I surely wasn't ready for such intimacy. I needed time.

'I am tired, Vish,' I said, pulling away from him.

Vish gently put me down on the sofa and sat down next to me maintaining a distance. He looked confused and asked me, 'Pari, what is it that you want from me? What is it that I can do to make things better? I am totally lost here.'

'Time,' I said, 'I need time. I need time to heal. I have to be able to love myself again to love you, Vish,' I continued.

'What do you mean, Pari? Do you not love me anymore?' he asked.

'I do, Vish, I do love you. But I am not the Pari you fell in love with Vish. We both need time for you to know and love the person that I am now,' I answered.

I knew that Vish wanted to hear none of the things that I was telling him. It was emotionally draining for me to see the hurt in Vish's eyes. But at that moment, I knew that I was doing the right thing.

I was feeling ill once again. I could feel the bile rising up my throat. I went to the bathroom and thought that I'd throw up. But I didn't. Maybe I needed some food or maybe I was just stressed out. The feeling of nausea persisted even after I lay down for a while. I rang the bell next to my bedside which would get somebody from the kitchen up to my room. Nanny came up and asked me if I needed anything.

Once I told her that I felt pukish but couldn't retch out anything, she came back with a glass of saline water which she asked me to drink up. I did as I was told and even before I could get through half the glass, I had my head over the wash basin puking my guts out. I felt better. Nanny always came up with home remedies that could easily give the best pharmaceuticals a run for their money.

I must have slept for a long time after that because my room was in total darkness when I opened my eyes again. I woke up with a knock on my door. It was Granny. I switched on my bedside lamp and asked Granny to switch on the top light in the room.

Granny looked at me, her forehead creasing into a frown, 'Pari, you don't look very well. It is all right if you don't wish to join us for dinner. I could ask Moses to send a tray up to your room.'

I told her that I wanted to go down for dinner and catch up with both Gramps and her.

'Up on your feet then. Dinner is about to be served. You can have a nightcap with us after dinner. Sixteen is the right age to start off on your first drink. It's celebration time after all,' she said with a chuckle and a cheerfulness in her voice. I washed my face, brushed my hair, and went downstairs to look for Gramps to see if I could just spend a few minutes with him alone before dinner. He was so excited about my grades when he arrived that afternoon, almost as though it was not I but he who had earned them. I found Gramps sitting in the garden with his drink. There was a chill in the air. His face broke into a smile when he saw me, and he got up to give me his bear hug.

Neither Granny not Gramps asked me about my father. Family and friends, apart from the Chaudhuris, knew that Mom and Dad had fallen out and so my father left home. But I wasn't sure if Granny and Gramps knew more. I pushed any thoughts of my father away.

While at dinner, we talked about the potential subjects I could take up next term. Gramps gave me his two pennies worth and said that I had a good head for numbers, so I should go with economics and mathematics. The evening ended on a peaceful and happy note. I kissed Mom and my grandparents good night and left for my room. Things were looking up slowly once again. I had all the people I loved under one roof that night and I had someone who would give his right arm for me as a boyfriend. With positive and happy thoughts in my mind after many days, I drifted off into slumber.

It was probably past midnight. I was restless suddenly. I felt queasy. I switched on my bedside lamp. I could feel the bile rising. I rushed to the bathroom and vomited the entire contents of my stomach.

I brushed my teeth and went back to bed. Someone knocked on my door. It was early morning. The room was no longer dark. I walked up to the door to unbolt it. It was Nanny bringing me tea, I thought. But when I opened the door, Vish was standing there in his jeans and a white T-shirt and floaters, a bouquet of flowers in his hand. It was not early morning. It was well past 10 o'clock. I overslept and forgot that I had a date with Vish. I headed to Mom's room to borrow a dress from her wardrobe. But Mom had left for work. Her briefcase was gone. Nevertheless, I helped myself to a yellow knee-length dress of hers which I had been eyeing for a long time. That day I decided to use the kohl and the gloss that had been lying unused on my dressing table for months.

I went down dolled up and ready for my date with Vish. Nanny had carried a cup of hot chocolate for me upstairs. I had a few sips of it, the taste of cocoa lingering in my mouth as I walked towards Vish who was sitting with Gramps in the living room.

Courteous as always, Vish opened the door for me to get into the car and then got behind the wheel himself. We drove out to see Vish's surprise for me. Among friends and family, a massive cake on a trolley, with unlit candles, was wheeled in—it was Vish's twenty-fifth, and I had forgotten all about it. How could I have!

Later during the party, I apologized to Vish over a hundred times for forgetting his birthday. But Vish just looked into my eyes and said that I was with him on his special day and that was the best gift that he could have received. I could feel his profound love for me, and that magical moment was most precious. Vish dropped me home before six.

That evening, I rang Siddharth, whose calls I had not returned in almost two months. I did not tell him about the traumatic incidents at home that had led me to shut myself off from the rest of the world. I lied to him and said that I had typhoid instead. I told him about Vish for the first time. Siddharth sounded genuinely happy to hear from me. He told me he would be visiting Guwahati for an interview and I told him that he was welcome to stay at home with us when in town.

Granny and Gramps, in the meanwhile, went back home. I was meeting Vish almost every day, getting closer and more comfortable with him each passing day.

While my emotional recovery moved steadily, I could not say the same about my physical state. I was often sluggish, troubled by certain smells, and continued to suffer from nausea. The stress that I had gone through had upset my regular flow of periods and that added to my mood swings.

Vish and Mom came with me to drop me to my college on the first day of the second term. There was a little party arranged by the seniors to welcome us back for the second term.

That evening, after the fresher's party, I threw up almost every thing I ingested, including water.

Studies and lessons were in full swing at college. But despite me enjoying classes, my condition worsened in the following week. I just could not hold anything in my stomach.

When I spoke to Mom about it over a call, she fixed an appointment with Dr Mason for the weekend. Guwahati was just about a three-hour drive from Shillong. Vish offered to take me to her clinic as Mom had meetings that she was unable to cancel at such short notice.

Vish collected me the next morning from my college and drove me to Guwahati to visit Dr Mason. I informed Nanny that Siddharth would arrive a little after mid-day for an interview—and that she should put him up in the bedroom downstairs, and make him feel at home till I returned.

At the clinic, Dr Mason greeted me warmly with her cheerful smile and said, 'What's up young lady? Heard you were sick after a party. Too much to drink?'

'Oh no, Dr Mason,' I said. 'No alcohol. It could be the fried snacks, though, I had just nibbled on some. I've been sick in my stomach for the last couple of months I'd say. Even the food that I love seems to be nauseating.'

'You look pale, Pari,' she said, beginning to scribble on her notepad. 'Hmm, no alcohol, I've heard that before.'

She directed the nurse to take my temperature. And after a couple of more questions, especially about my menstrual cycle, directed me to some more tests. Scribbling down everything on her notepad, she said, 'I am giving you some antacids till we get your test results. It could be jaundice. We don't want to take any chances,' she said.

I took the prescription and went out with the nurse after bidding Dr Mason goodbye. I was taken to another room for the tests. Vish dropped me home around half past eleven and promised to return by three in the afternoon to meet Siddharth.

Nanny was surprised to see me back home so early. She asked me about my visit to Dr Mason and I quickly briefed her, and ran upstairs to my bathroom. I threw up the antacid that I drank a couple of hours ago. I was sure that I had jaundice as suspected by Dr Mason. Siddharth arrived around 2 p.m. I was so glad to see him. I ran up to him and gave him a hug. As we sat chatting in the living room, I asked him, 'Where's your interview at tomorrow?'

'At the Public Works Department office. They have a vacancy in their accounts division. I had sent them my résumé. They are looking for a trainee on probation who, based on performance, will be confirmed as an accounts officer after six months,' he explained.

'How's the new term in college? Are you enjoying it?' he asked.

Before I could answer, I heard the doorbell. Vish had arrived. I thought I had heard his car driving in.

Vish came into the living room, nodded at Siddharth with his boyish grin, and looked at me, 'You feeling better, babe?' he asked.

He gave me a peck on my cheek. Vish then introduced himself to Siddharth.

'Vish Chaudhuri,' he said. 'Welcome home.'

Siddharth shook Vish's hand and said, 'Siddharth Das. Pleased to meet you, Vish. I've heard such good things about you from Indrani.'

Everyone in Shillong, including Siddharth, called me Indrani.

After feasting on sandwiches and lemonade, the boys agreed to meet at six with a promise that Vish would show Siddharth around town.

I went back to chatting with Siddharth about Shillong and our common friends. I told him about the fresher's party and how I was asked to parade with a peacock's tail clipped to my backside. Getting ragged in the second term of college was no doubt a bit out of sorts, but back then those were the norms. He burst out laughing. It was indeed good to see Siddharth.

The telephone rang, and I picked it up. It was Dr Mason at the other end.

'Hello. Dr Mason here. Can I speak with your mother, please?' she said.

'Dr Mason, this is Pari here. Mom is at the office. Shall I ask her to ring you?' I answered.

'Pari, you need to come to my clinic with your mother as soon as you speak to her,' she sounded serious.

'Do I have jaundice, Dr Mason?' I asked, worried that if I did, I'd be homebound for a while at least, which was definitely not my plan.

'We'll talk when you come. I have patients waiting. I need to go now. Make that call to your mother and get here soon,' she said and hung up.

I rang Mom immediately. She said that she was about to leave from work. I told her about my visit to Dr Mason in the morning and that the doctor wanted us to be at her clinic as soon as possible. Mom said, 'I'll be home in twenty. Come out when you hear the car.

We'll leave right away.' She hung up after that. I told Siddharth that I needed to visit the doctor with Mom.

On the way to Dr Mason's, I told Mom about Siddharth. I asked if he was not chosen for the job, would she care to hire him? I was making a pitch for Siddharth, talking about his loyalty and modest upbringing, telling her he'd be a good hand at her office, one she could rely on.

'Pari, you don't just employ people because they are your friends. There must be a demand before the supply, basic law of economics,' she said. I could not figure out whether the answer was a yes or a no. When Mom and I walked into Dr Mason's clinic, the doctor had a grave expression on her face. Mom looked at Dr Mason, worried. I could hear the nervousness in her voice as she said, 'Doc, you wanted to see us. Pari said that she may have jaundice. Is she all right?'

'Pari is pregnant. Her urine has tested positive for pregnancy,' Dr Mason announced.

I thought to myself: Has Dr Mason lost her mind?

'Mom, Vish and I haven't done it, you know. How can I be pregnant?'

Mom was silent. She looked as pale as a ghost. And then the penny dropped seeing the blood suddenly draining off Mom's face. Dr Mason's face was blurred, and everything went dark.

That evening my thoughts were in a disarray. On the way back home from Dr Mason's clinic, Mom looked as though she was in a state of shock as much as I was.

At home, we went into our own bedrooms confused, disoriented and beset by our fears. I did not know if Mom told Nanny anything at all but when Nanny came into my room that evening with the dinner tray, she said, 'Pari, sometimes things just happen. This will pass too.'

I asked her to take the tray back. Food was the last thing on my mind. I was sixteen and pregnant—what and how was I going to tell Vish? I would probably be ostracized by my friends for the rest of my life, I thought.

I was unable to sleep the entire night as the events of the last couple of years raced through my mind—the good, bad, and the ugly.

When I saw the first streak of daylight entering my room, I got out of bed and drew the curtains back, opening the window to allow the morning freshness in. I stood near the window and looked at the horizon where the orange sun was slowly rising while the light was dimming out from my life.

After I had regained consciousness at Dr Mason's the day before, she had said that I needed to return for a sonography to determine the age of the foetus, and get further tests done, if required. She also asked us to let her know whether we wished to terminate the pregnancy.

Mom's reply was an immediate affirmative, and she asked Dr Mason to give us all the necessary information and confirm a date for the same when we returned the next day. Mom and I, without speaking to each other, had decided that termination was the only option. The only difference was that Mom announced her decision to Dr Mason, whereas I was silent.

The next day, I woke up early and went downstairs to find Siddharth. I needed to speak to him; I had to let everything out of me. There was a slight chill in the autumn air. As we sat sipping our tea, I told him everything that had happened. I told him about how nervous I was about breaking the news to Vish and my decision to terminate the pregnancy. Siddharth listened quietly as I broke down in front of him. 'I am really really sorry for all that you have gone through. Termination is a good decision, the only choice that you have,' he said, his usually glazed eyes revealing emotions.

He continued, 'Don't get me wrong. Vish loves you. But if I were you, I wouldn't talk about the pregnancy to him.'

'Oh, but I can't not tell Vish!' I exclaimed. 'He knows that it's not my fault, he'd understand.'

'What is it that you would achieve by telling him when you are terminating it anyway? You've got a good thing going with Vish, don't mess it up. Look, that's what I think, but at the end of the day, it's your call,' Siddharth said and ended the conversation abruptly.

He was disturbed, I could see that. I also realized that what he said made complete sense. But I did not know what to do.

It was probably unthoughtful of me to have burdened Siddharth with my problems just before his job interview that day. But I had lost the ability to think anymore.

Mom held my hand throughout the journey, asking me not to be afraid. 'It will be sorted, my dear. I cannot imagine the pain that you must be going through. But right now, we have to get over this hurdle and I want you to be strong for that,' she said, squeezing my hand.

The sonography gave me the first glimpse of the life growing inside me, which I had been totally unaware of in the last few months. It was a hazy vision of a small tadpole with a loud heartbeat that I could see and hear on the machine for the first time in my life.

Mom was dumbfounded. She stared into the monitor that showed the pulsating foetus. How was Mom, or for that matter any woman, meant to feel or react to a situation like that? Was she angry with me? Or was she just disgusted with the turn of events?

All these thoughts crossed my mind as we drove to Dr Mason's clinic with the reports.

Dr Mason studied the reports and then put her hands up in the air and said, 'Can't be done. She is fourteen weeks pregnant. It's too late.'

'Pari,' she said, looking at me, 'we cannot abort. You have to go through the full term. Do you understand?' I didn't understand, I thought. I didn't want to understand.

'We can look at giving up the baby for adoption. Another six months, that's all,' she put her hand on mine across the table, her eyes softening.

It was no doubt a difficult task for her to break the bad news to us—one worse than the other on two consecutive days.

Dr Mason looked at Mom, 'You have to get her out of town in a month's time or earlier, the sooner the better, before she shows.'

Mom nodded, thanked Dr Mason, took my hand, and got up leading me out of her chamber.

I was in a daze wondering what it was that I had done to deserve this. What was I going to do? Did Dr Mason just say that I had to give birth? Was she serious?

I sat in the car and looked out of the window. I saw people walking on the pavement; people in cars, some driving, some mere passengers; people on bikes, some riding and some on the pillion. Everybody seemed to know what they were doing, everybody seemed to have a direction and purpose, except me.

When we returned home, Siddharth was not back from his interview, but Vish was waiting in the living room, sipping coffee.

A smile broke on his face when he saw me. But my heart broke into pieces when I saw him.

He walked up to Mom and gave her a hug and then he looked at me, 'You're not jaundiced, are you?'

Mom looked at me too.

'No, Vish, I am not jaundiced. I'm pregnant,' I said.

I tried to look into Vish's eyes, but he avoided my gaze. His shoulders dropped. Mom excused herself, leaving us alone standing in the middle of the large living room. Had it been any other day, Vish would have used that opportunity to give me a passionate hug or a kiss. But that day, he just stood there with his eyes lowered. Discomfited and awkward perhaps best described Vish at that moment. Stepping closer to him, I embraced him and sighed wearily, 'I'm sorry.'

He put his arms around me and murmured, 'I need to clear my head, Pari.'

We stood there in a tight embrace as time stood still. There was a hush outside. All I could hear were our hearts beating loudly.

As Vish slowly loosened his arms, I stepped back. I looked into his deep green eyes brimming with tears as I said, 'I love you, Vish.'

'Me too.' His voice faltered.

There was a long pause.

'And I always will. Goodbye, Pari,' he said, kissing my forehead.

He walked towards the door as I stood watching him get out of sight. He did not look back. Vish was gone ... forever.

I walked upstairs to my room. I lay down on my bed and stared up at the ceiling. I felt a strange emptiness inside me.

What was I supposed to do the next day—go back to Shillong, to college? Go somewhere else? Stay home?

I heard the doorbell ring. I shut my eyes, exhausted.

Nanny knocked on my door and walked in with tea and announced that Siddharth was home. As I slowly sipped my tea, I prepared myself to meet Siddharth.

It was past three. Mom and I did not have lunch. I went to Mom's room and knocked on her door. When she answered, I went in and saw her head lowered over a sheaf of papers on her desk.

'Mom, Vish is gone.'

Her wide despairing eyes filled up with tears as she looked at me. 'I know,' she said, the tears spilling onto the papers on her desk. 'Mom, can I sleep in your room tonight?'

'Of course, you can. Tonight and whenever you want to,' she said, wiping her tears with the back of her hand.

'Siddharth is back. I'll check on him. Mom, come and join us when you're done,' I said, realizing that she needed me as much as I needed her in this strange situation. I could see her buckling under grief. I needed to be strong for her and for myself.

I went down looking for Siddharth, leaving Mom to regain her composure. I was tempted to give her a hug and comfort her, but I did not. Mom was not the kind of person who would have wanted anybody to see her vulnerable side, not even her own daughter.

Siddharth entered the living room in a pair of shorts and a T-shirt, waved his hand when he saw me, and said, 'Hi, what did the doctor say?'

'Hi, how was your interview?' I asked, without replying to his question.

'Good, I think. They'll let me know in a month's time.' He sounded unsure.

'What did your doctor say? Has she given a date?' he asked again.

'Nope, can't be done. It's too late.'

'What do you mean? So, what now?' he probed, looking confused.

'I have to carry the baby to full term,' I said, feeling totally helpless even though I put up a brave front.

'What? Full term?' he exclaimed.

I nodded as he looked at me perturbed.

'You can't!'

'Siddharth, I have to. I don't have a choice. I don't know how I am going to go through with this, but I have to.'

He looked at me thoughtfully while I sipped my tea but said nothing.

'Would you like me to leave tomorrow?' asked Siddharth. 'You may want to sort things out with your family. I could stay back for a couple of more days if you want me to, though.'

Then he asked suddenly, 'When's Vish coming?'

'Vish was here and I told him. He's gone! I don't think he's coming back soon,' I said, feeling a lump in my throat.

Later, after dinner, I decided to sleep early. Mom looked at me with concern and said, 'You are sleeping in my room tonight. Get an early night dear. Don't wait up for me.'

'Goodnight, Mom,' I said, giving her a kiss on her cheek.

That night, as I drifted off to sleep, the last thought that flashed across my mind was of Vish's eyes and smile.

It was still dark when I woke up. Someone was on my bed … again. I screamed and jumped out of bed, and then I heard Mom's voice. 'It is all right, Pari. You had a bad dream.'

The lights came on. Mom held me and led me back to bed. I had forgotten that I was in Mom's room. I looked at the clock on the wall. It was past 3 a.m.

Mom put her arm around me after turning off the lights and getting into bed.

I was a nervous wreck. Everything in my life had fallen apart beyond repair. Tears were spilling out of my eyes. I was unable to cope anymore.

Mom was not in bed when I woke up again. I slid out of bed and went to my room. I felt a vacuum in my heart. I wondered once again what I was meant to do that day. I was in a daze.

I stood under the shower, becoming more aware of myself as the water sprinkled on my skin. I stood in front of the mirror after the shower. I turned sideways and looked at my reflection as I touched my stomach. Maybe there was a slight bump that was visible.

I changed and went downstairs to look for Siddharth and Mom. They were already at the breakfast table and they smiled at me as I walked in.

'Good morning, dear. Didn't wake you up. You needed the rest,' said Mom, sounding more cheerful than she had in the last couple of days.

'Good morning, Mom. Morning, Siddharth,' I said, pulling out a chair to sit down.

Moses came out of the kitchen and asked me what I'd like for breakfast.

'Just a cup of coffee and cornflakes please,' I said.

'Pari, Siddharth and I stayed up after dinner and talked. Let's go into the lounge and speak after breakfast,' Mom said, putting down her glass of orange juice.

Mom definitely sounded better than she had the previous day, almost as though she had found a solution to the mess in our lives. Something was brewing! I could smell it!

Mom led the conversation in the living room, 'Pari, you can go to college, lead a normal life and have the baby here itself. It doesn't need to be a secret. We can legitimize this whole thing.'

I thought my mother had lost her mind. With all that was happening in our lives, I wouldn't have been surprised if she did. 'Mom, how can we legitimize this?' I asked, annoyed with her.

Siddharth spoke, 'Indrani, the baby could be mine. I will give the baby my name. We can get married once you are eighteen, in a couple of years.'

'Siddharth, are you out of your mind? I don't want to get married to you in a couple of years, or ever! I don't want you to give your name to the baby! Have you both gone crazy?' I screamed, unable to control my voice or my anger at the ridiculous suggestions that Mom and Siddharth were making.

'Pari, please calm down,' said Mom, sounding irritable. 'Do you have a better plan? Tell us, and we'll go with what you say.'

Siddharth, on the other hand, sounded more composed. 'Indrani, two years is far away. We don't have to marry two years later when you turn eighteen, or ever. You are my friend and that has not changed just because you are pregnant. I cannot turn a blind eye and walk out, leaving you and your mother to deal with this now that I know.'

He looked at me and paused, probably expecting me to say something, and then continued, 'I will leave for Shillong today. I will talk to Maa, Baby and Shantu about you and that it all happened four months ago when you were just leaving after the end of your first term in college. They already know of you and, often, Shantu and Baby teased me about you.'

Shantu and Baby were Siddharth's siblings.

'Maa may not approve of the manner in which things have happened, but she will accept. She may blow my head off and blame me for it but she will love you and care for you once she gets to know you,' he continued with confidence.

I had never heard Siddharth sound so sure of himself. 'Call me tomorrow and let me know what you decide. If you agree, I will return with them on Saturday, so we can all meet,' he added, with a smile.

I cried listening to Siddharth because I knew that everything Siddharth had said was so selfless and made sense. I cried because

Siddharth offered me his support when I needed it the most. I cried because I did not want any of this from Siddharth. I cried because it was Vish who should have said all the things that Siddharth did, but he didn't.

I cried because I loved Vish and not Siddharth. I cried because life was so unfair!

'Pari, Siddharth is God-sent. He has come into our lives as your saviour,' Mom said, putting her hand over mine.

Mom and Siddharth were no longer speaking to me. They were planning my life in front of me as though I didn't exist. Clearly, my feelings at that moment were inconsequential.

I almost ran out of the room instead of walking. I was unable to deal with everything that was going on anymore. I realized that the story of my life was being scripted by my mother and my best-friend.

As Siddharth was about to leave, he looked into my eyes, held my face in his hands and said, 'I know that you have never thought me quite good enough for an equal. I know that I am not the knight in shining armour that you deserve. But I will do everything I can to give you the happiness that you deserve.'

I missed college for the next couple of days. I continued to sleep in Mom's room every night. Mom returned to work soon. I wondered what she felt when she met Dad at work and how she coped with it. She never spoke about Dad at home.

Siddharth came with his Maa on Saturday. The families met and it was decided that Siddharth would come back the week after, with all his belongings, and live with Mom and me. I was to continue college privately and the story to be told in town was that we were having a baby out of wedlock, but would register our marriage the day I turned eighteen.

My morning sickness had stopped gradually. Siddharth did not get the job that he had interviewed for. Mom helped him to set up a bakery. The three of us got into a routine, with me heading off for private lessons every day, Mom going to work and Siddharth working hard to fructify his bakery project. During weekdays, we met in the evenings at home for dinner and retired to our own rooms every night. One of the guest bedrooms now had all of Siddharth's belongings and it became his room.

Vish and his friends stopped speaking to me, so did Priya, except for a nod or a slight smile if we bumped into each other.

The dirty secret I carried with me was known to very few: just my mother's brother, Siddharth, Mom, Nanny, Vish. Even my grandparents were kept in the dark.

My friends thought that it was cool to be an unwed mother. But their parents did not feel the same. I was the girl with loose morals, to have become pregnant before marriage, as far as they were concerned. The men in my family, particularly my uncles, considered it scandalous. My aunts gossiped. But Gramps and Granny were supportive.

As the days passed, I gradually returned to my college books and focused on the well-being of the life growing inside me. Vish receded into the background, and I barely ever thought about him anymore.

By the time I was in my eighth month, I started feeling heavy and looked massive. My back often hurt with the growing weight of the baby in my womb.

Siddharth went with me for the doctor's appointments, listened carefully to the advice given and ensured that I religiously adhered to it. Mom gradually started taking a back seat as Siddharth took charge of my affairs.

I was in my last month. The college winter vacation had started.

On my visit to the doctor, I was told that I would deliver within the next fortnight.

A week later, my water broke. I was rushed to the nursing home that was nearby. Mom had already booked a room there.

I was taken to the labour room as soon as I reached and injected with saline to induce labour pain. But none came even after being on the drip for six hours. There was no water in my womb. I had no pain. Doctors announced that I needed a caesarean section to get the baby out.

I was wheeled into the operating theatre (OT) while Mom, Siddharth and my grandparents waited outside.

To the sixteen-year-old me, the OT looked menacing with cylinders, bright lights and equipment of all sorts that I had only seen in movies. I was terrified.

There was a flurry of activity in the OT as doctors and nurses in their green aprons, rubber hand gloves and masks prepared for the surgery.

I was made to lie down on a bed below a massive light, which looked down on me dauntingly. Dr Mason held my hand as the anaesthetist injected a liquid into the drip bag that was affixed to my arm. Dr Mason smiled at me and asked me to count to ten. Before I got to three, I was knocked out.

And then, my Sheena came into this world …

PART 3

2015

8

In the days leading up to my going to prison, I was in a daze. Things were happening around me and I had no idea how to make any sense of it. It was my lawyer Gunjan who first mentioned the possibility of me having to do some prison time. She said it would last a week, at most.

'We are doing everything possible to make sure this doesn't happen. But it looks inevitable,' she said. I heard the words, yet to understand completely what was going on.

On 7 September, I was handed over to judicial custody. After court, I was taken for the mandatory medical check-up. But, in reality, there are no check-ups—the accused are only made to sign a form when they are taken for a routine check every twenty-four hours to a government hospital. I could have been genuinely sick but no one bothered to check at all.

That evening, I was taken to Byculla Undertrial Jail. The white jeep that used to take me to court was no longer my transport from this day onwards. A blue truck with mesh on the windows was brought out to take me to prison. The cops from Khar police station were seated with me in the truck. It was late in the evening, after the prison bandi (lockdown) that happened at 6 p.m. every day. There were TV channel vehicles and photographers, scrambling to capture every tiny detail of my entry into prison. I was dressed in a pista-green salwar kameez with a dupatta.

My first memory of prison is the small door that takes you in. My head was covered with the dupatta as I entered. Prisoners have to always stoop when they walk in through that door—in a way, you have to bow your head to the supreme law of the land when you walk into jail. There was a bevy of cops inside. Perhaps, the cops accompanying me noticed how I had stiffened; a constable next to me reassuringly said, '*Dariye matt, kuch nahi hoga* (Don't worry, nothing will happen).'

I was taken straight to the office to sign documents. And from there, I was taken to the jharti (frisking) room. It was probably the most traumatizing part of being in prison.

'Take off your pants,' said the officer.

I took off my pants. 'Your knickers, too,' she said.

The first time you are taken to prison, you are stripped completely naked. The Police Inspector—PI—from Khar station was there, along with a jailer and female constable. I was in the company of an all-women team. And still, this felt like I was being stripped of my dignity, one piece of clothing at a time. It was scary.

They thoroughly checked my entire body for bruise marks. It was done to ensure that I wasn't assaulted at the police station. If there was an injury, they wouldn't have accepted me in the prison, as later this could become a legal issue for the prison authorities. The Khar cop was made to step out before they asked me, 'Did they hit you in prison?'

They hadn't. And I said so truthfully.

I was taken inside the frisking room again. During the second round of checking, they again pulled down my salwar to check for cash, drugs, or any other items. I had been told prior to coming to the station that I couldn't carry cash. Prisoners habitually bring in titbits of personal belongings hidden in their salwar. Frankly, the prison has everything—from kajal to hair dye, so one does not need to bring anything from outside. In the years to come, my hair dye would become a special topic of discussion.

Thankfully, over the years, I regained my sense of humour and would even laugh with my lawyer about it. 'Very soon, it would be in the supplementary chargesheet,' I'd tell her.

After all, my chargesheet did have the accusation that I was an ambitious woman. Why should my jet-black hair and some hair dye product lose out on its moment of fame?

And then I stepped into the main prison complex.

Byculla Jail is a two-floor complex. It has two units—Circle-1 and Circle-2. In September 2015, when I went in, the prison wasn't very crowded. Circle-2 housed pregnant women and women with young children—it is colloquially called the 'bachcha barrack'. Women are allowed to keep their children with them till they are seven years old. There are two barracks within Circle-2. Contrary to what one assumes about prison, the Byculla Jail is actually very well maintained. It has a beautiful garden, with flowers and beautiful plants.

I was put in Circle-1. This unit is where they keep regular female prisoners, and is much bigger—it has six barracks. On the first floor of the prison are four big barracks that function as common dorms. I was assigned to a barrack on the ground floor. The barracks are airy, with lots of fans to keep the inside cool. There are clean bathrooms that are washed by the inmates on duty, twice a day.

On the day I entered prison, the barracks downstairs were almost empty. Other than me, there were only two more people. I hadn't eaten anything that day. The prison constable, Wasima, was on duty that evening. She came to me and asked, '*Aapne khana khaya? Aap thoda doodh piyengi?* (Have you eaten? Will you have some milk?)'

I remember, I foolishly blurted out, '*Main raat ko doodh nahin peeti hoon.* (I don't have milk at night.)'

I was offered roti sabzi and some watery dal. When I was at Khar station, home-cooked meals stopped coming to me after the second day itself. My food came from restaurants, from biryanis to sandwiches to dosas. Even though I was not used to this food, by the time it arrived, I was somehow resigned to my fate. Or perhaps, I was really hungry. I didn't care what was in front of me. I simply ate. In a way, I was relieved to be in prison. At least, I was no longer cooped up in a tiny guard room. I liked the space. A strange sense of freedom took over me, even though the fear of what was going to happen to me stayed in my system.

For the uninitiated, prison is what they show in the movies. And so, I was fearful of what fate had in store for me. I didn't get much sleep that night. The tossing and turning continued through the night. Wasima was placed at the gate of the barrack. I was later given to understand that officials were instructed to keep a suicide watch on me. For inmates like me, the shift from a posh Worli apartment to prison is what rock bottom feels like. Add to it the high-profile nature of the case, along with the media attention—prison officials worry about the toll this may take on an inmate's mind.

I still remember the first time when I walked into the bathroom. I used the western toilet and realized there was no flush. No jet spray either. I came out and asked another inmate, Savitri [name changed], who was the designated kaamwali of that barrack, '*Flush kahan hai?* (Where is the flush?)'

She smiled kindly and told me, '*Nahin, didi. Aapko bucket se paani daalna padega.* (No, didi. You will have to use a bucket of water.)'

It might seem minor, but these things do add to the shock. In my life before prison, even as a toddler, I knew that when one turns on a tap water will flow out, and that this was something one does not have to think about as such. The concept of filling the bucket with water and using it was alien to me. I didn't even have buckets at home. As these thoughts swirled in my mind, I took the bucket, filled water in it, and used it to flush the toilet.

I spoke to Savitri at one point in the night, when we were both not getting any sleep. She, too, was being tried for a murder case—the murder of her stepmother—and had been in prison for four years at that time. Her father and husband were in prison, too. After serving so much time, she was eventually acquitted in 2017. It is a sad truth of the Indian legal system that people suffer for years in undertrial prisons only to get acquitted in the end. Savitri had two little girls who were with her in-laws. After she came to prison, her family simply abandoned her. They didn't send her money, so she had to work in prison to cover her basic needs. She was paid 1600 rupees a month for working as a kaamwali. Her grouse was the same as most women in that prison—her husband had a steady flow of cash coming from the family while she was simply left to fend for herself. The world is harsher for women in every strata of society even inside a jail.

After much tossing and turning, I slept for a couple of hours. By the time I had got to my assigned barrack on the first day, it was evening. Next morning, I got a better view of the prison. As I looked around, I saw a team of officers waiting to talk to me. I was handed a bottle-green saree to wear.

When a female prisoner is accused of murder under Section 302 of the IPC, she has to drape a green saree over her regular clothing on the occasions when she has to step out of the jail circle for mulaqats, which are meetings with family or lawyers, or to go to the canteen or the dispensary, a practice that has continued since the British era. I later understood that the colour coding was perhaps designed to allow prisoners to get a sense of the severity of the charges. The chances of a murder-accused getting bail are very low. In a way, the saree signifies that the inmate has to stay for much longer, a symbol that the prison has given them shelter. The spirit of it might come from a pure place but my immediate thought was: Everyone will think I am a murderer. Of course, I hadn't realized then that everyone in the world outside the prison walls had already labelled me as one.

At first, I was nervous and anxious when I was told that I had to wear that saree. The guard sympathetically said, '*Aapko aadat par jayegi* (You will get used to it).' I draped the saree on top of what I was wearing. Every time I had to go for Monday morning inspection, office visits or mulaqats, I would wrap that green saree around me.

Superintendent Chandramani Indulkar met me in the office. It was my first time meeting him.

'*Aap kab aaye* (When did you arrive)?' he asked me.

'*Kal raat* (Last night),' I said.

'*Kya kalam hain aap pe?* (What are the charges against you?)' he asked.

Of course, he knew the criminal sections I was charged under. The whole country did. But it is a part of the procedure, where prisoners give their details. I was asked for contact numbers, and I gave Peter's.

With these formalities out of the way, I was formally entered into the prison system of the Byculla Undertrial Jail as prisoner number 1468.

My lawyer, Gunjan, came to meet me at around 10 a.m.

'What do you need?' she asked me.

I looked at her, my eyes still hopeful, and said, 'When am I getting out?'

She stayed quiet.

I continued, 'I have two sets of clothes. If I am going out in a week then these will suffice. If not, I will need some more clothes.'

She finally broke her silence. 'We have to wait for your chargesheet to be filed.'

It had already been fifteen days since my arrest and there was no chargesheet in sight.

Gunjan told me that Rakesh Maria's order was out and he had been moved to the home guards. I then remembered what he had said to me in the Khar police station in the presence of several officers, 'You would be hung to death.'

Gunjan told me that Javed Ahmed, who was my friend, had become the new commissioner of police, Mumbai. I had known his wife Shabnam for several years, too, as long as I had known him. They were a lovely couple and good people. There, I thought, there's hope for things to get better soon!

The conversation returned to getting clothes and other basic items from home. Gunjan hesitantly said to me, 'I don't know what's up with Peter.'

I sniggered and said, 'Tell him to come and meet me. He must be nervous. Why hasn't he come to meet me?'

Gunjan let my questions linger, and then said, 'Don't worry. He will come soon.' I guess it was her way of reassuring me so I didn't sink further into depression.

The mulaqat area where Gunjan and I met was heavily guarded. While I was there for the meeting, all other prisoners were kept away. I realized later this wasn't because they doubted me, or Gunjan, for that matter. They had consciously kept me away from the hardened criminals to protect me from extortion demands and threats, and the curiosity of other visitors who would have been sitting close to Gunjan on the other side and might have gossiped about what they heard once they left the prison. My face had, after all, been plastered on every newspaper, magazine and TV screen for the last fifteen days, with stories about me that even I was hearing for the first time. I suppose every Tom, Dick and Harry would gladly participate in making my story more sensational and juicier just for a moment in the sun.

After Gunjan left, I was taken for my medical test. Dr Khan and Dr Nivedita were the doctors who manned the prison infirmary. They were really good to me. They took great care of me through my prison days and, in the end, I became good friends with them.

Breakfast was brought to me that day. It was some inedible upma which I couldn't swallow. It wasn't so much the food as my own emotional state. With the first spoonful in my mouth, I broke down. I cried for a long time. At the Khar police station, I had cried for the first few days. But after that I hadn't. But now, it was different—there was too much inside me, waiting to burst out. In the first days of prison, I was overwhelmed.

Lunch too was equally inedible. I couldn't eat it. Lunch is served around 10.30 a.m. Some people ate it hot, while some took it inside and ate it around 1 p.m., during the rest time. After lunch, the guards locked the cells between 12.30 to 3 p.m. It is the time the shifts change for the guards. So, as an added security measure as well as to ensure the prisoners take their rest, they lock up the barracks. People lie down, watch movies or soaps on television and read books. Each barrack has a TV and everyone loves watching movies in the afternoon. At 3 p.m., the gates are opened when everyone is served tea. And dinner is served at 5.30 p.m. The other inmates had to stand in a queue for their meals but, in my case, they got it for me inside. Right from the beginning, they were protective towards me, never wanting to endanger me.

I was instructed by the prison guards to not discuss the case with other inmates either. I was alone in my cell after tea when the guards came and informed me that I would be moved to another single-occupancy cell the next day. I didn't want to move though; I was petrified to be alone. In the few hours that I had been there, I had sensed the warmth of the other inmates too. They weren't hostile. One of them had come and asked me if I wanted some pickles, and another one came and said hello. I didn't mind sharing a cell with someone.

In my heart, I was still waiting for Peter. The second day passed and there was no sign of him. Then the third day passed. And then the fourth day. I had no visitors, and only possessed two sets of clothes, a toothbrush, toothpaste, a bar of soap, and no money. I would wear one set and wash the other. I repeated this process for the whole of the first week. I wrote to Peter several times in the first few days. The other inmates offered me envelopes and stamps. I asked the jailer if I could make a phone call. She told me patiently that phone calls were not allowed in Indian prisons. The only way a prisoner can communicate with people from the outside world is through letters or family visits. I didn't know that. Crestfallen, I returned to my cell. I wrote to Vidhie as well, not knowing how to send the letter to her; I didn't have a UK address for her and there was no one to give me any information.

Lawyers are allowed to meet their clients twice a week—I saw Gunjan again on the sixth day. Two people from the British Consulate—Daisy and Nawaz—also visited me in the interim. They wanted to check if I was doing all right. I told them to ask Peter to come to meet me. They looked at each other and didn't say anything. I felt everyone was withholding something from me.

My eyes lit up when I saw Gunjan. Finally, a familiar face! She came with a bag of clothes for me. When I saw her, the first thing I said was, 'Peter hasn't come to see me.'

She calmly looked at me and said, 'Indrani, I am not sure of the direction Peter is moving in ...'

I looked at her, puzzled. 'What do you mean?' I asked.

She changed the subject and said, 'Here are some clothes I have brought for you. What else do you need?'

My mind went back straight to Nawaz and Daisy's faces. I knew something was amiss.

'Is there a message for Vidhie or Peter?' Gunjan asked.

I repeated, 'Gunjan, please ask Peter to come to meet me ... I need to see him!'

Finally, Gunjan said sombrely, 'Indrani, you shouldn't rely on Peter.'

I was aghast. 'What do you mean? He is my husband. He will do anything to take me out. He loves me, for God's sake.'

Gunjan's expression wasn't very reassuring.

'He must be rattled. He will come,' I continued.

'No, Indrani. I don't think he is rattled at all. I think he knows exactly what he is doing. I think you mustn't bank on him. You tell me what else you need.'

She had purchased some clothes from FabIndia. Marks and Spencer had just opened so I had told Gunjan to ask Peter to go there and purchase some undergarments for me. I remember saying, 'I hope Peter has sent the right sizes!'

'No, Peter hasn't sent these. I have got them,' came Gunjan's flat answer.

I couldn't understand why we were buying new clothes when there were wardrobes at home stacked with clothes. Why couldn't Peter just send them over? Maybe because those were too flashy for prison. A lot of them were sleeveless. I reasoned with myself.

I couldn't figure out why Peter would not come and see me. He knew I was innocent. I obviously hadn't done what I was accused of.

Had Peter faced such an adversity, I would have never left his side. I had a zillion questions and no answers in sight. But the solitude of a prison barrack can have a meditative impact on you. Eventually, it is here that I found the answers I was looking for.

Somewhere, it dawned on me, that perhaps Peter never loved me the way I loved him. Unconditional love doesn't fall apart under the most strenuous situations. From the day I set foot in the prison, I was on my own. But this realization only hit me later.

9

A few days later, I was moved to a cell in barrack one. In each barrack, there are forty inmates. The prison staff was under instruction to keep me separate from the others. I had not lived alone for a long time; the last I had lived on my own was twenty-five years ago, when I was in Calcutta. I was fearful and uncomfortable with the idea of being on my own in a cell. They emptied out a full barrack upstairs and put seven people inside. The people whom I was sharing the barrack with were accused of, or being tried for, less serious crimes like cases of bounced cheques or theft.

In prison I would sleep on the floor for the first few weeks. I wouldn't talk to anyone. I would sit in a corner and cry for hours sometimes. I suppose my wails became worrisome because the guards called for the on-call psychiatrist to come speak with me. To add to it, I wasn't eating properly. It was a combination of too many things—loss of my daughter, abandonment by my family, and this life in jail. I would spend hours praying for Sheena: Was she alive? The question kept coming to me. My heart said something, the cops were saying something else altogether.

Now that the solitude of prison gave me time to think, questions started slowly entering my mind. If Sheena was dead, how did Peter speak to her? Peter's absence was haunting me. I was starting to piece together the larger story, but could not see the whole picture. The jail authorities would give me newspapers to read but would cut out all the articles about my case. In my barrack, there were strict instructions to not put on the news channels. Every time I asked, I was told, 'It is not allowed. Just entertainment channels.' They didn't want me to get disturbed. In those months, every news channel was reporting my case, events from my life, things about my family; they put out any and every version they could about me. Everyone, from acquaintances to former employees, was dragged onto national television to offer their two bits about me. Later, I would get to see how some used it to settle scores, too. Even people whom I didn't know from Adam shared stories and their opinions about me.

When I met the psychiatrist, I told her, 'I want to go home. I miss my family. I miss my daughter.' It was Vidhie's first few days at the university. I wanted to be with her. The shrink was rather useless and I am not sure what counselling she really did. It did not help me.

On 20 September 2015, I found out from the news, that had slipped through scrutiny, that the case has been moved to the CBI. Gunjan confirmed this when we met that week.

While I was in police custody, the Khar cops had made an announcement that they had excavated a body. There was a big story about how I was a greedy woman who committed this murder; that, coupled with moral objections I had about my daughter's relationship, led me to commit the crime. My chargesheet was laughable. I allegedly killed Sheena because she was dating Peter's younger son, Rahul. Peter loved Rahul so much that all our assets and property would be given to Rahul and, by proxy, to Sheena. I killed Sheena to stop it all. When I read it, I joked to my lawyer,

'Wouldn't it be easier to just kill Rahul? Why Sheena?' It was all assumed—Rahul might marry Sheena so I killed Sheena to take over the property. What about Peter's other son, Rabin?

For a murder accused, a chargesheet has to be filed within ninety days. The CBI was racing against time; they perhaps didn't have enough time to do a thorough independent investigation prior to filing my chargesheet. I assume that the story in the first chargesheet didn't fly because most of the discussed assets were in my name. I didn't need to kill anyone to get access to them. They realized later that earlier in 2015, both Peter and I had made a will which stated that if anything were to happen to either of us, everything would go to the other spouse. But the stakes weren't equitable—more common assets were in my name.

From the time I was arrested to the end of September, I had lost 18 kilos. I went in at 61 kilos and went down to 43 kilos. This was discovered at one of my medical check-ups and it was alarming for the prison authorities, too. I was grieving the loss of Sheena, and the loss of Peter, too. I was emotionally in a bad space. I had barely been eating. I had written to Peter every day in that month and there was no response.

On 1 October, I got up at 4 a.m., like I usually did. I prayed, like I did every day, and then I passed out. I was rushed to JJ Hospital in a semi-conscious state and admitted to a critical care unit. I remember waking up five days later, though I was told that I had regained consciousness late at night on that very same day. When I woke up, I was surrounded by cops. I asked for some coffee. It took me some time to register the fact that I was in the hospital. For a brief period, I had cognitive memory loss. I had forgotten the entire prison episode. The doctors asked me my name and I couldn't even recollect who I was. When they called me by my name, Indrani, I wouldn't respond—my own name wasn't registering. All the while, the doctors kept checking my vitals and my responses. I wasn't talking to anyone. I wasn't able to remember who I was. I, apparently, asked for my mother. Throughout my time at the hospital, I didn't ask for Peter or Vidhie, I just asked for my mother in my sleep.

Later, I got to know that my mother had died of a heart attack on 30 September. In Hindu mythology, we believe the spirit exists after death. It was so strange. I was unconscious around the same time that my mother passed away. We hadn't spoken in a few months. In my state of semi-consciousness, I remembered my mother and my first day of school. Prison authorities even checked if I had somehow heard about her death from the news. But I hadn't. I guess a child and mother are connected by instinct. It doesn't matter if they are physically together or miles apart.

Another shocking fact came to the fore after scores of tests were done—it appeared that perhaps somebody had made an attempt on my life. A sample of my blood and urine was taken to Hinduja Hospital for further tests. The head of medicine in JJ Hospital, Dr Wiqar Sheikh, who eventually became almost a guardian to me, was convinced that something was amiss. Dr Sheikh used to visit the prison every Wednesday to check on inmates suffering from hypertension and diabetes. He had checked me at the prison earlier, before I was moved to JJ Hospital, and noticed that my pupils were constricted. It was he who recommended I get admitted. But the doctors knew I needed to be protected. Dr Sheikh insisted that I be kept in the CCU throughout my stay at the hospital. The blood samples from the Forensic Science Lab (FSL) report came out clean but the report from Hinduja Hospital showed a drug overdose. In prison, the only people who are allowed to give you medication are the prison guards. They make you have the medicine in front of them.

But I wasn't destined to die that day. Enquiries were made and everyone around was questioned.[1] The lady who gave me the last medicine I took was suspended briefly. I was usually given a sleeping capsule because I couldn't sleep. I am convinced the hospital visit was the result of a deviant attempt. It was all eventually hushed up. A full body check-up showed I had cerebral ischemia—a blockage in the brain. The prison authorities put it out in the media that the brain blockage had caused my collapse. Even after this, there was no sign of Peter.

On 6 October, I was brought back from the hospital. Gunjan came to visit me three days later, on 9 October. We did not meet in the regular mulaqat room that day. She was brought inside the jail dispensary. The prison staff requested her not to tell me about my mother so I would not get further distressed—they were really good to me. But Gunjan knew she had to tell me about Mom. Upon hearing it, I broke down. I was shattered. I didn't even get the chance to meet my mother before she passed away. Gunjan asked if I wanted to apply for temporary bail.

I asked her again, 'Why hasn't Peter come yet?'

I was pining for Peter in those days. When I was in JJ Hospital, a senior doctor at the hospital, Dr Rana [name changed], told me Peter was holidaying in Goa.

I asked him, 'How do you know?'

He stayed quiet for a bit and then said, 'Forget about what you've done or not. You could be the worst criminal there is. But he is your husband. And he isn't here.'

The doctor asked me, 'Do you still want me to call him?'

I was crying hard by then. But I said, 'Don't call him.'

'Indrani, you have to fight this battle alone. And you are alone. The reason I am telling you this is that you are going back to prison. I am not sure what others have told you but you should know who is not showing up for you. You have been on the list of the world's most powerful women. You can fight this. And you have to fight this till the end. Never stop believing in your own strength. Just don't give up! *Jiska koi nahin hota hai, uska uparwala hota hai* (Those who don't have any one, have God looking out for them) …' he trailed off.

Dr Wiqar Sheikh fought for me with the prison authorities and he spoke without fear about what was the real cause of my sudden collapse. He was someone who took care of me. He didn't let the prison administration suppress what had happened. As a result, additional security was assigned to guard me once I returned to prison.

My conversation with Dr Rana was playing in my mind when I asked Gunjan about Peter when she came to see me at the dispensary. I knew she wasn't telling me something. I did receive a letter from Peter a few days later. It was a typed letter and did not bear his signature. It was a strange one in which he wrote about the chargesheet and promised that he would come and see me soon. The letter asked for some documents to be signed by me. It felt like a cruel letter, as the first letter received by a spouse who is rotting away in prison. I couldn't help but think about the document being asked for—it would grant rights to everything I owned, transfer the signing authority for my bank accounts from me, and transfer the assets I own.

It was a strange time. I was physically recuperating, emotionally battling the grief of whatever was happening to me, the loss of a parent, and the confusion of what was happening with my family.

I was still gullible. The letter stated that it would be easier for Peter to handle everything from the outside. In it he indicated that I would most likely be in prison for a very long time and that he didn't have money to pay the lawyers. It wasn't making any sense to me. He was Peter Mukerjea. How could he not have money? We never had a paucity of money. But as foolish as it sounds, my instant reaction was to ask the jailer if I could sign the documents.

The senior prison jailer didn't allow it at that time.

He later called me to his office and said, '*Pehle toh aapko sign karne ke liye court permission chahiye* (You will first need permission from the court to sign). They are property-related documents.' And then he took a pause, before saying, 'But I have a request. *Aap meri behen jaise ho. Aap itne saral ho. Aap humein bilkul tang nahin kar rahe ho.* (You are like a sister to me. You are so simple. You don't bother us at all.) I want you to wait for three months before signing this. *Aapke paas abhi bas ek hi taqat hai—aapke paise ka taqat. Filhaal aapke pass aur koi nahin hai, aur kuch bhi nahin hai. Aapki izzat aapke khud ke gharwalon ne mitti mein mila diya hai. Hum aapko batate nahin hai, taaki aapko aur takleef na ho. Aapke pass aaj ki tareekh pe bas aapka paisa hai aur aapka manobal hai. Aapko ye ladai larni hai.* (You only have one strength—the power of money. Nothing else. Your reputation has been dragged through the mud by your family. We have kept this from you so as to not cause you pain. As of now, you only have money and your resilience to stand by you. You have to fight this battle.)'

I stood there thinking: Yes, I was 43 kilos. I had a near-death experience. But I argued with him saying, 'You don't know my husband. He loves me very much.'

But I knew somewhere even then that I had to stop denying it all. It wasn't my time. I had to wait for my time. And, until then, money and mental strength were all I had. People who are innocent eventually get out and it is they who have the last laugh.

10

When I didn't sign the documents, Peter wrote several letters to me. A lot of our properties and bank accounts were in my name alone and he couldn't access them. It was mid October when the team of officers from the CBI, who were investigating the case, applied to meet me in prison. They requested to interrogate me over a period of four days.

I was still frail from the hospital stint. On the first day, only two people came to meet me. I cried throughout the questioning. Even though they were kind to me, it was traumatic to relive everything.

In the second interview, one officer asked me, 'Are you aware that Peter has taken all your things out of the house?'

I didn't know.

And then came the shocker: the jewellery, all sixty-nine sets—which were rightfully Sheena's and Vidhie's—were now in a locker under Peter's and his sons' names. Except for three among those, which Peter had gifted me during our wedding, everything else was my own.

I finally sat there thinking about all of it from a more pragmatic place. The questioning went on for a few days. It would start at 11 a.m. and would carry on till late evening. After a couple of hours of interrogation, the prison guards would take me back to my cell to ensure that I ate something before having the heavy medication that I was on. The CBI officers were polite. They asked me about Sanjeev and my marriage to him. I was hazy about the timings of events but my story remained the same. During the interrogation, one of the questions that came up prominently was: Did Peter know that Sheena was your daughter?

In my first written statement to the Khar police, I had written about my first caesarean surgery, and the second one and third one. But, men being men, did not register what I was driving at. But one of the female cops during my CBI investigation, which was roughly two months after that statement, stopped me mid-sentence while I was again narrating it, and said, 'Madam! You've mentioned the C-sections?'

I said I had.

'If you don't mind, can you come to the frisking room?'

I asked her why. She looked at the men in the room, perplexed, and announced, 'Peter is lying ... how is it possible he didn't see the scars?' She took me to the jharti room and saw the marks for herself. She came out and told the men, 'She is telling the truth! There are prominent marks.'

You can't be with someone for sixteen years and not know something as big as this. Peter would later confess to the media, in a TimesNow interview, that Sheena herself had told him about her birth mother. Rahul's grandmother gave an interview confirming Peter knew that Sheena was my daughter.[2] Mekhail, too, confirmed the same to the CBI. It was during the CBI interrogation that I started to see through Peter's lies.

I later found out that while I was at the centre of this raging storm, Peter gave media interviews saying he did not know Sheena was my daughter and that he was shocked by the brutality of the crime.

My husband, who made love to me so passionately for so many years, never stopped to notice my prominent caesarean scars. Newer generation scars are below the bikini line but in my case they were prominent. Peter's brother and sister-in-law gave an interview to *Mumbai Mirror* saying that I was secretly having an affair with my ex-husband. I called him to Mumbai to my home to spend a dirty weekend. Everyone made it a point to ensure my doom.

While in prison, I also questioned the choice of Khar police station. Our home was under the jurisdiction of Worli police station. If, according to the cops, the last time I met Sheena was in Bandra, I could have been taken to the Bandra police station as well. There were many pieces of a large jigsaw puzzle all around me. It was only in prison that I began to put these pieces together. A lot of what happened to me then is only beginning to make sense to me now.

On 18 October, Vidhie was called back from England. The CBI wanted her statement, too. Vidhie had left for England in the first week of September and, during this time, I had neither seen her nor had any communication with her. This time when she came, she insisted on meeting me. And so, Gunjan brought her to see me in prison, accompanied by Peter and Shangon. Vidhie and I broke down on seeing each other. The mulaqat room was a long corridor separated by a mesh wall with prisoners on one side and those who come to meet them on the other. You can see those who come to meet you, but you can't touch them or hold them. I couldn't hug Vidhie through the mesh that separated us. They were there for twenty minutes. Peter assured me he will come to meet me every week.

I told Vidhie that day: 'I may be inside but I want you to remember I am a strong woman. And I am not going to take this lying low. I will come out. All of this will be over soon. Just remain strong and I want you to be a good person till I am out there to take care of you.'

I got the feeling that she wanted to tell me something, but she held back because there were people around.

On 20 October, I was taken to the court.

On 19 October, Peter was arrested at 6 p.m. During this period, the CBI team was coming in to meet me regularly. Talking to them reassured me a bit. I would still cry a lot but I was settling into prison life. There was no chargesheet to read until then. I was naive enough to believe that once the chargesheet was filed, I would get bail and go home. I was counting the days, until one day I stopped chasing what wasn't going to happen for me. At least, not then. Days became months and months became years.

I wasn't aware of Peter's arrest until I was taken to the Esplanade (Killa) Court. The matter wasn't committed to sessions. This is a magistrate court. There was high security. The press had crowded the place so the van couldn't get to the court. I remember giving a byte to a television channel. Reporters shouted at me: 'Have you been framed?' The cacophony was piercing my eardrums. During the first two months, the media had lashed out at me because of the stories. Now everyone was beginning to question what was going on. I remember looking directly into the TV Today camera and saying, 'Yes, I have been framed!'

Pat came the next loud statement: 'Did Peter frame you?' I kept quiet at that. By then, I felt that Peter had some kind of role to play in what had happened to me.

Just then, a voice from somewhere shouted, 'Now Peter has also been arrested. What do you have to say?'

The words hit me hard. I broke down in the van. In some ways, I felt vindicated. No one knew if I was guilty or not, but I had to bear the burden of being shamed all by myself. That day, I told the police guards who escorted me to the court not to cover my face—it was normal practice to cover the face of the accused being brought to the court. I wanted to fight this! My message to the world that day was: I was alone but I wasn't going to give up easily.

I didn't meet Peter that day.

I got my chargesheet in court. My lawyer took it and I was escorted back to prison. When I finally sat alone in my cell, my system was shocked. Tears rolled down my face. So much had happened that day. I requested the jail authorities to let me watch the news. I saw the scenes on the TV in a haze, of Peter being taken away into CBI custody. One of the female cops in prison hugged me and asked me to stay strong.

Something shifted in me that day. It was a strange sort of turning point where my faith in God was restored. Somewhere, something was karmically corrected. It was divine intervention. Peter was going to turn sixty on 21 November. Earlier, I had received several letters from him about how he was planning his birthday bash and how he would be thinking of me while cutting an elaborate cake.

That's where it all started for me—the phase where the phoenix rose from the ashes.

PART 4

1980s

11

Sheena was born in 1987, on a cold winter afternoon after a C-section procedure.

As I regained consciousness, and the effect of the anaesthesia gradually wore off, I felt an excruciating pain in my abdomen.

I was still disoriented and could not figure out why my stomach hurt so badly. My mouth was dry and my tongue felt like sandpaper.

I could hear my mom's voice somewhere in the distance.

'Mom,' I screamed, unable to bear the pain.

'Pari,' it sounded like Dr Mason, 'you've had a baby girl. Open your eyes sweetheart.'

Dr Mason, Mom and a nurse were standing around me in a room that was unfamiliar and smelt sterile as I lay on my back on a bed, with a drip in my arm.

They were all beaming with smiles as they looked at me.

Mom pushed the hair away from my forehead as she said, 'Pari, she is beautiful. She looks just like you did when you were born.'

'Mom, my stomach is hurting badly,' I cried.

Dr Mason instructed the nurse to inject something into the drip and held my hand saying, 'The pain will go away in the next five minutes. Whenever you feel the pain return, just ring the bell and sister will give you the medicine.'

She gave a list of instructions to the nurse before departing.

When she saw me licking my dry lips, she said, 'You can have a spoon of water every hour. From tomorrow you can start on liquids.'

She smiled at me as I asked, 'How's the baby?'

'She's in the nursery. You'll see her in a bit.' She blew a kiss at me and left the room.

Siddharth, Gramps and Granny were shown in by the nurse who had left with Dr Mason.

Siddharth smiled at me. 'Sheena—that is what we will name our little girl. Mom's choice.'

Mom looked pleased that her suggestion for the baby's name was made official by Siddharth.

Gramps exclaimed, 'Sheena sounds great!'

Gramps and Granny were both fawning over me and declared that the baby looked identical to Mom the day she was born.

All of them were over the moon.

The baby was brought into the room wrapped in a hooded white towel. The nurse put her next to me on the bed as Gramps, Granny, Mom and Siddharth all hovered around waiting for their turn to hold her.

She was pink and almost bald with just a few light strands of hair on her scalp. Her eyes were shut, and I thought I heard a slight snore in her heavy breathing. It was as though she had done all the hard work and not me.

I could not sit up to hold her, so I gently pulled her closer to me into the crook of my arm. My heart was overflowing with a sensation that I had never experienced before. I was overwhelmed. I was in love, really in love with this little person next to me.

'Sheena!' I exclaimed.

We returned home with Sheena four days later.

In the two months before Sheena's birth, Dad's bedroom was stripped out and converted to a nursery, refurbished with a baby cot, pink curtains and powder blue paint on the walls. Mom had gone overboard with Sheena's welcome and filled the nursery with every possible toy she could lay her hands on, baby oils, creams, powders, nappies and clothes enough for fifty infants.

A crib was placed next to the bed in my room. I wasn't sure what Mom had in mind, but we were ready with supplies for Sheena for the next two years.

Nanny took charge of setting Sheena's routine with massages, baths and timely feeds. I did not lactate, so Sheena had to be put on formula milk from day one.

Sheena was a night bird from the day she was born. She slept throughout the day and stayed awake at night. But she was a contented baby. She cried only when she was hungry, or when her nappy was soiled.

Most of the time, when she was awake, she kicked her legs, flayed her arms, made gurgling noises, and looked at whoever held her or sat next to her through her beautiful eyes. She smiled often, at times wide enough to reveal her toothless gums. She was adorable!

I loved holding her and watching her fall asleep in my arms as I rocked her. I was often dismissed by Nanny and, at times, by my Mom as they felt that I was encouraging bad habits and spoiling Sheena by picking her up from the crib even before she could cry.

Sheena and the crib frequented Mom's room as well. Mom loved Sheena. Sheena became her world. I often wondered if Mom had loved me as much when I was a baby.

Winter vacations were over when Sheena was almost two months old. It was time for me to return to college if I chose to.

Siddharth had finally set up the bakery. It was inaugurated with much pomp and pleasure. Sheena was proudly introduced to all at the opening ceremony. There was a huge gathering of family and friends.

Tongues stopped wagging and all the people who gossiped earlier decided and announced that Siddharth, Sheena and I made a perfect family.

Siddharth was not a hands-on father. But he liked having Sheena around.

Sheena brought the lost joy back into our lives. By the time Sheena was four months old and able to hold her neck up, Siddharth was less nervous about carrying her. Gradually, he warmed up more and more to Sheena. Siddharth and I also bonded more as we raised Sheena.

Siddharth moved into my room when Sheena was four months old. We had not had any physical intimacy apart from holding hands, not even a kiss, up until then.

I was extremely fond of Siddharth but was never attracted to him either physically or intellectually. He was my saviour but by no stretch of the imagination the man of my dreams.

Intellectually, I never thought of him as quite good enough for an equal. But I was indebted to him; he had legitimized Sheena's existence, with no expectations from any of us. I owed everything to him.

But as time went by, we became closer, and Siddharth and I finally went all the way when Sheena was just shy of five months. In the meantime, I studied and worked hard and fared well in my tests and assignments with good grades.

Siddharth and I were now a couple in the real sense. Sheena was six months old when I was pregnant with Siddharth's child.

When I missed my period, I went to meet Dr Mason and as luck would have it, I tested positive for pregnancy.

'Dr Mason,' I said to her, on my visit the next day, 'I am not ready for another baby. Sheena is only six months old!'

'Pari, I think you should have the baby. It will be good company for Sheena, and they will grow up together. You've just had a caesarean six months ago. I'm not sure if it's safe to go ahead with an abortion this soon. Besides, it's good for you to get over with having children now and complete your family. You will be free after that to pursue your own goals,' she said, looking into my eyes.

She smiled at me after that, probably realizing that she may have pressed her opinion too hard upon me, and added, 'Talk to your mother and Siddharth, and see what they have to say. If you still decide that you would rather not go ahead with it now, Siddharth and you can come back and let me know. We'll see what can be done.'

'Dr Mason, I am sure that I am not ready. But as you say, I will talk it through with Siddharth. I am sure, he too isn't ready for another baby. We are still not married! Anyway, thank you for your advice. Can we visit you tomorrow please, after I have spoken to Siddharth and Mom?' I urged, without considering her hectic schedule and appointments.

'You sure can, Pari,' she said, picking up the receiver of the intercom to speak with her secretary to check for an available slot for my visit the next day.

'6 p.m. tomorrow. Bring Siddharth with you,' she insisted after putting the receiver down.

'Thank you, Dr Mason, for accommodating us,' I said, getting up.

I returned home that afternoon from Dr Mason's and waited for Mom and Siddharth to arrive.

Siddharth arrived first. He came and kissed me on the cheek when he saw me in the living room.

'Siddharth, we need to talk,' I said, trying to put on a smile as he sat down next to me on the blue upholstered sofa.

'I went to see Dr Mason yesterday. I am fifteen days late. I had a urine test done yesterday, and today when I went to see her again, she told me that I am expecting.'

Siddharth broke into a smile that warmed up his eyes and said, 'You mean that we are pregnant.'

I nodded, 'Yes, Siddharth, that's what she said.'

Before I could finish what I was going to say, Siddharth stood up, picked me up, and said, 'Oh baby, I am so happy. This is the best news that you could have given me.' He was overjoyed!

I had not heard Mom's car driving in. But in the middle of it all, Mom walked in and said, 'Hey, what's it that I have missed out on, Siddharth, fill me in.'

'Mom,' said Siddharth beaming, his eyes dancing with happiness, 'we are going to have a baby.'

'You mean, baby Sheena's going to have a playmate,' she said and smiled.

Siddharth nodded, unable to stop smiling, almost laughing with happiness. 'Yes, Mom! Indrani has been to Dr Mason's, and it is confirmed.'

Maybe Dr Mason was right, I thought. Sheena needed a sibling.

Siddharth did not take my breath away whenever I saw him. His touch did not put me on fire as Vish's had. But Siddharth cared for me. I decided that I was going to have the baby and make my relationship with Siddharth work. I would love him one day the way I loved Vish. I thought that if I could get over Vish, I could perhaps fall in love with Siddharth some day. And Siddharth deserved it all—my love and the baby that I was carrying in my womb.

The next evening, Siddharth and I went to Dr Mason at 6 p.m. but not to discuss abortion as I had thought the previous day.

The moment we walked into her chamber, Siddharth greeted her with a broad smile, 'Good evening, Doc. We are all so happy. Indrani is in your hands now for the next few months.'

Dr Mason looked at me, smiling, probably relieved that I had decided to have the baby after all.

She wisely made no mention of the discussion that we had had the previous day.

Dr Mason congratulated Siddharth and gave us a list of dos and don'ts, and a date for the sonography.

Sheena was soon almost a year old. She was the most gorgeous baby in town. She was no longer bald or toothless. She had a few teeth evenly set, pink lips that smiled often, dreamy eyes, and a crop of golden hair on her head. She was the centre of attraction wherever she went.

The second time around, I did not suffer from morning sickness like I had when I was pregnant with Sheena. Siddharth was extra attentive towards me and my needs. He was always fawning over me, which, at times, I found stifling. It was probably my hormones.

Gradually, for absolutely no fault of his, Siddharth started getting on my nerves. Everything that he did or said irritated me, but I did not reveal my annoyance to him or to anyone else. And all that time, I hated myself for feeling this way.

I busied myself as much as I could with Sheena and my studies so that I had little time left to spend with Siddharth.

Every evening, Siddharth would come home with ice creams or pastries that I loved to eat. My heart used to break seeing him try so hard to please me and keep me happy.

Mom constantly monitored my diet and ensured that I ate enough for two, and stayed agile and fit. Nanny followed her instructions diligently.

Meanwhile, I was on a serious guilt trip for being unable to love Siddharth the way I should have, despite his kindness and apparent love for me. Sadly, Siddharth knew how I felt even though I never let my guard down. But I could tell that he knew.

I was seven months pregnant when Mekhail decided that he wanted to take on the world. I once again had to undergo surgery after my water broke, as despite being on the drip for several hours the doctors had failed to induce labour pain.

Mekhail was born prematurely. He barely weighed 1.8 kilos when he was born and had to be kept in the incubator at the hospital for over a week.

Everyone celebrated the birth of a baby boy and also declared that my family was now complete. Free advice was flowing in, a dime a dozen, on how I should now get my tubes tied, or cut, or use a copper T. I was eighteen years old then.

Mekhail came home when he was ten days old. Mom converted another room into a nursery for him, this time the curtains were blue and the walls were painted white. Mom was a bit more sensible this time around and did not fill Mekhail's wardrobes with clothes and supplies for fifty babies as she had done for Sheena.

Several of Sheena's toys that she did not play with anymore, or jumpers that she had outgrown without wearing even once, were moved to Mekhail's nursery.

Mekhail was a tiny baby with a crop of black hair on his head, hair on his back and big eyes. This time, too, I did not lactate. So, he was on formula. Unlike Sheena, he slept a lot, throughout the night and almost all day.

Sheena was thirteen months old when Mekhail was born. Her gurgling noises had graduated to a few monosyllables. She had visited me a couple of times with Mom when I was in the hospital. She was excited to see me every time she came. I missed her terribly as that was the first time I stayed away from her.

When Mekhail arrived home, Sheena was intrigued. She stood near his crib and looked at him, probably with mixed emotions. Her monosyllables and glances shifting from Mekhail to us probably meant, 'Who's this new kid in town? What's he doing in my territory?'

Nanny had her hands full with Sheena waddling about the house and Mekhail's routine of massage, bath, feed and sleep.

Siddharth was nervous about Mekhail's fragile health in the beginning but, as the doctors had predicted, Mekhail turned into a healthy baby by the time he was thirty days old.

Sheena was initially troubled by the divided attention after Mekhail's arrival. But slowly she started accepting his presence as she began to participate in little tasks with Nanny, Mom and me while we gave him a bath or powdered him.

I had thought that Mekhail's birth would act as a bonding catalyst for Siddharth and me. But it was quite the opposite. I had post-pregnancy blues and became irritable at the slightest of things. I drifted away from Siddharth even further. I was repulsed by the thought of his touch. I knew that it was unfair, but my thoughts and feelings did not change.

I moved to Mekhail's room with the excuse of his premature birth and the need for constant care. Mekhail was adorable and a content baby despite being born two months before time.

While Mekhail slept, I prepared for entrance tests for further education. My final under-grad exams were over, and I was awaiting the results. Sheena often spent the entire day with Mekhail and me in his nursery, while Mom and Siddharth were out at work. I loved my time with both the babies. They filled my heart with joyousness that more than made up for the mishaps and compromises in my life.

The under-grad results were announced. Once again, I had topped in almost all the subjects, which was celebrated with pride by my grandparents, Mom and, even, Siddharth, who by then had very little to do with me, even though we lived under the same roof.

People in town who had taken pleasure in gossiping about me when I was pregnant with Sheena and discussing my loose morals were now full of compliments about what a good egg I was. Everyone cooed at Mekhail and Sheena whenever they saw them.

Spring was setting in. The trees were exploding with blossoms. Mom decided to organize a Sunday lunch at home for family and close friends. Mom's and Dad's families had all been invited except Dad. It was then that I overheard Dad's brother giving Mom his spiel about how much Dad missed her and how keen he was on a reconciliation with her. Dad's sister joined in with her two bits about how upset the entire family was about Mom's callous disregard towards his feelings. Guests at the lunch were enjoying themselves. But the family was there with an agenda, as always.

I could see Mom tearing up, clearly unable to give them an explanation.

Once all the friends left, family members huddled in the garden for a conversation that, by the looks on their faces, appeared grave in nature. After a while, Siddharth and I were beckoned to join in.

'Pari, you've done really well. We are all proud of you,' said Aunt Neena [name changed], one of Dad's sisters. She had vilified me the most when I was pregnant with Sheena.

'Let's now plan the big wedding,' she announced, pleased with herself as she sipped on her vodka.

Everyone nodded and applauded.

Siddharth looked uncomfortable as he knew very well what was going on in my mind and was probably apprehensive about my reaction.

'Whose wedding?' I asked cheekily, even though I knew what Aunt Neena was referring to.

'Yours, of course, silly,' she said, smiling broadly, revealing some spinach stuck in her teeth.

'Siddharth and I have no plans to get married,' I said with a firmness in my voice that wiped the smile off her face.

'Oh, but you are over eighteen now. You said you would get married once you are eighteen. Wasn't that the plan?' asked Dad's brother, looking first at me and then shifting his gaze to Mom.

'I never said that I wanted to get married at eighteen, or to Siddharth,' I said defiantly.

Siddharth and his mom looked embarrassed at my outright declaration.

Gramps, sensing the mounting tension in the air, said, 'Let's keep this discussion for another day. Today is for a drink and a smoke and a good laugh. What do you say, folks?'

The Sunday lunch finally came to an end at 7 p.m. Gramps and Granny left with Mom's brother who lived not more than ten minutes away from us. Maa stayed with us that night and planned to leave the next morning for Shillong. That evening, Mom came into Mekhail's nursery just as I was falling asleep. She kissed Mekhail on his forehead and sat next to me on the bed.

'Pari,' she said, 'Neena thinks that Dad and I should get back together.'

Her eyes looked at me pleadingly.

'What do you think, Mom?' I asked, looking straight into her eyes.

'What is it that you want, Mom?' I continued.

Mom burst into sobs. I knew her answer.

'I don't know, dear. But there are times I do get lonely,' she said, sobbing.

'You have your own family now, Pari,' she continued, wiping her tears.

'And is this family that I never planned, not yours? Where on earth do you have time to be lonely, Mom? Dad can't come back!'

'He needs me, Pari. Have we not punished him enough? I cannot shut him out from my life forever.'

'What about me, Mom? What about my feelings, my life?' I said, with too many thoughts racing through my mind. 'Mom, you meet him at work every day. Why does he need to come home to be with you? You have not shut him out of your life. Mom, I can't and will not be under the same roof as him,' I said.

Mom's response changed my life, and the decisions that I took subsequently.

'This roof belongs to him.'

'Goodnight, Mom, I'm tired,' I said, sinking my head back into the pillow.

Mom left, whispering goodnight, sobbing at the same.

That night I lay in bed, awake, thinking about my life. So much had happened in the last five years, often breaking me to pieces. Yet, every time I managed to pick up the pieces and take the next step, something else would happen to take me back a few paces.

Despite the tragic turn of events in my life, I had never broken to the point of no return. I was an achiever. I worked hard and topped my exams at school and college. I had made not just my family proud of me but also my teachers and professors, who believed that I had a bright future and was capable of accomplishing anything that I put my mind to.

I knew that if I could muster the courage to step out of the cocoon that I had been in for the last nineteen years, I could make it. That was my moment of awakening. I decided that I could not, under any circumstances, get trapped in a loveless marriage with Siddharth to save the honour of another man who had ruined my life. I dared to dream. And so, at barely nineteen years of age, I planned the great escape.

As I had suspected, Mom succumbed to the pressures put on her by Dad's family. A couple of days later, Dad's belongings arrived home, which was a precursor to his arrival shortly after. I failed to understand how Mom was so easily persuaded to allow him to return home despite the upheaval that he had caused in our lives, particularly mine. Was she not afraid that it could happen again?

Siddharth did not react when I told him about Mom's conversation with me, or when Dad's bags arrived a couple of days later. While Siddharth's relationship with me was already fraying at the edges, he was well settled in his bakery business that Mom had funded, and he was earning well. He did not want to upset the apple cart by giving her his point of view. He was, by then, in a rush to set a wedding date: to probably secure his own future.

When I spoke to Mom's brother, who knew everything, instead of empathizing with me or advising Mom against letting Dad into the house, he just asked me about my wedding plans.

Clearly, nobody wanted to talk about the elephant in the room.

I knew that I had to leave Siddharth and my home, once and for all. I decided that I would leave town with Sheena and Mekhail before Dad returned to live under 'his roof'. He was due to arrive in a couple of weeks.

University admissions for post-graduation had started. I needed to get admission and accommodation sorted for myself and the babies, in whichever town or city I chose to move to.

I was barely nineteen and had five thousand rupees in my bank account, which was a joint account with my mother. How I was going to survive in another city with two kids and no money if Mom refused to help was something that I had not dwelt upon before going to have a conversation with her about my plans.

Mom was still in bed when I went to speak with her. We had not been speaking much after the face-off that Sunday evening.

I made myself comfortable on the brown leather couch in her room.

'Tea, Mom?' I asked, not knowing where to begin.

'Not for me, Pari. You can have some if you like. I can ring the bell,' she replied sitting up.

'Thanks, Mom. Not now,' I said. 'I'd like to move out.'

I paused for a while as Mom got out of bed to draw back the curtains.

'Calcutta University has responded that they will consider admission after a personal interview. I know that I can crack it, Mom,' I continued. 'Mom, if you can organize our tickets, we can leave in two days. We can stay at Aunt Leena's till my admission and till we find a place to live in.' Aunt Leena [name changed] was my mother's cousin.

'And who is the "we"? You are surely not expecting Siddharth to shut the shop and move to another city, are you? And when did you apply to Calcutta University and why?' She looked at me as though I was speaking Greek.

'Mom, I don't want Siddharth to come with me. I will go with Sheena and Mekhail. I need to go far away, Mom—from Siddharth, from this house, from this town,' I said, trying to sound as calm as possible even though I felt turbulence brewing inside.

'Pari, you don't know what you are talking about. If you want to move out, fine! We will organize a place here, close by, where Siddharth and you can stay, and the children can come and go. You don't have to come home till you are ready to,' she said, giving me a look of bewilderment and slight annoyance.

'Mom, I don't want to marry Siddharth. I just want to leave with the kids and make a fresh start,' I said, tears brimming in my eyes. 'Please, Mom, I want you to understand that I need to go away from this town.'

'And what happens to Sheena and Mekhail when you go to your classes? You cannot take Sheena and Mekhail away from me, from Siddharth. And what's wrong with Siddharth now? You guys are getting married soon—the families already have one foot out of the door to dance at your wedding.' Mom bombarded me with questions I had no answers to.

'Mom, I have tried. I have tried harder than you can imagine to love Siddharth the way I should and mentally accept him as my partner, but I have not been able to. We have nothing in common, Mom, nothing at all. I thought that Mekhail would be the reason for us to bond. But things have become worse. I can't bear to be with Siddharth anymore. And then there's Dad. I can't do this anymore. I just can't,' I pleaded, in the hope that she would understand.

Mom was silent. She looked at me and then out of the window. There was a gentle breeze blowing and birds chirping outside.

'Pari, I will let you go and study in Calcutta. But the kids stay here,' she said, looking back at me after gazing out of the window pensively for a good few minutes.

'Mom, it's not just about higher education. I want to move cities, bag and baggage, with Sheena and Mekhail. A nanny can come with us. She will look after them when I go for my lessons. We can get a cook who will prepare our meals, buy a car, and get a driver, or I can learn to drive. We can buy a house or rent one. Mom, people move cities all the time. You can come and settle us in,' I implored, believing that everything that I said made sense and was possible.

'Yes, Pari, you are right. People move cities all the time. But those people have jobs, they earn, they pay rent, their nannies, their cooks, their drivers. They are not teenage students with toddlers,' she almost sounded sarcastic.

I could not hold myself back any longer.

'Mom, these people also did not need to beg their mother for help because they had been raped by their mother's husband at fourteen and then again at sixteen. These people had the good fortune of a normal childhood. I didn't! Mom, I know that I don't have a job, I earn nothing, and I know that I can't raise Sheena and Mekhail all by myself, which is why I am asking for your help. If I had a job, we would not be talking about all of this, would we?' I asked partly angry, partly sad, and feeling totally helpless.

'Pari, it's your call. If you go, you go alone. The children stay here. And that's final.'

She continued, 'You decide what you want to do. We will talk again when I am back from work.'

Mom got out of bed and walked into her bathroom. That was the end of the conversation.

It was going to be a tough day for me, I thought to myself. My conversation with Siddharth would be as difficult as it was with Mom, probably even more. But I had to tell him about my feelings, my dreams and my plans now, sooner rather than later.

I walked down to Mekhail's nursery where he was sleeping peacefully like an angel in his crib. I looked at his little fingers clutching the flannel that covered him. As I kissed his forehead, he shifted and made a groaning sound, as if to say, 'Please do not disturb me.'

Sheena was probably in the kitchen or the garden with Nanny. I felt the sudden urge to hold little Sheena close to me.

I called out for Sheena as I walked out of Mekhail's nursery to the kitchen. Sheena was not there, but I asked Moses for a cup of tea.

Sheena was in the garden sitting on the swing as Nanny was feeding her porridge.

She jumped off the swing and came running to me when she saw me. I picked her up and held her in my arms as tightly as I could, as though if I didn't I would lose her forever. Probably it was a premonition.

I felt a lump in my throat. I went back into the kitchen to get my tea and asked Moses if he could find Siddharth and ask him to join me in the living room.

Siddharth came into the living room. 'Good morning, did you sleep all right?' he asked with a nervous smile. He probably knew that what he was going to hear wouldn't be music to his ears.

'Good morning, Siddharth. I didn't sleep much. And you?'

'Yes, I did, thank you. What's up?' he said, sipping the tea from the mug that he had carried with him when he came. Siddharth just stood by the window without bothering to sit down, as he normally did when he drank his tea.

'We need to talk,' I said, feeling sorry for him but at the same time relieved that, finally, I had brought myself to tell him what I should have done a long time ago.

'Siddharth, I am leaving,' I said, '…leaving town. I've been called for an interview in Calcutta.'

He listened without looking at me and said nothing after I paused.

I continued, 'I can't marry you, Siddharth. I feel terrible. You have always been so good to me. I owe my life to you. But I just don't feel the way I should. Forgive me for not being able to return your love. I know this is not how things should be, particularly after Mekhail. But this is how things are. I am sorry, I really am.'

Siddharth finally sat down on the sofa opposite me before saying, 'I knew this was coming. I just kept hoping that it would never come. Indrani, you are not able to love me because you are still in love with Vish!'

I could not believe my ears. I flew off the handle, which I never did with Siddharth no matter how irritated I was with him.

'How dare you!' I said tersely. 'I am not in love with Vish and will never be in love with you. I don't have to be in love with anyone else to be not in love with you. I am not in love with you because of the way you are!'

I finally did it. It was all out in the open.

Siddharth looked shocked more than hurt at my blatant outburst. And then, gradually, his eyes returned to being glazed as always.

'I'm sorry, Indrani. I shouldn't have brought up Vish's name. I know it probably still hurts you,' he said.

I just got up and left the room. As I walked back to the nursery, I felt like a load was off my chest.

When Mom returned from work that evening, I told her that I would leave town on my own, as she had suggested, and I'd return every three months to Gramps's and Granny's, where I could spend time with Sheena and Mekhail. I wouldn't sign up for a life of farce, live in a loveless relationship or be under the same roof with my rapist for any longer than I already had.

'Mom,' I said, 'I'll take Sheena and Mekhail with me after I finish my university and maybe even earlier if I am able to get a job while I am studying.'

Mom looked at me in a way that I knew what I was going to hear next was not going to be good.

'Pari, we need to sort out a few things before you leave,' she replied. 'Sheena and Mekhail are getting looked after here very well. And so are you. Yet you have chosen to go far away not just from

Siddharth or this town, you have chosen to distance yourself from your kids. You are abandoning them for the freedom you seek. And freedom comes with a price, always.'

'No, Mom, that's not true! I have not chosen freedom over Sheena and Mekhail. I just can't afford to take them with me without your help. I will meet them every quarter, Mom,' I said, pleading with her to understand my feelings.

Why was it so difficult for Mom or Siddharth to understand why I wanted to leave, I wondered.

'Pari, you are free to go, do whatever you wish to. I will take care of Sheena and Mekhail. I will adopt them, both Dad and I. I have spoken to him. The kids cannot be here without a mother and no legitimate father. They will face questions they will never have answers to, for the rest of their lives. Had you and Siddharth got married, things would have been different. What I am proposing is the only solution and in their best interest.'

My mind was not working anymore.

'I will get the affidavits made that you and I will sign in court tomorrow,' she declared.

My head was spinning. I thought to myself that Mom had started it all by agreeing to get Dad back home.

'Fine, Mom,' I said, surer than ever that I needed to get far away from here. The next day Mom and I went to court where I signed the affidavits that declared that my parents had adopted my children, Sheena and Mekhail, both toddlers, and that I had, out of my free will, given Sheena and Mekhail to them for adoption.

I did not cry. I had dared to dream and this was the price I had to pay. This realization had sunk in all too quickly. But I was not going to let anyone make me feel guilty for anything. The affidavits were just pieces of paper. I would get Sheena and Mekhail back soon.

Mom and I spoke to Aunt Leena that evening. She agreed to pick me up from the airport and host me till my admission was done and I found a place to live in.

Mom gave me seventy-two thousand rupees and an airline ticket for the following Saturday, which was three days away.

I packed a bag of clothes and kept it near the door of Mekhail's nursery. Nanny teared up every time she saw me. I did not call Gramps or Granny. I spent the next three days holding Sheena and Mekhail close all day and all night. Siddharth stayed away from me.

And then Saturday came. It was time for me to go.

I held Sheena and Mekhail close one last time before I left. Sheena ran back into the house when I let go of her, clueless as to what was going on in her life or mine. Mekhail fell asleep in my arms and Nanny carried him back to the nursery.

As I stood with the door of the car open, I looked back at the house with the green roof, the white walls with ivy climbing on them, the house I lived in as a child, the house where I fell in love with Vish, the house where I was defiled and raped twice by my father, the house where I brought Sheena and Mekhail when they were born, the house where I spent almost nineteen years of my life—the house that I planned never to return to.

But as the car moved away, my spirits lightened and rose. I was free at last! I decided that I was going to return to this city only when I had made something of myself. I was going to return to take Sheena and Mekhail when I could give them the life they deserved. I was never going to enter the same roof that my father was under, ever again.

That was the first time I was going to fly alone. The flight attendant showed me to my seat in the aircraft. Soon after, we were strapped in and the announcements were made for take-off. The aircraft slowly gathered speed on the runway, my heartbeat speeding at the same pace as excitement and euphoria kicked in.

I woke up when the passenger seated next to me tapped me lightly on my hand and said, 'Sorry to wake you up, we've been asked to put on the seatbelts. We are landing.'

My heart started beating faster as the aircraft descended and touched the tarmac. I had arrived, at last, in Calcutta.

Aunt Leena was waiting at the arrival for me. She greeted me with a warm hug and a wide smile that lit up her eyes, which were so similar to Mom's. She had arrived in Calcutta almost fifteen years ago to study law. But before she barely completed her first year, she caught the fancy of Rajesh Seth [name changed], the son of a wealthy business family, and got married to him instead. Their home was a mansion with a sprawling garden, even though not quite as big as the gardens we had back home. She had two children, Raj and Reena [names changed], who were shy kids then.

As Aunt Leena and I drove out of the airport into the city, I immersed myself in the visions of the crowded streets. The sea of people with a perfect litany of movements and activities was an overwhelming sight when one came from a small city with fewer people, as I did. There were red flags and banners with communist symbols everywhere.

We were greeted at the door by Raj and Reena, who were eagerly waiting for the arrival of their older cousin, of whom they had hardly any memories. They were both around eight to ten years old, Raj being the older of the two.

The children followed my aunt and me to the room where I was meant to stay, where my bags had already been placed. After my aunt left to check on other things, Raj and Reena both sat down on the rug in front of the bed with clearly no intention of leaving the room.

'Mom said that you have a baby brother and a sister. When are they coming? Do you have their photos?' Reena squealed.

I froze listening to what Reena had said. I wondered if I had heard correctly.

All day, I had felt a vacuum somewhere in my heart despite my euphoria. I was missing my babies; I had just not realized how much. 'They are not my brother and sister. They are my babies,' I said.

Unsure about what story Aunt Leena had fed them, I thought it was best to distract their attention with something else till I spoke to my aunt.

'Reena, why don't we first take out the chocolates I have got for you. You can take me to your mom after that.'

Aunt Leena's conversation with me during the drive from the airport was all about my admission to Calcutta University. It had not struck me earlier that Aunt Leena had not asked me about Sheena or Mekhail on our way home even once. I decided that I had to find out what was going on.

We found Aunt Leena in the kitchen where she was giving instructions to the man standing next to her, whom she introduced to me as Maharaj, their cook.

'Would you like some tea?' asked Aunt Leena.

'Yes, please. We need to talk, Aunt Leena,' I said.

Aunt Leena gave a few more instructions to Maharaj before we left the kitchen. We went to the garden, which had comfortable, cushioned caned chairs, and sat down.

The sun was beginning to set, turning the sky into shades of pink, orange and indigo. Aunt Leena's in-laws were nowhere to be seen. But I decided that I was going to ask after them only once I had some clarity on the muddled conversation I had had earlier with her children.

'Aunt Leena, Reena and Raj think that Sheena and Mekhail are my siblings. They have clearly misunderstood.'

'Oh, but they have not misunderstood. That's what I've told them,' she said firmly, for a minute almost sounding like Mom.

She looked at me and continued, 'That's what Babuji and Maa also know,' referring to her father-in-law and mother-in-law.

'But why? Why have you told them that Sheena and Mekhail are my siblings?' I asked, perplexed.

'Pari,' she said, looking at me, her eyes softening. 'Your mother spoke to me for a long time last night. She has told me that your father and she have adopted the kids so that you can start your life again without any baggage.'

'Aunt Leena, Sheena and Mekhail are not baggage. They are my children!'

'But you gave them up willingly for adoption, didn't you? You wanted a fresh start without your kids, didn't you? They are now the children of your parents. Pari, you cannot have the cake and eat it too. It is magnanimous of your parents to have taken the responsibility of your children and legally give them rights and recognition. You must allow everybody a fresh start when you have chosen one for yourself!'

'Aunt Leena, I wanted to bring Sheena and Mekhail. But what happens to them when I go to my classes? Mom decided to keep them with her because I did not have answers to several questions, this being one. I had pleaded that Nanny be sent with us to look after them. Mom did not agree,' I said, trying hard to make Aunt Leena see the real picture.

'Things are not what they seem like', I continued, holding back my tears. 'I fled from home because of some terrible things that had happened to me, and I felt suffocated. Those wounds pervade my body and my soul,' I said, unable to stop the tears now.

Aunt Leena took my hand in hers. 'Sweetheart, you must believe that everything that your mother is doing is with the best interest in her heart for you, Sheena and Mekhail. She is your mother.'

She looked beyond me pensively and then added, 'Not everyone gets a second chance in life. You have got it. You are young, intelligent and you have your entire life ahead of you. You can conquer the world, but you cannot do it with two babies in tow and that too as an unwed mother.'

She paused briefly, and then continued, 'How does it make a difference whether Sheena and Mekhail are your siblings, or you call them your children? Will you love them any less if the world knows them as your younger sister or brother?'

I did not give the answer that Aunt Leena had probably wanted to hear. I asked her instead, 'What have you told Uncle Rajesh?'

'He knows, Pari. But he too believes that you cannot be an unwed mother to Sheena and Mekhail. He thinks that you could have married Siddharth and continued your life back home with Sheena and Mekhail as your children. But, now that your parents have already adopted them, you should stay here and complete your education. It's a new city, new life and you can meet Sheena and Mekhail whenever you want to. You are barely nineteen, they could easily pass off as your siblings. Nobody will bat an eyelid. Babuji and Maa didn't think twice when I told them that they were your siblings.' She looked at me with reassurance.

Hearing her speak with so much passion, I wondered if she regretted not completing her own education and getting hitched instead. But I also wondered if she knew the truth about Sheena.

By the end of the day, I was exhausted, physically, mentally and emotionally. I kicked off the slippers that I was wearing and slipped into the sheets without bothering to change or brush my teeth. As I sank my head into the pillow, I fell asleep. It was a long day, one of the longest in my lifetime.

The next day, I went to the university with Aunt Leena for my interview. I was given a set of forms to fill up. I started writing the details that included my name, qualification, grades, home address, name of parents and name of siblings, if any. In that column, I wrote: 'Sister–Sheena; and Brother–Mekhail.'

Just then the usher outside the interview room called out my name.

I was no longer nervous or sad. The fact that Sheena and Mekhail were my siblings became the gospel truth for me, even though it was only a half truth. I etched it in my mind for it to become my truth, too. I was going to live and let live, I decided. I breezed through the interview. We were told to return the next morning to check the results. But I knew I was in—and I was right.

My life in Calcutta truly begun that day.

Around 3 p.m., I proceeded to try my luck at the YWCA hostel—I couldn't stay at my aunt's forever.

I looked at myself in the big mirror in my aunt's lobby and thought that I appeared quite presentable and casual at the same time in my grey skinny jeans, white shirt that was slightly oversized brown suede loafers and hair tied back in a ponytail.

The taxi dropped me right outside the YWCA, which was a triple-storeyed building with a massive door at the entrance of the ground floor.

My meeting with Mrs Mandal, the hostel warden, went well and she told me there was one room available.

'The single room that is still available will cost you two thousand rupees per month with breakfast and dinner. Payment for the month needs to be made in advance. If you want to just go with bed and breakfast, it will be twelve hundred and fifty rupees per month. The night you want dinner, you can inform in the morning and pay twenty-five rupees at the reception. The gates are locked at 11 p.m. and if you wish to return any later, you need to inform at the reception by 5 p.m. No guests, male or female, including relatives, are allowed inside the premises.'

Curfew time is 11 p.m.! Things were getting better by the minute, I thought.

The room that I was shown was not more than ten by eight feet, if it was really that. It had a single wooden bed with a mattress and a pillow, a wooden wardrobe, a desk and a chair. There was no air conditioning, and the bathrooms and toilets were for common use. My boarding stint at Shillong was going to be helpful now, I thought. Hostel life was not alien to me. At least, I had a room to myself. I learnt that there were only five such single rooms out of the hundred. The remaining rooms accommodated two women per room.

I thanked Linda, Mrs Mandal's assistant, after she gave me a set of keys, one to the main door at the entrance and two to the padlock on the door of my room.

I stepped out onto the pavement of Garden Street having made the first deal of my life.

I hailed a taxi back to Aunt Leena's with the assurance of a roof over my head, a meal a day, till I obtained a master's degree or a diploma of recognition.

I was left with just about enough money to last me for the next few months. And if I got carried away at any point and overspent, it could almost mean that I would be begging on the streets. Scary, I thought, but I knew that I was going to find a way. The first step towards freedom for me was costly, to say the least.

Aunt Leena was in the kitchen instructing Maharaj when I arrived. She thought that I got a great deal when I told her that I spent over fifty thousand that day and paid for my entire lodging, breakfast and tuition for the next three years. I knew that I had made the right decision. My aunt and uncle gave me some household stuff that was enough to get me started.

My life was sorted, for now.

The next morning, after breakfast, I bid adieu to the Seth family—I left with my bags for YWCA.

By the end of the day, I was settled in Room No. 10 at YWCA with my clothes neatly hung and folded in the wardrobe, clean linen on the bed, other items placed on the racks, and a framed photograph of Sheena and Mekhail placed on the small shelf next to the mirror on the wall. I was set to begin my new life in Calcutta, all by myself.

That night, when I lay down on my bed after turning off the lights and kissing Sheena and Mekhail goodnight, I thanked the Almighty for giving me the inner strength and resources to start again despite all odds, despite a lie that I would have to live with for the rest of my life, despite a dirty secret that was buried deep in my heart, despite the skeletons in my closet that would stay with me forever.

I woke up with the morning sunlight entering through the louvres of the window next to my bed.

There was a knock on my door.

'Hi, there,' a female voice said in a friendly tone.

I got out of bed and pushed the door open, which I had not locked the night before. A fair, plump and not very tall girl with a short mop of curls and a broad smile stood outside the door, holding two mugs of steaming brew in her hands.

'Good morning, I'm Vidya,' she said. 'Care for some tea?'

I took an instant liking to Vidya.

Vidya and I chatted over tea, introducing ourselves and Vidya offering to give me a helping hand for anything I needed. She was twenty years old, a computer engineer from Tamil Nadu.

'Calcutta is one of the best places for higher education. You will like it here. So, who are these cuties?' she asked, her gaze moving from me to the photograph of Sheena and Mekhail.

She stood up and went to the shelf where the framed photo was placed to take a closer look before I could reply.

'The blondie is your kid sister. She looks just like you!' she said looking back at me. 'And the little bundle, another sister or brother?'

'Sheena and Mekhail,' I said, without giving a direct reply to her.

It was one thing to write in a form that they were my siblings, but it was quite another to have to actually say that out loud to someone else. I could feel the colour draining off my face.

'How cute!' she exclaimed. 'You are lucky to have a kid sister and brother. I wish I had a younger sister, always wanted one. Hey, listen, I better get going. I'll get late for work. I'll see you in the evening. You will get to meet a few more girls then.'

She picked up the mugs and left me in a state of anguish, even though she had asked the most well-intentioned questions, unaware of the skeletons in my closet.

'How am I going to deal with this?' I thought to myself. I knew that it was going to be a task to get used to the fact that my children now legally belonged to my mother, and she had become their custodian and parent, even though I was their biological mother. I knew that I had to get my head around it sooner rather than later.

The first couple of weeks were hectic for me, restarting my life, settling in at YWCA and making new friends there.

Vidya and my morning cups of tea became a routine affair, at times in my room and at times in hers. As time passed, I got used to the idea of my two siblings whenever an introduction of Sheena and Mekhail came up in any conversation with someone. Gradually, I started believing in it myself and soon it became the reality of my life.

It was a good decision to stay in a hostel that had working women, apart from students. Whenever vacations started, all the students would return to their hometowns and families, except me. The working girls had no college vacations like we did. Except for their work leaves when they went home, most of them had to stay in the hostel as they had jobs they needed to attend Monday to Saturday.

Gradually, I started confiding in Vidya and Pratibha, who was a student in another college and lodged in the room next to mine. They knew that I had left home because I had issues with my parents, even though they were not aware what those issues were. They knew that I was tight on cash and had to live within a stringent budget.

Pratibha was an exotic beauty from Nepal and was about my age. She was slightly built and had straight and shiny black hair cut in a bob that complemented her heart-shaped face. She was a fun girl and both of us got along like a house on fire.

I lived on a street which was full of life all day long, every day. The restaurants and cafes were packed during the day and evenings, and the clubs and discotheques were packed at night.

I was very often invited by friends in the computer centre that I had joined for a year-long programming course instead of the university as well as in the hostel for a nosh-up in the late evenings, or to shake a leg in the clubs at night. Sadly, none if it came cheap. With the shoestring budget that I had to survive on, all I could afford was instant noodles every night and just about enough to indulge myself with a Sunday brunch every fortnight at Flury's, the most sought-after cafe in town.

Needless to say, at times I was almost envious of the gang who used to gussy up and leave for the night clubs and party till morning.

I did not hear either from Aunt Leena or Uncle Rajesh, neither did I contact them after I moved into the YWCA. I was totally cut off from all blood ties. In the initial days, I missed having no contact with my family. I missed Sheena and Mekhail like crazy. But as time passed, I learnt to live with my new situation. I was determined not to return home till I was financially capable of bringing my kids back with me.

Park Street was festooned with lights by mid December, getting ready for Christmas and New Year celebrations. Many of the students in the hostel left for their hometowns to ring in the New Year with their families, all but me. That was the path I had chosen, and I had to walk on it till I reached the cul-de-sac.

One evening, Vidya popped into my room while I was about to prepare my regular dinner, instant noodles.

'Hey, listen,' she said. 'How about us going out tonight?'

'Wow,' I thought. Was I hearing what I was hearing? Vidya wanting to go out at night?

'Vidya, I have got sixty bucks on me. I can't go out tonight. You know that I would love to go out and have a blast like everyone else. But I just can't!' I replied, frustration simmering inside me.

'We can,' Vidya said, sounding defiant. 'Let me foot the bill tonight. You can pay me back your share whenever you want to. I'm only saying that because otherwise you'd bite my head off. What I'd really like to do is to treat you to a good night out. What I'd like is for you not to pay me back. What I'd like is for you to swallow your pride just this one time!'

I smiled at her, a sudden euphoria taking over my senses. This was going to be my first night out after a year and a half in Calcutta.

I rushed to the bathroom with my soap and shampoo. For a glimmery evening wear look I chose a short beige dress with sequin work on it. I wore a pair of brown leather Roman sandals that I could lace right up to my knees. I brushed my long hair that fell straight and glossily up to my waist after a good shampoo and conditioning.

I had no other make-up with me apart from the lip gloss and the kohl pencil that Mom had given me more than three years ago, which I had brought with me.

Park Street looked spectacular with a myriad light decorations in different shapes and themes. My spirits soared to heights that I had not experienced before. I was mesmerized by the breathtaking beauty of the art in the lightworks and how very enchanting it made this part of the city look.

Good old Vidya had planned it all and I couldn't thank her enough for the evening of a lifetime. Our first stop was a restaurant named Sky Room, where Vidya had already booked a table for us.

Sky Room had a spectacular ceiling which had the night sky painted on it with tiny star-shaped lights twinkling around clouds. The restaurant had strict guidelines of not entertaining guests below the age of eighteen after 9 p.m. I was allowed in only after I showed my ID. There was a live band playing and a crooner with blonde hair in a short black dress whose looks and voice could have given Madonna a run for her money.

We were shown to a corner table with a good view of the band without the music blaring straight into our ears. Sky Room had a posh and lively ambience without being ostentatious. All the tables had either couples or larger groups of guests. Oddly, Vidya and I were the only two girls dining without male company. And, yes, we did turn a lot of heads.

The chicken tetrazzini and chicken á la Kiev were supposed to be the signature dishes. I settled for the tetrazzini and Vidya asked for the vegetable au gratin.

'White or red, ma'am?' asked the waiter while taking our orders.

Up until that evening, I had never had a glass of wine or a drink in the real sense, apart from occasionally having a sip of liquor from someone's glass back home.

Vidya looked confused at the waiter's question. I quickly said, 'Two glasses of red, please.'

The waiter continued, 'The house wine or anything from the menu that I can recommend?'

I was lost too by then. I was no wine connoisseur. I couldn't tell the difference between a wine and a lager!

To be on the safe side, I replied, 'The house wine, please.'

The waiter was clearly in no mood to give up.

'Can I get you an aperitif before the wine? And just a suggestion, with the tetrazzini and the au gratin, a glass of chilled white wine would be more complementary,' he said politely, probably hinting that red was the wrong choice of wine.

I was totally clueless about what 'aperitif' meant, and I could tell from Vidya's confused expression that she knew no better. Was it meant to be a culinary word for starters, I wondered, but never asked for the fear of being looked down upon as an amateur by the knowledgeable waiter who was serving us.

'We will have our reds now and the whites with the meal please,' I said, trying to sound as confident and well versed as I could, as though I went out to fine-dining restaurants every night.

The moment the waiter left, Vidya blurted out, 'What the fish! I don't drink. We will both pass out on our dinner plates.'

'We won't, Vids,' I chuckled. 'Gramps would always tell me that you can only get as drunk as you think you want to be. And, tonight, we will pass out only on our beds back in our rooms. Trust me on that.'

The knowledgeable waiter was back with two glasses of red and a bowl of nuts, which he placed on the table with a smile and said, 'Enjoy the evening, ma'am.'

Vidya and I clinked our glasses, with Vidya saying, 'Cheers to our first glass of wine!'

'Cheers!' I said. 'To a blast tonight!'

The first sip of wine tasted horrid! The second sip left a tingling sensation on the tongue. And as the number of sips grew, so did the sensations on my palate. The last sip was divine, leaving me wanting for more.

Our meals arrived and so did the glasses of white wine. Vidya and I were both chatty and happy by then. A couple of young gentlemen who were sitting two tables away in a big group, beckoned our waiter. They were watching us for a while and had smiled at us a few times.

'This is the life!' I said. 'Vids, I must get myself a part-time job. We need to do this more often.'

That night, I clearly tasted blood.

After our meal, Vidya and I hailed a taxi to go to the Grand Hotel in Chowringhee Lane, where Pink Elephant, a popular nightclub, was located.

I had never been to a nightclub before, nor had Vidya. Pink Elephant looked pretty much like the nightclubs that I had seen in the movies. There was a long bar with a sea of young people where drinks were being sold and a dance floor where everybody was swinging to '*Staying Alive*' as we entered.

We had to wait for our turn to get a table.

'This is the life,' I thought once again that night. I was light-headed from the wine that I had drunk and the excitement of being in the stratosphere of the good life; it was all that a nineteen-year-old could wish for with just sixty bucks in her wallet. That night my wishes were horses, and I was riding!

I had no recollection of how Vidya and I got into our hostel and reached our rooms. My last memory before I passed out on my bed was that of an orange sky, which meant that we partied all night till daybreak on our first 'night out' in Calcutta.

'Gramps would have been proud of me!' I thought as I passed out in my beige sequin dress and brown Roman sandals to wake up in time for dinner. I had slept all day after partying all night!

That first night out sparked a fire in my belly to look beyond my academic prowess. I no longer wanted to go to university. I wanted to make money, I wanted to make lots of money—to be able to pay my friends back, to be able to have more than my instant noodles every night for dinner, to not only window shop for dresses but to be able to buy a dress, to stop worrying about the dwindling savings in my bank account, to be able to go for a night out on my own steam, to be able to elevate myself from my hand-to-mouth existence.

I scoured through the advertisements in the newspapers, but alas all vacancies looked for nothing less than a master's degree in something. But I kept searching and searching, till one fine day not very long after, I saw: 'A walk-in interview for freelancers to sell the Diners Club card on commission only. Applicants need to be over eighteen years of age, smart, well-groomed and eloquent.'

I ticked all the boxes, I thought, as I walked into the office of the Diners Club as if I owned the place. I was strangely not as nervous as one is supposed to be at an interview. The interview lasted for not more than twenty minutes after I handed over my handwritten résumé. I was asked to come for an orientation and training programme the Monday of the subsequent week. I was given an appointment letter by the secretary of the manager who had interviewed me after a half hour wait in the reception area.

'Well done, Indrani! You will go great guns,' said Vidya, excited at the news of my job.

'You will be my first customer,' I said, giving her a hug and a peck on her cheek.

The orientation and training session was all about learning the ropes of selling a comb to the bald. The ownership of a Diners Club card was no doubt a status symbol. Flashing out the plastic Diners Card anywhere instead of a wad of paper money, or any other plastic currency, meant that you were a higher mortal. Hence, selling the Diners Club card was all about stoking one's vanity and ego boosting. That was the essence of the training session.

Despite my freelance sales job, I knew that I would still have time to spare, so I enrolled myself for lessons in computer programming, which kept me busy for four hours a day, Monday to Friday. I needed to have a bit more on my CV than just an economics graduate degree.

Freelancers had to report to the office once a week to hand over the filled-up and signed forms along with the hefty membership-fee cheques of the customers. I opted for Friday afternoons as my computer lessons on that day were only until midday.

I left the office of the Diners Club after a briefing session with the sales manager, Shrikant, with a bunch of one hundred forms. We were told that the commission on sales would be paid to us on the second of every calendar month and that we would be paid four hundred rupees for every new member who enrolled with Diners Club through us.

On the first day itself I bagged my first customer: Vidya Swaminathan!

Very often, I went out on cold calls as I still barely knew anyone in Calcutta. By the end of the month, I had fifty-eight new Diners Club members to my credit. I was the top-performing salesperson, not just among the freelancers but also the full-time executives who were on the company's payroll.

Shrikant, the sales manager, announced at the month-end meeting, looking at no one in particular at first, and then with his gaze fixed on me, he continued, 'A round of applause for the youngest sales exec in our team, Indrani!'

Everyone in the room clapped.

Shrikant said in his booming voice, 'Indrani, you have beaten us all with your sales numbers! Well done! Come back on Tuesday to pick up your cheque. You have a job waiting here for you when you complete your studies.'

Moving his gaze to the team of freelancers and full-time sales execs he said, 'Eat your hearts out, guys! You ought to learn a lesson or two from Indrani.'

Shaking my hand with a firm grip and congratulating me, Shrikant exited the room, leaving me with a lump in my throat.

I returned the next Tuesday to collect my first pay cheque of ₹23,200 that I had earned in twenty-five days of work.

There was no looking back for me. I was clearly good at selling. I studied hard, topped my programming class, sold Diners Club cards in my spare time, and partied every weekend from night till morning with my besties. Life was good, the heavens were smiling upon me.

I learnt at the age of nineteen that the gift of the gab, together with a sharp intellect and a go-getter spirit, conflated to success as far as making money went. I sold all the time, everywhere and anywhere, till I was able to make money out of nothing.

As I stood with Vidya and Pratibha in Park Street that New Year's Eve, at the stroke of midnight, the skies above Calcutta were ablaze with the most spectacular display of fireworks.

When I looked at the lit-up heavens and amidst the celebrations around me, I thought of Sheena and Mekhail, whom I had not seen for almost two years, that special bond and connection that I had with them, that fine line of letting them go but never quite being able to cut the cord. For a few brief seconds there was a silence inside me amidst all the chaos outside, and the images of all that I lost and all that I gained in the twenty years of my life flashed across my mind.

On account of my outstanding performance, the Diners Club had awarded me with a two-year free membership, and I was the proud owner of a Golden Diners Card that I could flash at Sky Room or Pink Elephant instead of a wad of crumpled notes.

Dressed up in an orange and black outfit, black high heels, artfully done-up eyes with black liner and mascara, pink gloss on the lips, a generous spray of perfume, I headed off to Vidya's room. Pratibha was already sitting there in her favourite short black dress.

We were headed to Peter Cat, a restaurant in the building next to YWCA that served the best chelo kebabs in the city.

We met Vidya's friend Astra on our way out. When we stepped out with Astra leading the way, there were three men, all very well groomed, one with a fractured arm, and a young lady standing outside waiting for Astra.

'Are these really Astra's friends?' I wondered. 'They are a class apart.' But I kept my thoughts to myself.

Astra introduced her friends D.P., Taran, [names changed] Sanjeev and Philo.

Sanjeev was a bespectacled man; there was an air of distinction about him. His chiselled face had a moustache, which was otherwise clean shaven. His left hand was encased in a plaster cast, supported by a sling.

The other two men were older than Sanjeev, and even though they looked distinguished, they did not have the sparkle in their eyes as Sanjeev did. Sanjeev had a pleasant smile, firm handshake and courteous conduct.

When he shook my hand, I felt an erotic charge that definitely made his subtle behaviour more appealing. After Vish, that was the first time I felt drawn towards another man. I liked what I saw and what I felt. I knew that this was not the last time I was going to meet Sanjeev. There was instant chemistry between us; once our eyes were locked, the rest of the people were cropped out of the picture.

'Would you care to join us for a drink?' Sanjeev asked us.

I wanted to, but declined instead and said, 'We've got a table reserved for dinner. We are already late. Maybe some other time.'

'What about after dinner?' Sanjeev pursued.

I could see Vidya getting restless and for fear of getting smacked on my head I said, 'Not tonight. Maybe we can meet for a cup of coffee tomorrow afternoon?'

His face lit up while Vidya gave me a dirty look.

'6 p.m. tomorrow at Big Max,' he said.

'Done, 6 p.m. sounds good,' I said, as my heart skipped a beat.

Pratibha, Vidya and I walked to the next building to Peter Cat while Sanjeev and his friends left in two cars to wherever they were going.

We spent a happy evening eating, drinking and reminiscing about the good times that the three of us had together.

Next day, I showered and changed into a pair of navy-blue trousers and a crisp white cotton shirt, all set to go for the sales calls that day. I no longer made cold calls. In a year's time I had built a diverse set of clientele and I managed to add newer clients almost every day through references only. Better still was the fact that I had quite a few job offers that I could choose from the day I completed my programming diploma.

I was excited the entire day with thoughts of 6 p.m. at Big Max and not as focussed on work as I usually was.

Big Max was the most popular fast food joint on Garden Street before the arrival of the likes of McDonald's, Pizza Hut, Burger King and Barista. Big Max was all of these rolled into one.

When I arrived at Big Max, Sanjeev was already seated at a table for two. He stood up as I entered and flashed a smile at me.

He was dressed in a pair of navy-blue trousers and a crisp white cotton shirt tucked in, the same combination of clothes that I was in.

He held his hand out to shake mine and said, 'Good to see you, Indrani. I was afraid that I was going to be stood up.'

'How could I not show up?' I replied. 'I was the one who invited you, remember?'

I sat down on the chair facing him across the table and, on an impulse, I pinched his hand which was resting on the table and said, 'Same pinch, blue and white.'

Sanjeev looked at me, surprised, and laughed out loud. He had a hearty laugh; I liked the sound of it.

'I noticed,' he said. 'Telepathy. Great minds think alike. Would you like to eat something?'

'A chicken burger and a Coke please. And please let's go dutch,' I said.

'Oh, don't be silly. You can pay when you are out with your girlfriends. Ladies don't pay when there's a man at the table.'

He got up and left for the counter to pay and returned with a token till our number flashed on the screen.

'Astra mentioned last night that you've been at the YWCA for a while. What do you do Indrani?' he asked.

'I just finished my exams last week. I'm also working, rather freelancing, with the Diners Club, in sales,' I said.

And before I could stop myself, I blurted out, 'Hey, do you have a Diners Club card?'

I could have kicked myself after that. I had absolutely no plans to hustle. But clearly 'sales' was now ingrained in my brain cells and had become my second nature. I couldn't resist the temptation of selling even on the date which I had been so looking forward to the entire day.

I was saved by the number that flashed on the screen, which summoned us to get our food from the service counter.

Sanjeev went across to the counter and returned with two burgers, fries, Coke, coffee and a bottle of water.

'Here you go,' he said, placing the tray of food on the table with one hand, the other still slung in a cast.

Sanjeev started talking about himself as we munched on our burgers. He was twenty-seven, had attended a private boarding school in Rajasthan, graduated from a university in Calcutta, and joined the family business with his uncle after that. He said that he had lost his father when he was barely three and, ever since, along with his mother and younger brother Vivek, he lived with his grandmother, uncle, aunt and two very young cousins.

'And no, I do not have a Diners Card,' he said suddenly. 'But now I will if you sell me one.' He seemed amused.

I could feel my ears turning hot. I knew that I was flushed with embarrassment and was red in the face.

'You don't have to. I wasn't trying to sell you one. I just asked,' I replied hoping that he'd leave it at that.

'Give me a form. I'll take it with me. Let's meet tomorrow. I'll bring the cheque for the fee.'

And just as I opened my mouth to say that he'd got it all wrong, he added, 'I insist.'

I meekly nodded and smiled.

'Thank you. Shall we meet after work tomorrow? To go out for dinner?' he asked.

'Let's meet here at five tomorrow. Or I can come to your office, if that's okay. My friend is leaving town in a couple of days. I'd like to spend time with her in the evenings,' I replied, even though the invitation for dinner with Sanjeev was tempting.

In the couple of hours that I spent with Sanjeev, I realized that he was a man who was probably entrenched in the patriarchal norms of society and believed that women should be ensconced within these norms for safety.

Even though I differed in my thinking, I did not express my opinion. I liked Sanjeev. I had already goofed up by selling the card to him, two minutes after we met. The last thing I wanted to do was to have a debate on my first date about a woman's place in society, with a man whom I was attracted to, after so long. That conversation could wait, I thought.

He pulled out a card from his wallet which had his office address and phone numbers, and handed it to me.

'Sanjeev Khanna,' I said aloud while reading his business card.

I gave him my Diners Club business card and we both rose to leave.

'I'll walk you back to your hostel. It's dark. My car is anyway parked close to YWCA,' he said.

'How are you driving?' I asked, looking at his bandaged arm.

'I am not. I've got a driver. Let's go,' he said.

We walked back to YWCA and as he had said, his driver had parked the car almost in front of the hostel gates.

We shook hands before I went into the lobby, and he waited till the door closed behind me.

Sanjeev was not a Greek God with Adonis-like chiselled features and six-pack abs. But he was handsome in a different way which I liked. He had a good sense of humour and was intelligent.

That evening, Sanjeev and I did not discuss my family, even though he spoke about his. As I walked up the stairs to my room, I wondered if Sanjeev could draw me, in the near future, into a conversation, where I'd talk about my life back home, about the dark secrets that I never shared with Vidya or Pratibha in the years that I had spent with them.

I opened the lock on my door, entered my room and turned on the lights. Taking a deep breath, I looked at myself in the mirror. And then looked at Sheena and Mekhail's photograph. I felt tears rolling down my cheeks. There was something about him and the evening that I had spent with him that touched me somewhere deep down and aroused emotions that I had thought I would never experience again, particularly with a man.

The next day, I visited Sanjeev at his office, which was unprofessional, but it did not stop me from pushing the envelope. Sanjeev was taken aback, no doubt, but equally delighted by my surprise visit.

His face broke into a smile that reached his sharp eyes when he saw me waiting in the lobby of his office. He shook my hand with a firm grip and excitement gleaming in his eyes.

The office was filled with a motley collection of furniture and paintings. 'Awful interior design!' I thought but kept my thoughts to myself as Sanjeev led me to his cubicle.

'Here you go!' he said, handing over the form that I had given him the previous day along with a cheque for the membership fee for the Diners Club.

I thanked him and got up from the chair to leave. 'I'm sorry to have barged into your office without checking with you. I should have called. Let me not hold up your work any longer.'

'No trouble, whatsoever,' he said with a smile. 'It's almost lunchtime. There's a rooftop cafe close by. Why don't we grab a bite together?'

My head said 'no', but my heart said otherwise. I knew that I was giving into temptation, which could be a blunder, as my soul was still scarred, the wounds had not healed, and I was probably still unprepared to reciprocate the emotions that I saw in Sanjeev's eyes that afternoon.

'Oh yes, lunch sounds great,' I said instead.

The cafe was two buildings away from Sanjeev's office and was on the terrace that opened up to the winter sky. The lunch crowd was just pouring in as we reached, so we managed to get ourselves a table for two in the corner.

The staff seemed to know Sanjeev and came to attend to him the moment we sat down.

'Two chana bhaturas, two Cokes and a bottle of water,' said Sanjeev as the waiter scribbled the order on his little notepad.

'I am a vegetarian on Tuesdays and Saturdays,' Sanjeev announced after placing the order.

'I'm not,' I said before I could stop myself.

'I'm sorry for ordering for you without checking with you first,' he said looking apologetic. 'The chana bhatura is really good here. But we can get you something else if you would like.'

'I'd like to have the same as you,' I replied putting on my best smile.

Our Cokes had arrived and as we sipped, Sanjeev suddenly asked, 'Tell me about yourself, Indrani. Do you have someone back home?'

I froze. I did not have an answer to his question! What was I going to tell Sanjeev? That I had a daughter whose paternity I was not at ease to disclose, and that I had a son whose father was a bête noire, that I had a mother who was now the mother of my children—the list just went on.

I was saved by the arrival of the chana bhaturas. But I knew that I could not live a lie with the man across the table for as long as I had with Vidya, Pratibha and the rest of the people I knew in Calcutta.

'It's delicious!' I said after a bite.

'You're not upset anymore that I didn't ask you before I ordered, are you?' Sanjeev asked with an impish grin.

'I'm not in touch with my family back home. If it is okay, I'd rather not talk about it,' I said replying to Sanjeev's first question.

'And I'm glad to be sitting here with you and eating the most delicious chana bhatura that you have ordered for me without asking,' I continued, answering his second question, with a smile.

'I don't mean to prod. And if you do not wish to, you need not answer. But why are you not in contact with your family? These things happen, you know. But at the end of the day, family is family. And you ought to mend your ties, no matter how difficult the proposition may appear to you now,' he said.

'No man is an island. And you are incomplete without your family,' he went on, suddenly grasping my hand, and giving it a squeeze.

'I can be an island as I am not a man,' I replied, peeved at his assumptions without knowing the facts and the tragedy that crippled my soul and my entire existence.

'Mom, Dad, sister and brother,' I said to stop him from prodding further. 'The rest of it in our next meeting.'

'Date!' he corrected me, with a wink and a smile that touched my heart.

Sanjeev liked me a hell of a lot, I could see and feel it. And the danger was that I liked him too, a hell lot!

We decided to meet the next evening for dinner at Sky Room. I chose a pair of white palazzo pants and a white crop top for my date with Sanjeev. Adding on a pair of silver danglers on my ears and slipping into a pair of brown stilettos, I walked down to the lobby to wait for Sanjeev to arrive.

'Poodle,' said Sanjeev smiling at me, 'you look great!'

'Hey, did you just call me "Poodle"?' I asked, surprised at being addressed as a canine.

'I sure did. Dogs are man's best friend. I love dogs. I've got three at home. They are adorable. I'll take you home to meet them,' he replied, with his infectious smile lighting up his eyes.

'Can we just stick to Indrani?' I said without acknowledging his love for the canine species.

'Sure, Poodle,' he replied. 'Let's go. We'll walk down to Sky Room. It's just a stone's throw away.'

Sanjeev stretched his hand out to hold mine as we walked down Garden Street towards Sky Room. The way Sanjeev protectively and firmly grasped my hand filled my entire being with a feeling of warmth and affinity towards him which I had not experienced with anyone after Vish.

That evening I had made up my mind to not let the fears of my past cast a shadow on my newly found happiness.

Sanjeev had booked a table for us and when we entered I realized that he was one of the favoured clients in the restaurant, clearly a frequent diner there. It was uncanny that I had never met him earlier at Sky Room since it was my favourite haunt, and I went there very often.

Our drinks had arrived, Sanjeev's rum and Coke, and my vodka and soda along with a bowl of nuts.

'Cheers to the good life. Cheers to our friendship. Cheers to many happy days ahead!' said Sanjeev, raising his glass.

I thought that there was an honesty in his eyes that was quite evident even though I barely knew him for me to have come to that conclusion. I felt guilty about not coming clean with him about my past and the life that I had left behind.

'Penny for your thoughts! I seek your full attention tonight. No drifting away,' Sanjeev nudged me, bringing me back to that present moment, back to Sky Room.

'Sorry,' I said, 'Sanjeev, I can't do this.'

I gulped down my vodka almost at one go, fervently hoping that it would give me the strength to give a complete disclosure to the man sitting next to me, who had clearly fallen in love with me, unaware of the baggage that I carried.

'Can't do what? I'm lost here,' Sanjeev asked, looking puzzled.

'Can I please have another vodka?' I asked without looking at him, fearing that I'd burst into tears before I could tell him anything.

'You sure can. Are you all right, Poodle?' There was a note of genuine concern in his voice as he asked me.

I nodded, as he beckoned the waiter standing in one corner trying to be invisible till called for.

'Another round, please. Can you please hold on to the mains for a while till we are ready?' he told the waiter, who politely bowed and agreed.

'Spill it out, Poodle, whatever it is. Is it that you don't like me? It is all right if that's what it is. We can enjoy our meal tonight and not meet again, even though I will think about you a lot after that,' he said.

'I do like you, Sanjeev, a lot. That's the problem! There are things that I have not told you about myself. Once I do, you'll probably never wish to meet me again.' I was about to start talking about that frightful evening eight years ago that scarred me forever when the waiter arrived with our drinks.

As I sipped my vodka, I slowly narrated my saga to Sanjeev amidst sobs. All the pent-up grief inside me poured out, which I had buried deep down for all those years.

Sanjeev listened to every word that I said in silence, looking intently at me, his eyes at times revealing shock and at times empathy.

'And that is how I ended up in YWCA and that is why I cannot be with you. My life is a mess, you deserve better,' I said, wiping my tears with the serviette and sobbing at the thought of never seeing Sanjeev again.

When I had stepped out for dinner that evening, I had no plans to disclose my past to Sanjeev. All that I wanted was to have a good time, maybe even a wild night out with him. But I had ended up ruining that one evening that I was so looking forward to by letting out the dark secrets of my life, I thought to myself.

I excused myself to powder my nose, leaving Sanjeev at the table to nurse his drink.

My tears had washed out the kohl from my eyes, leaving black marks all over my cheeks. I thought I looked like a mess when I saw myself in the mirror on the wall in the ladies' room. The cold water that I splashed on my face brought the colour back and the confidence to return to Sanjeev and enjoy the evening as I had planned to.

Sanjeev smiled at me warmly when he saw me walking back to the table.

'Are we ready for dinner?' he asked, taking my hand in his.

'Yes, Sanjeev, I am ready,' I said, not just replying to the question that he had asked but also to the question that he had not asked.

'That's my girl! Wine with the mains or the same?'

'Vodka, please,' I answered, squeezing his hand. 'Thank you, Sanjeev, for hearing me out and for understanding. I'm sorry for not telling you the truth earlier.'

That evening Sanjeev and I talked over dinner and shared stories about our lives that we had never spoken about to anyone else before. We bonded like we had known each other for a lifetime.

'Let's go home,' he said suddenly as he pulled out his wallet to pay the bill.

12

It was almost midnight when we reached Sanjeev's house. There was pin-drop silence, and the lights were out in the big bungalow that Sanjeev lived in with his family. Sanjeev's bedroom was a flight upstairs.

His dogs, Cleo, Toby and Snoopy ran around Sanjeev in excitement and sniffed at me on and off to check whether I was a friend or a foe of their lord and master. Once satisfied with my intentions, they retreated to their corners.

Sanjeev held me in his arms and kissed me on my mouth, slowly and sensuously, making me crave for more. Caressing me gently, he undressed me and himself, whispering sweet nothings into my ears.

Next morning, Sanjeev suggested we have dinner with his folks.

'Sanjeev, I'm not ready to meet your family. I'm not sure that I want to share my past with anyone but you for the moment,' I said, feeling sorry for turning down his dinner invitation to meet his family.

'I need to sort out a few things in my life. I don't know where I stand as of now with Sheena and Mekhail. I hope you understand,' I said, holding back tears.

'That's cool. We'll do as you say. I'll pick you up for dinner at eight. We'll still have dinner, just you and me,' replied Sanjeev, his eyes on the road ahead as we meandered through the traffic back to my hostel.

When I unlocked my room door, I went to the shelf next to the mirror where Sheena and Mekhail spent the entire night alone without me in Room No. 10 at YWCA. I picked up the photo frame, held it close to my chest and let the tears roll down, tears that I had held back in the car on my way to YWCA with Sanjeev.

My tryst with Sanjeev the previous night started a fundamental and consequential shift in my life. And whether I was ever going to be able to normalize this new approach to life with all the baggage that I had, was a big question mark in my mind. I knew that it would be an arduous, if not impossible task.

Sanjeev, no doubt, captured the nuances of my feelings but could I expect the same from his family members, I wondered. I was clearly in the tricky landscape of getting into a relationship with Sanjeev. But it was also likely that expectations from his family could be sky high whilst I was still neck deep in my own issues that still needed resolving and closure.

As planned, Sanjeev picked me up at eight for dinner. We decided to meet every evening for dinner and for lunch, including bank holidays and Sundays. Over the next few weeks, I was introduced to several of Sanjeev's friends at the clubs, restaurants and get-togethers that we attended.

Sanjeev grew up in Calcutta's upscale locality of Hastings and belonged to an affluent family. His father was in the construction business like him and was murdered when Sanjeev was still a child. He grew up in a joint family and studied in Mayo College, Ajmer. Sanjeev was a member of several elite clubs in Calcutta and a regular at the car rallies and races. He spent most of his time either with me or at work or at the Calcutta Cricket and Football Club.

As the days passed, Sanjeev and I became a couple in every possible manner, just short of being wedded. My results were announced. My hard work had paid off. I had yet another meritorious achievement to add to my academic records. It was time to move to the next phase of my life and look for a job which was more meaningful and holistically rewarding.

By then, I had moved out of the YWCA hostel to an accommodation closer to Sanjeev's place. Vidya and I met rarely after I moved out of YWCA as her free time was reserved for Hormez [name changed], whom she was dating then, and mine for Sanjeev.

Sanjeev had finally decided that it was time that I at least meet his mother, as his protracted absence from home, almost every night and on days when he was off work, was becoming a point of contention with his family, particularly his uncle, Gour Mohan Kapur. Sanjeev believed that his uncle was well-meaning but was a strict disciplinarian, who disapproved of Sanjeev's lifestyle.

Sanjeev and his mother, Sudha Khanna, came to fetch me one evening to go out for a meal together. Everyone in Sanjeev's family was aware that he had a woman in his life, which was the reason for his frequent and prolonged disappearances from home. They coaxed him often to tell them if he had chosen a partner and had any plans to settle down. However, Sanjeev was clearly not in a position to give them an answer that they wanted to hear. Sanjeev had disclosed to his mother all that I had shared with him about my life, after we agreed that it was best to tell her everything. Based on my next steps, we could reveal as much as we chose to, to the rest of the family.

Sudha Khanna, Sanjeev's mother, was a beautiful woman with a wheatish complexion. She was clad in a brown sari, had pinned up her hair and had a dignified air about her with a pleasant smile on her lips. But I noticed a deep sadness in her eyes even at the first glance.

Sanjeev had booked a table in a restaurant at Hotel Hindustan, which was more well-lit than the cosy restaurants that we frequented. Only after I placed my order of food and drinks did I realize that

Sanjeev's mother was a vegetarian. She, unlike my folks at home, did not drink alcohol. I thought about how different she was from Sanjeev in all respects. But she was kind, gentle and there was a connection that I felt with her instantly even though we were poles apart as far as our food habits went.

'Indrani,' she said, 'Sanjeev has told me everything. What we know can stay between us. My mother is eighty and has orthodox and conservative views. She may not take all of this in the same spirit as I have. What one doesn't know doesn't hurt them. Sanjeev is happy with you. His happiness is everything to me. We ought to find a solution, which takes care of everyone's sentiments while we look at both of you tying the knot.'

What Sanjeev's mother said surely resonated with me but how pragmatic was the solution she offered? That was definitely a big question mark in my mind. I loved Sanjeev and was willing to be a part of his life as his wife, but I wondered if there really was a way out that could take care of everyone's sentiments—of the Khannas and the Kapurs. Her suggestion and opinions towards finding a solution generated more questions than answers in my mind.

I was, however, touched by the kindness beaming from her eyes even while she was asserting her point firmly as to how Sanjeev and I could possibly get married. She, no doubt, left me a lot to ponder over. Once she put her point across without mincing words, she deftly moved the conversation to my academics, future career plans and to her own life, putting me at ease for the remainder of the evening. She spoke about Sanjeev's father, who was brutally murdered because he did not succumb to the pressures of ruthless contractors who had tried to persuade him to sanction the use of poor quality material for construction of a dam and a bridge that were under his charge as the chief engineer of a reputed German firm. She reminisced about her short time with him, her voice imbued with an affection and passion as she spoke about him. But her eyes revealed a grief almost as though even after almost twenty-five years of his departure, there had been no closure for her.

The evening with Sanjeev and his mother was a meeting of minds and souls. I did not know then whether Sanjeev and I would eventually get married. But I was certain that I shared a bond with him and his mother that would stay with me for the rest of my life, and one that I would cherish no matter where I was or where life led me.

That night when I returned home, I looked at Sheena, whose photograph was now on my bedside table and felt a sudden sweeping urge to go to her, hold her as she looked at me with her large brown eyes. I needed to return to Guwahati, where I had left behind a part of myself in Sheena and Mekhail, without whom I was incomplete.

Apart from my degree in economics, I now had a diploma in computer programming—I knew, in the long run, my programming knowledge would give me an edge if I were to seek a decent job with a multinational company or look at starting any business of my own.

Within the next couple of days, and surprisingly without much effort, I bagged a job at a Computer Training Centre as an academic counsellor where I was offered a decent salary and the freedom to use the computers and train in more advanced programming skills. The job entailed selling training courses and packages to prospective clients, which I thought was a good opportunity to hone my marketing and sales skills with a different product in the comfort of an air-conditioned office, without having to step out.

I had accepted the job offer and was due to join the firm in two weeks, which gave me ample time to visit Sheena and Mekhail. I had decided to bring them back with me and arrange for a nanny who could look after them while I was at work.

After almost three long years, I headed off to an STD booth to make a call to Gramps and Granny. My heartbeat accelerated as I heard the long ring buzzing through when I held the receiver next to my ear.

When I heard Granny's voice saying 'Hello' after a few rings, I could almost see her standing in front of the console table in the hallway of their cottage where the black and brass telephone was kept from the time I was three years old.

'Granny,' I said, with a lump in my throat and tears brimming in my eyes.

'Pari! Oh, my darling, where have you been? How are you?' Granny recognized my voice instantly despite not having heard from me in such a long time.

'How are you, Granny? How's Gramps?' I was overwhelmed with emotions and longing for my family, a feeling that I had buried deep down for the last few years.

'We are both good, sweetheart. Why have you not called us?' Granny's voice was a combination of relief, concern and joy.

'Gran, I am fine, thank you. Can I please visit you and Gramps, like stay with you for a week?' I said without spelling out that I had no intention of going home where my father lived.

'What a silly question, Pari! You sure can stay with us for as long as you wish to. This is your home. When will you be coming?' I could hear Gramps's voice somewhere as Granny spoke to me.

'It's Pari,' Granny said.

Gramps came on the call and his otherwise heavy voice was like music to my ears. 'Princess, how dare you ignore Granny and me for this long?' he barked into my ear.

'Gramps, I miss you. I will come visit you and Granny soon. Maybe in the next couple of days. I will tell you everything when we meet. Let me buy my ticket and I'll call you back in the evening,' I said, almost wishing that I had wings and could fly to my grandparents at that very moment. I had not realized how much I missed them up until I spoke to them that day.

Time had not muddied my memories of the love and support that Gramps had always given me unconditionally whenever I sought refuge.

I rushed to a travel agent and purchased a return ticket for myself, a ticket for Sheena, aged five, and Mekhail, aged three, from Guwahati to Calcutta.

I was scheduled to leave in two days and there was plenty to do before I left. I had my hands full with my own packing and buying goodies for Sheena and Mekhail before Sanjeev reached at eight to fetch me for dinner. Sanjeev arrived, looking as cool and chilled out as he always did in the evening in his faded blue denims and a pink shirt that added colour to his radiant and ever cheerful face. We were invited for dinner to his friend Rakul's house which was close by, which meant that I had very little time to break the news to Sanjeev about not just my travel plans but my decision to bring Sheena and Mekhail to live with me. I had no desire to let my glorious past stare Sanjeev in his face, but it was essential for both of us to come to terms with the truth, no matter how brutal it was, even if it meant that we could not be together. That was the essence of it all.

'Sanjeev, I am going to visit Gramps and Granny the day after. I have booked my flight,' I said and waited for Sanjeev's reaction.

'Hey, that's good. What time your flight? I'll plan my day accordingly. I'll drop you to the airport,' he said, not sounding surprised even if he was.

'Are you sure though, Poodle?' he asked. 'Are you sure that you want to go back? I suppose it'll do you good.'

He looked at me and smiled, melting my heart. I said no more. I had to tell Sanjeev that I was planning to return with Sheena and Mekhail.

Mukul Agarwal, a few years older than Sanjeev, was the youngest sibling of the Agarwal family, who were a part of the toffee-nosed gentry in Calcutta. That evening a fight broke out at dinner amongst the Agarwal siblings. With the big news I had to break to Sanjeev, I almost let out a sign of relief when Sanjeev got up to leave.

On the way back to my place, which was just a short drive from Mukul's, Sanjeev jabbered continuously about anything and everything, which left me with very little room to tell him about my own plans. When we reached home, I invited Sanjeev inside so that I could get my news out of the way, sooner rather than later. He seemed pleased at the invitation clearly expecting way more than a simple chat.

Once indoors, Sanjeev ked off his loafers and lounged comfortably on my bed while unlaced my Roman sandals before sitting next to him.

'Sanjeev, I am going for ad a week. I am planning to bring Sheena and Mekhail back wie.' I looked into Sanjeev's eyes as I spoke and paused for his real and response.

'Oh! For how long? I tht you will be starting your new job in the next couple of w You will barely get any time with them before you have to go to drop them. Why don't you just spend a couple of extra day th them while you are with your grandparents. That's more pral and will save you a lot of hassle,' he said, pushing a tendril of l behind my ears.

'Sanjeev, I don't plan to t Sheena and Mekhail back. I am bringing them with me for go They'll stay here with me.'

'Poodle, you can't be serid' he exclaimed, looking at me in disbelief.

'I have to. I have made up iy mind,' I replied, praying in my heart that he would understand

'Poodle, you are a paying guest here. You can't have two young kids living with you in this room. And what happens to them when you go to work?' Sanjeev was now beginning to sound almost annoyed. His words brought back memories of my conversation with my mother three years ago when I had announced that Sheena and Mekhail would move with me to Calcutta.

'And what happens to us?' he continued in an exasperated voice. 'Badi Maa may not take this well.'

'I don't know, Sanjeev. I don't have an answer to your question now. All I know is that I love you more than you can imagine. I don't want to lose you. But I need Sheena and Mekhail as much as I need you. I do not expect you to understand but things can work out if we really want to be together. We can and will find a way. Please, just bear with me!' I pleaded.

But Sanjeev sat still. He did not pull me into his arms, nor did he look into my eyes. It was as though he was shell-shocked and numbed by the turn of events.

Sanjeev got up and slipped on his shoes. Kissing me on my forehead, he said, 'Let's sleep over it, Poodle. We both need a good night's rest to clear our heads. Let's meet for breakfast at quarter past nine. I'll come to get you. Nightie night.'

I got up to see him off, but he quickly added, 'I'll see myself out.' With a wave of his hand, he walked out of the door without looking back. I got out of bed, changed into my pyjamas, washed my face, and climbed back into the sheets. Maybe I was disappointed with Sanjeev's reaction, but my belief persisted that everything was going to be all right the next morning. And I was right. When Sanjeev returned in the morning the next day, he beamed when he saw me. He did not look upset anymore. I almost felt as though I was glowing with a borrowed radiance from the smile that lit up his face.

At that moment I knew that no man could ever love me as much as Sanjeev did.

'You win, Poodle,' he said, as I slid into the seat next to him in the car.

I clasped his hand and whispered into his ears, 'Thank you, Sanjeev, for understanding. Thank you for loving me for who I am and what I am. I love you, Sanjeev.'

The next day Sanjeev took the morning off to drop me to the airport. He held on tight when we embraced before I entered the terminal gates.

'See you soon, Poodle. Call me once you reach your grandparents' home. I'll call you every morning and at night if it is okay with your folks. I'll miss you but I know that I'll see you soon. Love you,' he said, holding my face in his hands.

Gramps was waiting for me at arrivals when I landed. He looked the same, smelt the same and his joy knew no bounds when he saw me walking out of the exit doorway.

'My princess,' he said gleefully and as though I was still a ten-year-old, he scooped me up in his arms, 'welcome home!'

It was indeed heartwarming to touch and feel family again. The drive up to Gramps's cottage was a journey down memory lane— the familiar roads, the air as fresh as champagne, the fragrances of the flowers and trees that lined the streets and the stories of how Gramps and Granny still bickered over the same old things. Gramps filled me in about Sheena and Mekhail, and how quickly they had both grown in the last three years.

'Sheena is almost your clone. Even her mannerisms are similar to yours. There's always something or the other going on in her little head, plenty of questions and always eager to know more.

Mekhail follows her around like Mary's little lamb. Sheena is sure the bossy boots amongst the two,' Gramps said, with his laugh and twinkling eyes.

He made no mention of Dad or Siddharth. 'Your mom has got her hands full with the duo. Pari, sweetheart, you should have at least called us. Granny was worried about you even though Leena had said that you had settled in well. Granny really missed you. Are you doing all right?' he asked me, after talking about Granny and Mom.

'Gramps, I've got a job now. I'm now ready to take Sheena and Mekhail with me. Are they already at your place? I can't wait to hold them in my arms. I can't wait to meet Granny,' I said, excited at the thought of seeing Sheena, Mekhail, Granny and even Mom, and catching up on everything that I had missed out on in the last three years while I was away building my own life.

I could see Gramps's brow creasing into a frown. 'Your mother is planning to come down with the babies tomorrow. Till then catch up with your Granny, let her spoil you silly. She has made your favourite Sunday roast. Look how skinny you've become,' he said, lifting up my hand as though to inspect whether I had any flesh around the bones.

'How is Siddharth, Gramps?' I asked, curious that he had made no mention of Siddharth in the last couple of hours.

'No idea, Pari. He left a week after you did. Ever since, we have never heard from him. We've not seen him at all,' he said dismissively.

'And what's happened to the bakery?' I probed.

'Your mother decided to shut shop after Siddharth left,' Gramps answered as we entered the beautiful avenue that led up to their cottage, the most picturesque view etched in my mind.

Granny was delighted to see me and she burst into tears when she hugged me. 'Gran, I missed you both. Why did you and Gramps not visit me? You knew where I was. Why did you not make a trip when you missed me, Gran?' I finally asked the questions that I had had no answers to in the last few years. I always wondered why my grandparents, who were such inveterate travellers, chose not to visit me even once in Calcutta.

The room was fraught with silence. She looked at Gramps, her eyes still moist and as Gramps nodded, she returned her gaze to me and said, 'For you, Pari. We did not go to you because you were not ready. To start afresh you needed to be away from everyone and everything that could trigger off memories which you left behind.'

'All right, girls, that's enough! Pari, honey, go and freshen up. Let's meet in an hour. I'm parched and starved,' Gramps deftly intervened before Granny got more embroiled in a conversation that could have led to a debate of emotions rather than a cosy family reunion.

My bags were already in the bedroom that I always used, whenever I visited my grandparents. Granny had picked the roses from Gramps's garden and put them in a crystal vase on the dresser of my room. The freshly plucked roses let out a heady fragrance. The mellow light of the setting sun seeped into the room as I unpacked and hung my clothes in the wardrobe that Granny had probably emptied out for me. I felt blissful.

That evening I enjoyed the perfect reunion that I could have asked for. Gramps raised a toast to me for having secured a job. Granny raised one to me for having returned as a woman with an indomitable spirit. While, I raised a toast to beloved Gramps and Granny.

Later, as we slipped into the evening, the phone rang. Granny took the call and yelled out, 'It's for you, Pari. Someone named Sanjeev is asking for you.'

I rushed to the telephone, grabbed the receiver from Granny and spoke to Sanjeev, who was hundreds of miles away from me,

'Sanju, I miss you. I'm sorry I didn't call you earlier. I planned to, after dinner, so that we could speak peacefully without Gramps and Granny hovering around. How are you?'

Sanjeev's husky voice boomed through the receiver into my ear, 'Poodle, I miss you. I am good. All okay with you?'

I told Sanjeev all about my evening back home.

Both Gramps and Granny gave me curious glances when I returned to the dinner table but they refrained from asking me any questions.

'That was Sanjeev, my boyfriend,' I said, relieving them of their misery.

Gramps was taken aback by my upfront announcement and Granny couldn't hide her excitement. She blurted out, 'I knew it. We have a lot of catching up to do, Pari.'

Granny followed me to my bedroom once dinner was over. She made no bones about wanting every juicy bit of information about Sanjeev and my relationship with him. Washed and changed into my pyjamas, I climbed onto the bed which was neatly made with crisp white sheets. I gave Granny the complete low-down on Sanjeev and my meeting with his mother.

'Pari, I am at a loss. Why do you want to take Sheena and Mekhail with you now? Get settled first and gradually get them into your lives. At least that's what I think would work well for everyone,' said Granny pensively.

Without answering her perhaps sensible question, I asked, 'Gran, what time is Mom coming tomorrow? I can't wait to see Sheena and Mekhail.'

'Don't know, my dear. Maybe by midday. You get a good night's rest now. Gramps would want you to be at the breakfast table at eight. The old man hasn't changed at all,' she said smiling.

Kissing me goodnight, Granny turned off the lights in my room and left. I was exhausted after the flight and the long drive home from the airport. As my head sunk into the soft pillow, with the thoughts of the next day when I would get to meet my children whom I had not seen for three long years, my eyes shut only to open the next morning.

As I sipped on my morning tea the next day, I had butterflies in my stomach, excitement taking over my senses as I thought of Sheena and Mekhail running into my arms in a few hours' time.

I got out of bed and opened the bag which was packed with all the goodies and toys that I had purchased for Sheena and Mekhail. Finally, I would touch and feel my babies, and not just their framed photographs. Finally, they would be in my arms. Finally, they would be a part of my life. Finally, I would wake up with them every morning. I realized that I was smiling as their wonderful thoughts crossed my mind. The countdown had begun to when I would finally have a life with the three people whom I loved the most— Sheena, Mekhail and Sanjeev …

I got into a pair of grey stone-washed denims, a pink lace top and a pair of flip-flops after my shower. It was yet to be eight and I had enough time to make a call to Sanjeev before breakfast. I walked down to the hallway where the telephone was placed and quickly dialled Sanjeev's number to speak to him.

Gramps and Granny were already at the table. Gramps rose to give me his bear hug as he wished me. I kissed Granny and took my seat next to Gramps like I always had from the time I was three years old.

Gramps looked at Granny and said, 'Why don't you ring your daughter after breakfast and check whether they'll be here in time for lunch? I'll get some ice cream for the munchkins. Pari come along with me while Granny organizes lunch,' he said, turning towards me.

Food was one of the primary factors in Gramps's existence. He was the kind of person who would plan the menu for dinner for the next day while eating breakfast today.

I followed Granny to the hallway with my cup of coffee, once we had finished breakfast.

Granny went up to the console table where the telephone was placed and dialled Mom.

'Angel is here. What time are you arriving?'

Granny paused to hear Mom's response from the other end.

'Oh,' said Granny, 'why don't you have a word with Pari? She is eager to meet the kids.'

Granny handed over the receiver of the telephone to me. 'Hello, Mom,' I said.

'Hello, Pari. How are you?' Mom asked.

'I'm fine, Mom. How are you? How are Sheena and Mekhail? When will you reach?'

'I'm good. Sheena and Mekhail have both gone to school,' Mom answered.

'Mom, why have they gone to school today? Aren't you supposed to be leaving for Granny's soon?' I asked, surprised that instead of getting all set to visit me, Sheena and Mekhail had gone to school.

'I've got a couple of meetings that I need to finish. If it gets late, we'll come tomorrow. Didn't make sense for them to miss school today needlessly,' she replied.

'Mom, I've been waiting since yesterday. Please get here today as soon as you can,' I pleaded.

'I will try, Pari. I'll get there as soon as I can. See you. Bye.' With that I heard a click, and the line went dead.

'What's going on Granny? Did you not give Mom my dates? You said that you would,' I demanded.

'Pari, I called her the moment you confirmed your flight details. Maybe she's caught up with work. They'll be here by evening.

Why don't you run along with Gramps and get the ice cream?' she replied.

I nodded and headed off to look for Gramps. I told him that Mom and the kids would probably not arrive in time for lunch, but Granny wanted us to get the ice cream anyway. As Gramps drove his car, I looked out of the window and soaked in the sights and smells of the greenery and then the shops of the bakers, tailors, tinkers and grocers as we entered the mazy lanes in the marketplace. The delay in Sheena and Mekhail's arrival was uppermost in my mind. I somehow felt that Mom was being evasive but brushed it off as an overreaction on my part.

By the time we returned it was almost six o'clock in the evening. I restlessly and eagerly waited for Mom to arrive with Sheena and Mekhail. However, there was no sign of them whatsoever. I thought of ringing Mom but then changed my mind, fearing that my father could pick up the call. I wanted to speak with Nanny or Moses and find out what was going on. But I couldn't, lest my father answered the call when I rang.

When it was close to dinner time, I urged Granny to ring the house once again, even though in my heart I knew very well that there was fat chance of seeing Sheena and Mekhail that day. I stood next to Granny, as I did in the morning, when she rang Mom, hoping that Nanny or Moses would answer the call and tell her that Mom and the kids were on their way to visit us. But no such luck.

Nanny answered the call and said that Mom was still at her office and the children were already tucked in to bed. I spoke to Nanny after Granny and, unmistakably, I could hear a sob at the other end as we chatted. I asked Nanny to come along with Mom and the kids, to which Nanny replied, 'Pari, I shall ask Madam if I can come. I'd really like to meet you. I miss you. You may be able to speak with Madam on her office line unless you want to leave a message with me.'

'Nanny, please ask Mom to bring Sheena and Mekhail first thing in the morning tomorrow. And you too must come. Please give my love to Moses,' I said.

Gramps, Granny and I had dinner that evening in awkward silence.

The two days rolled to three and then to four, five, six and seven, but Mom did not show up with Sheena and Mekhail. Gramps was livid with my mother's conduct and reproved her on the last occasion when she once again made up some excuse for the delay in the scheduled visit. Granny, too, was clearly upset with Mom and despite always being warm and understanding, I could see that she was filled with cold fury. Sanjeev continued to reassure me that Mom must have genuinely had some reason for the delay and was not procrastinating.

It was on the eighth day that I decided to drive down to my house, where I had vowed never to set foot ever in my life after I walked out three years ago. The kids and I were booked to travel in a couple of days to Calcutta. I could no longer stay in suspended animation.

I packed my bags and requested Gramps and Granny to take me to Mom's house to meet and bring back Sheena and Mekhail. Granny was hesitant. She thought that it was a bad idea and that my visit could trigger an undue showdown at home. Gramps, on the other hand, was supportive and all set to give his daughter a piece of his mind in person for causing me so much grief. Granny reluctantly agreed to accompany us.

It was close to midday when Gramps got his car out on the driveway. And as Granny and I were about to get into the car, I saw a white saloon driving in with Sayeed at the wheel and Nanny in the passenger's seat. My heart started pounding frantically as the car came closer and finally halted. Sayeed and Nanny smiled affectionately at me.

The rear door of the car opened, and out jumped Sheena with her beautiful mop of hair and twinkling eyes, looking arrestingly beautiful. Behind her trailed young Mekhail with jet-black cropped hair, obsidian eyes, a tanned complexion and a beatific smile. For a moment, everything stopped and stood frozen in time.

I kneeled on the ground and stretched my arms out as Sheena and Mekhail excitedly ran towards me. Finally, I thought, the heavens were smiling upon me, and I would hold Sheena and Mekhail in my arms and close to my bosom, where they could hear how my heart beat for them all the while I was away from them. But alas! My arms stayed empty. Sheena and Mekhail ran past me and jumped into Granny's arms.

I stood up and looked at them, my heart overflowing with all the love pent up for so long. I smiled at Sheena and opened my arms once again to her, but she just stared back at me. Mom had alighted from the car and come towards me by then, and Mekhail quickly took refuge behind her when I turned towards him.

The brutal truth dawned upon me only then—Sheena and Mekhail had perhaps no clue who I was. I felt dizzy. I was not prepared for the eventuality that Sheena and Mekhail would not recognize me! That was my retribution for leaving them behind when self-preservation and survival were the only imperative for me almost three years ago.

I hugged Mom and Nanny. Mom's familiar floral fragrance and Nanny's warmth filled my senses with emotions that had become alien to me for the last few years. Mekhail ran up to Gramps as he got out from behind the wheel to pick him up. It was a family reunion all right except that Sheena and Mekhail had no inkling that I was a part of the family, and their mother.

Ironically, I was an interloper in this much-awaited family gathering. Sheena and Mekhail were finally with me and yet not with me. That was the price I had to pay for giving wings to my dreams and for choosing to go as far as I could from the man who had hurt me.

I helped Granny's house help, Natasha [name changed], bring my bags out from Gramps's car and back into my room so that I could quickly take out the goodies that I had brought for Sheena and Mekhail. Hearing Sheena chatter in her mellifluous voice and seeing the sparkle in Mekhail's eyes melted my heart. Sheena avoided any eye contact with me, and Mekhail winced as I ruffled his hair; I was just a stranger to them. My attempts to draw them into a conversation with colourful toys, presents and chocolates were futile. There was no doubt that Mekhail worshipped the ground that my mother walked on. He did not leave her side even for a moment. Sheena was clearly Nanny's pet and more of an extrovert than Mekhail.

'Hello, Sheena,' I said, taking her little palm in my hand, just as she finished narrating a little episode about her friend to Granny.

Sheena did not take her hand away from mine but did not respond either with a smile or any words.

'Sheena, I'm your mother,' I said, hoping that there would be some reaction from her after my statement.

She looked at me with her large doe-shaped eyes with a strange expression. But before she could say anything, Mom interrupted, 'Sheena! Mekhail! Why don't you both go with Nanny and play outside in the garden?'

She looked at Nanny and before she could say anything, Nanny instantly ushered both Sheena and Mekhail out of the room.

Mom turned to me once the children had left. 'Pari, I am really happy to see you. Don't get me wrong, but we had agreed on a few things before you decided to leave. You are not supposed to confuse the kids. I brought them here so that you could at least meet them once before you go. Pari, the kids are happy. Their life is with us here, with their friends at school, with their cousins. They know nothing about you or Siddharth.'

'Mom, I'm their mother. I am taking them with me,' I was almost in tears as I spoke.

'You were their mother, Pari. You are not anymore. You stopped being their mother when Mekhail was a little baby. You had given up your rights when we signed the adoption papers. Pari, you chose to go away, no one had asked you to.' Mom's eyes were icy, and her words were like a knife.

'Mom, that's a piece of paper! You can't stop me from taking my kids with me!' I screamed, upset that my mother was talking gibberish and somehow didn't get my point.

'I sure can, Pari. They are not your kids!' Mom replied, sounding exasperated.

'That's enough girls!' Gramps cut in, raising his hand up.

Gramps turned towards me and said, 'Pari, my princess, I know that what I am going to say is not what you want to hear. I also know that it will hurt you. But she is right. You can meet Sheena and Mekhail whenever you want to but not as their mother. For all that counts, they have been for almost three years now, and will continue to remain, the children of your parents. Sheena and Mekhail are happy here and you must not upset the apple cart if you really care for them. And I know that you do. You must see reason and do what is best for them.'

There was a firmness in Gramps's voice even though he spoke gently. Gramps had always, in the past, supported every decision that I took in life, trivial or major. But this time, the writing was on the wall. I didn't have his support because he did not have faith in the convictions I had—that it was possible for the kids to make a fresh start, that I could be a good mother to Sheena and Mekhail, that they would eventually settle down with me and be as happy in no time as they were with Mom now, that Sanjeev and I could give them the love they deserved, that I could work at the same time and take care of their needs, as would Sanjeev. Gramps had made up his mind that Sheena and Mekhail would not go with me.

Through the window that looked into the garden, I could see Sheena and Mekhail running around the fountain gleefully, with Nanny and Sayeed seated on the stone bench, keeping an eye on them. Maybe Gramps was right, that they were happy here and this was the life they knew, and I had no right to disrupt it. That piece of paper that I had signed three years ago was a finality and a binding constraint that was impossible to undo or overcome as of now.

Unable to speak, my heart heavy with despair, I nodded in silent acquiescence. I could see Granny's eyes welling up with unshed tears, even though she said nothing.

Sheena and Mekhail returned to the living room shortly after, with Nanny trailing behind them. They ran to Mom for a quick cuddle. Mekhail jumped onto Gramps's lap and Sheena on Granny's after that, both giggling with infantile excitement which diffused the tension in the air.

Sheena finally looked me in the eye and gave me a smile that took my breath away and stayed etched in my memory for days to come.

Nanny shortly announced that it was nap time for the kids and that lunch would be served when we were ready. Mekhail was already yawning despite his excitement. They didn't need much cajoling to retire for the afternoon nap.

Everyone spoke very little at lunchtime. Each one of us was lost in our own thoughts that emanated, perhaps, from our conversation that afternoon.

Once lunch was over, everyone decided that an afternoon siesta was much needed to soothe our nerves after the intense discussion that we had a little while ago. I asked Mom if it was all right for me to lie down with Sheena and Mekhail. Mom nodded in agreement. It felt strange that I was seeking permission to spend time with my own children.

When I entered the bedroom where Sheena and Mekhail were asleep, Nanny was pulling the sheets up to cover them snugly. They looked like little angels, peace radiating from their beautiful faces. I lay down next to Sheena and held her tight as though if I didn't, I'd lose her forever. I put my hand out to touch Mekhail's face and, as I touched him, he smiled in his sleep. I knew that I had very little time with them as Mom had planned to leave the next day.

I did not know when I fell asleep but when I woke up, Sheena was still asleep in my arms. I slowly pulled my hand out and laid her head on the pillow. I got up and walked to the other side of the bed to sit next to Mekhail, who snored slightly in his sleep. I stroked his hand and pushed back the lock of hair that covered his forehead. Suddenly Mekhail opened his eyes, instantly wide awake, stared at me, and started bawling. Sheena got worked up hearing his cries and Nanny came running into the room. Sheena sat up on the bed and looked at me with fury.

'Go away,' she screamed. 'Don't touch my brother.'

Not wanting to upset the children anymore, I got up and left their room feeling helpless and hopeless. I went upstairs to my room and cried into my pillow, muffling the sobs that I did not want anyone else to hear. Once I was more composed, I went to the hallway to ring Sanjeev, who I hoped to catch before he left office. I called him on his direct line that he picked up after just one ring. When I heard his husky voice at the other end, a new hope started flowing within me. There was someone who was waiting for me, someone who loved me enough to make me a part of his life and his family despite the manifold complexities in my life.

'Sanjeev, I love you,' I said the moment I heard his voice. 'I am coming back the day after and alone. I'll take a taxi from the airport. If I don't speak to you tomorrow, I will see you at eight for dinner the day after. Come and fetch me. We'll go to Sky Room. Please reserve our corner table.'

'Will do, Poodle. What about your Mom and the kids? Have they not come yet? Sorry, baby,' he replied.

'They are here, Sanjeev. The kids don't know who I am. Nobody here wants them to know who I am. They are happy, all of them. I can't bring the kids. They are not mine anymore. I have no right, apparently.' I was getting more hysterical as I spoke.

'Come back soon. Love you. I'll call you at night. No more tears, promise me,' he said.

'I promise,' I said, 'and thank you for loving me.'

I returned to my room and placed my bags near the door even though I still had two more nights to go. For the remainder of the evening Sheena and Mekhail stayed miles away from me and, for some reason, Mekhail cried whenever he saw me. I was disappointed but there was nothing that I could do. All my plans had gone awry and all I hoped for at that moment was for time to tick away as quickly as possible so that I could be on my flight back to Calcutta.

Sheena and Mekhail had dinner a couple of hours before us, and Nanny took them to their room to be cleaned up and tucked in. Gramps, Granny, Mom and I had a couple of drinks before dinner.

When Mom asked me about my plans, I was in no mood to tell her anything about my job or Sanjeev. Mom had stitched me up. She had deliberately delayed her trip to deprive me of the time that I could have spent with Sheena and Mekhail, and deprived them of the opportunity of getting to know their mother. I was not going to allow her to cause me any more grief, I decided. I could not perhaps blot out every image of the past, but I was going to try hard, I made up my mind.

Once dinner was over, I said gravely, 'I'd like to have breakfast in my room tomorrow, if it is not too rude. I'll come down after Mom leaves with Sheena and Mekhail. Goodbye, Mom.'

Gramps said it was fine. Granny said that she would send breakfast up to my room at eight as she wiped the tears that rolled down her cheeks. Mom wished me luck. I rose from my chair and walked up to Mom.

I gave her a kiss and spoke before I could stop myself, 'Mom, I shall never come back unless someday you need me. Sheena and Mekhail are yours. You need not worry that it will be any other way. You have my word on that.'

I could see the tension easing out of my mother's face. I knew that I had done the good deed of the day albeit at the cost of my own happiness. I popped my head into Sheena's and Mekhail's bedroom, which was dark except for the faint light from the night lamp. I turned on the top lights to have a look at little Sheena and Mekhail, who were my little babies but not mine anymore, who I knew I was not going to see for many years to come, or perhaps even forever, after that night. They both slept soundly in the comfort of the duvet, unaware of the complexities that surrounded my life and that could possibly catch up with them some day when they were old enough to ask questions. I walked up to their bed, prayed for their well-being, blew a kiss to each of them without touching them, turned off the lights after that and tip-toed out of their room, closing the door behind me.

Nanny came up to my room to say goodbye before they all left. I was pained by the turn of events, but I was going to be okay. I no longer felt guilty for daring to restart my life three years ago, far away from the rut that I was in. At seventeen, I had the belief that I could have taken care of Sheena and Mekhail while I studied. I was not allowed to. My belief persisted. I returned at twenty to once again take Sheena and Mekhail with me. I was yet again not allowed to. But my belief persisted. One day Sheena and Mekhail would come to me, I knew that.

On the day of my departure, Gramps and Granny came to drop me at the airport. With promises to stay in touch, which I decided that I was going to honour, I walked into the departure terminal of the airport and looked back to wave to Granny and Gramps, who stood there till I was out of sight.

As the aircraft took flight, I looked down at the cluster of homes scattered sparsely around the runaway. I was bidding goodbye to Guwahati, a city in which I had several ugly memories but where now parts of me were alive and growing everyday in the form of Sheena and Mekhail. The journey somehow seemed shorter on my way back to Calcutta. As the wheels of the airplane touched the tarmac, I thanked the Almighty for giving me the fighting spirit that I possessed in a world where there had never been an easy time to be a woman.

After I picked up my bags and walked out to the arrivals to hail a taxi, I saw Sanjeev standing right in front of me with his arms outstretched and his unguarded smile. I dropped my bags and ran into the comfort of his strong arms. I knew that a new chapter of my life was about to begin, and it was high time that I accepted with gratitude what life had in store for me.

On our way to my accommodation from the airport, I filled Sanjeev in on the nitty-gritties of my futile visit, and the grief that came with it. My room had been tidied up and I could smell the sweet fragrance of potpourri that was kept in a bowl on my bedside table. On the table, were also the framed photographs of Sheena and Mekhail that I had looked at and kissed every morning after I woke up and every night before I fell asleep in the last three years. Placing my bags on the floor, I opened the wardrobe to pull out a fresh change of clothes before I went in for a shower. On two shelves of the wardrobe lay all the things that I had purchased for Sheena and Mekhail prior to my trip for their use when they moved in with me. I felt dejected at the sight of those things that Sheena and Mekhail would never use.

To preserve my sanity, I had to let go of the last vestiges that reminded me of Sheena and Mekhail and numbed my heart with anguish. Almost like an involuntary reflex, I pulled down an empty bag that lay atop the wardrobe and packed in it all the things that I had kept for them, along with their photographs by my bedside. I took the bag out of my room and put it in the storage. That was my way of healing—out of sight, out of mind, I thought.

I put on a long black dress that reached my ankles, with a tall slit on the left that gave a decent peek of my thigh. No pantyhose, I decided. After my hair was washed and blow dried, a careful application of pink lipstick, eyeliner, eye shadow and mascara, I felt my confidence return and spirits sore up again to face life with grit and tenacity, on a fresh note without letting the blows from my past bog me down any longer. I decided to have a good time that evening with Sanjeev and let go of all my worries.

When the doorbell rang at five past eight, I slipped on my black stilettos, sprayed a generous dose of perfume and, with my chin up, I walked out of the door to meet Sanjeev.

Sanjeev remembered to book our favourite corner table at Sky Room as I had asked him.

The band was playing retro songs with full gusto to the delight of the diners. Sanjeev ordered his rum and Coke, and a vodka tonic for me to start the evening. Sanjeev was his cheerful self, as always. As we clinked glasses to start the evening, instead of his usual 'salute', Sanjeev surprised me with a decent proposal, 'Poodle, to us! To our love! Marry me!'

He did not ask. He commanded with affection and faith in the love that we shared.

'Your wish is my command!' I replied saucily.

Sanjeev spent that night in my room after dinner. Needless to say, we were both burning with desire after being away from each other for ten long days.

In another three days, I was to start work as an academic counsellor. I needed to inform my employers at the Diners Club office that I would not be able to freelance with them any longer. I had informed the sales head, Shrikant, about the job offer that I had accepted before I travelled to Granny's. Shrikant tried hard to dissuade me and insisted that I'd be bored soon in the confines of a computer centre. My response to Shrikant was, 'Make me an offer that I can't refuse!'

After Sanjeev had left that morning, I changed into a pair of cream slacks, a pink shirt and my brown low-heeled work shoes and headed out to the Diners Club office to handover the cheques and the filled-up forms of new members that I had signed up but did not have enough time to submit prior to my travel to Granny's. I knew that I was going to miss the team of people I worked with there, but I also knew that selling credit cards was not my endgame. I needed to continue my search till I knew what my calling was.

Shrikant rose from his chair as I entered his cabin to say goodbye.

'Indrani, good to see you. How was your trip?' He greeted me with a firm handshake.

'It was good. Thank you. How are you, Sir?' I answered.

'Indrani. Please take a seat. I have something for you,' he said with a smile.

'I have an offer for you that you can't refuse.' The fervour in his voice indicated that he was on a mission to sell a comb to the bald, on this occasion the 'bald' being none other than me.

He buzzed the intercom and asked for two mugs of coffee to be sent in, along with the offer letter.

The coffee arrived first and then the letter that Shrikant handed over to me in an envelope with my name written on it.

'Open it.' There was a tone of authority in his voice.

I did as I was told and as I read the letter, I sat up on my chair, my eyes almost popping out of my head seeing the salary, which was thrice the offer that I had signed up for, with perks of free computer lessons at a centre of my choice and a huge incentive scheme. Clearly, Shrikant had taken my words seriously and made me an offer that I would find impossible to refuse!

I was gripped with euphoria at the realization of my worth; I was awed by the plethora of choices that I had in front of me in my professional life at the age of twenty.

'Thank you, Sir,' I said. 'I am overwhelmed. I am grateful for this amazing offer. But I can't. I have accepted an offer; they are expecting me at work on Monday. And I don't wish to sell credit cards any longer. I am bored, Sir!'

I was forthright and, perhaps, too open for Shrikant's liking. But I had to say what was on my mind at the cost of Shrikant's ire. He looked at me aghast.

I folded the letter, put it back into the envelope, placed it on his desk, and looked him in the eye. 'Sir, I have learned the tricks of the trade from you. I, perhaps, will never have a superior as good as you. I can't thank you enough for hiring me when you did. I survived the last two years because you believed in me. You honed the skills that I had; I will always be indebted to you. But it's time for me to move on. I apologize if I have disappointed or offended you. But I must go.'

With that, I stood up and put my hand out with my best smile on. Shrikant stood up, shook my hand, and said, 'Best of luck, young lady. You'll go a long way. Your Diners Club membership expires next year. Don't forget to renew it!' His face broke into a smile as he winked at me and let go of my hand.

'Aye, Sir!' I said, relieved that I could wriggle out of the awkward situation that I was in.

That evening I was due to meet Sanjeev's extended family at a dinner at his house. Sanjeev had asked me to wear an Indian outfit, if possible, a salwar kameez or a sari. Since I owned none, I went shopping for something appropriate.

Sanjeev was going to pick me up at 7 p.m. and after the previous day's long travel, not sufficient sleep throughout the night and a hectic day, I was exhausted by mid afternoon. But I was exhilarated at the prospect of meeting his family, particularly his young cousins, whom he spoke of very fondly.

Sanjeev's mother greeted me with a hug and a smile when we entered his house, 'Welcome, Indrani, please feel at home. Take a seat. I'll let everyone know you are here.'

Sanjeev made a sweeping gesture and said, 'Mom, you sit with Indrani. I'll call everyone.'

A man of around Sanjeev's age walked in before Sanjeev could leave the living room to call the others.

'Vivek, this is Indrani,' Sanjeev said, introducing his brother to me.

'Welcome home!' Vivek's face brightened up as he gave me a smile. He was darker and taller than Sanjeev. In fact, he looked a lot like their mother. There was a certain mellowness about him while his eyes blazed with intelligence.

He was followed by Nikhil, Sanjeev's cousin who was around ten, with chiselled features and the longest eyelashes that I had ever seen. At his heels was a young toddler, Nikita, Nikhil's baby sister, with curly black hair and large eyes, who coyly peeped from behind him and smiled at me. I handed out the chocolates that I had brought for them, which Nikita took after slowly approaching me, looking down and smiling shyly every time she made eye contact with me.

Sanjeev returned in a few minutes with his grandmother, 'Badi Maa', and uncle's wife, Aunt Uma. Badi Maa was clad in a white sari as traditionally worn by women of that generation after they lost their husbands. She had silver hair which was pinned up in a bun and the sweetest smile ever. She was a tiny woman compared to the rest of the family. She patted me on the cheek when I joined my hands in a namaste to greet her.

Aunt Uma was a tall, fair and plump woman, probably in her thirties, who had a cheerful face and a warm smile. 'Indrani,' she almost squealed in excitement. 'So pleased to meet you, at last.'

'Same here. I have heard so much about all of you from Sanjeev. Thank you for inviting me for dinner,' I replied, touched by the welcome air in the household.

Sanjeev's uncle finally arrived just as the drinks were being served. Gour Mohan Kapur, alias Uncle GM, who Sanjeev was in complete awe of, was dark, tall and heavily set, with a strong face and stormy black eyes that radiated power. It was the first time that I noticed that Sanjeev's body language changed upon his arrival, from confidence to edginess.

Sanjeev's mother introduced me to Uncle GM who greeted me politely when I rose to greet him. 'Please sit down. Is there any particular drink that you prefer?' he asked, looking at the Fanta on the table next to me.

I said that I was fine with my drink. He walked to the wooden bar and poured himself a whiskey and asked Sanjeev and Vivek if they would like one as well. They walked up to the bar and helped themselves. It was very apparent that Uncle GM was the patriarch of the house, and he called the shots.

Uncle GM and Aunt Uma asked me about my family, my educational qualifications, my job, hobbies, likes and dislikes, while Badi Maa smiled throughout our conversations and looked dotingly at her son GM.

Dinner was a sumptuous vegetarian meal cooked at home along with a few non-vegetarian dishes of lamb and chicken brought from outside. Sanjeev had briefed me earlier that Badi Maa was a staunch vegetarian and did not approve of any meat or fish being cooked at home. Apart from eggs which were allowed to be cooked in their kitchen, any other non-vegetarian item had to be catered from outside. I was pleasantly surprised that she made no fuss about everyone else digging their teeth into the chicken legs at the same table. She was clearly lenient with her orthodox views and let the family relish without any guilt a meal of their choice.

The evening ended with warm hugs and 'goodnights'. Sanjeev's family invited me to drop in whenever I wished to, without hesitation. I thanked them for their kindness and for the wonderful evening that I had with them.

As I was on my way out, Uncle GM unexpectedly said, 'Indrani, you must understand that Mummy is a lady from the old school of thought. Sanjeev and you must get engaged shortly and get married after that as soon as possible. I'd like to meet your father.'

That was a bolt from the blue. I could not help but notice the startled look on Sanjeev and his mom's faces. I quickly tried to regain my composure after being suddenly seized by a sense of helplessness and nodded in agreement without saying anything.

Sanjeev drove me back home. I studied him for a moment. He was in deep thought, perhaps trying to figure out a way to deal with the awkward situation that Uncle GM had unwittingly put me in. Then in a profound whisper, he said, 'We will do what we can to sort this. I can hear the wedding bells and I can see you being the most beautiful bride. I love you, Poodle.'

That night, I stayed awake for a long time reliving the past, which I rarely thought about any longer. The past and the present seemed to diffuse into a blur. Suddenly, I found it difficult to breathe. The walls seemed to be closing in on me. I was afraid that Dad would once again be the reason that I would lose a love of my life, like I had lost Vish.

Sanjeev and I did not talk about how we were going to arrange the meeting between Dad and Uncle GM in the next couple of days when we met. I joined work in the Computer Training Centre as per plan. I was briefed the first couple of days on the courses and the programmes to suit the different needs of students and work executives that I would counsel and finally convince them to pay a hefty fee for the programme, without which their lives would be worthless. I was good at it and almost every person whom I counselled ended up as an earnest student in the centre. During the lunch breaks or any free time that I had, I sat with the programmers and trainers, and honed my skills in programming.

After three months went by, Badi Maa again nudged us about a meeting between our parents. I finally had to make that call to my folks that I was dreading. Gramps, I thought, would make a good mediator, and could speak with Mom and Dad and brief them about my relationship and future plans with Sanjeev. I rang Granny and shared with her my concerns about Uncle GM's insistence on meeting Dad to discuss the wedding plans and that he was unwilling to settle for any other male member from my family for the discussion. In his view, it had to be the father of the bride and himself who had to have the first meeting before the others in the families met. I could not see the rationale behind his decision but there was not much that either Sanjeev or his mother could do to change his mind without revealing the facts and the issues.

Two days later, Granny rang me at my office and confirmed that Dad had agreed to meet Sanjeev's uncle and that he would travel to Calcutta over the weekend.

Dad arrived on a Saturday morning and called me on my landlord's landline after he had checked into Hotel Taj Bengal. Hearing his voice after so many years gave me goosebumps and sent a chill down my spine. But Sanjeev was too precious for me, as was his family, who had in the last three months filled my life with a happiness that had eluded me for a long time. I needed to make peace with my enemy to enter the next phase of my life.

'Pari, how are you?' he asked, when I came on the line.

'I am fine. Thank you for coming to meet Sanjeev's family. It means a lot to me,' I whispered, with mixed emotions of relief and apprehension.

'Pari, I am sorry. I know that I am unworthy of your forgiveness. But if it makes any difference, I am truly sorry for the pain that I have caused you. I hope that you do find the happiness with Sanjeev that you deserve. What time are they expecting me? Give me the address, I'll be there.' Dad sounded genuinely apologetic and seemingly intent on putting his best foot forward.

'Sanjeev said that he would send the car for you. If you can please be ready to leave at 7.30.'

'I'll be at the lobby on time. Give me the car number so that the front desk can let me know once the car is there. See you in the evening. Is there anything you would like to tell me before I meet Sanjeev's family?' he checked.

'Gramps would have briefed you. Sanjeev's mother knows everything. The rest of his family knows nothing. That's really all. They expect the wedding to happen as soon as possible,' I answered.

With that, we said our byes for the moment and disconnected. I felt dizzy. I went and lay down hoping to catch a few winks, which I thought would perhaps calm my frayed nerves. But sleep was remote.

For the meeting, I wore a mauve salwar kameez that I had purchased earlier but had not had the occasion to wear till then. Sanjeev looked handsome in an orange linen shirt and a pair of khaki slacks. At Sanjeev's home, everybody was dressed up for the evening ahead. They were all set to extend a warm welcome to the father of the bride. In that moment of joy with Sanjeev's family, the pain and grief that I had experienced in the past on account of my father's misdeeds somehow disappeared into oblivion.

Dad arrived shortly after. Sanjeev and I went out to greet him. He looked tired and much older than when I had seen him five years ago. His cream shirt and brown trousers hung loosely on him. I was no longer angry with him. I had forgiven him, which, in turn, had released me from the pain that gnawed at me deep inside, time and again.

When I introduced Sanjeev to Dad, he courteously extended his hand out, 'Hello, Sanjeev, pleased to meet you.'

'Hello, Sir. Welcome! Thank you for coming home to meet us,' Sanjeev replied earnestly with a smile that lit up his face.

Uncle GM, Sanjeev's mother and Aunt Uma were waiting in the living room for Dad. They all rose as we entered and greeted him warmly when I introduced them. My heart was pounding heavily, and I was afraid that everyone in the room would hear it if it did not stop.

When we had all sat down in the living room, Uncle GM said, 'Mr Bora, we are really glad that you were able to visit us. We have been looking forward to meeting you.'

Dad smiled and replied, 'I was told that you wished to meet me to take forward the friendship between Indrani and Sanjeev. Please feel free to discuss and ask any questions that you may have.'

I could see Sanjeev and his mother exchanging glances and then looking at me. I could not tell what was going on in their heads, but I hid my worries in an air of insouciance. Thankfully, both Uncle GM and Dad's conversations for the next half an hour was confined to their business and work interests, which, perhaps, was their way of gauging each other and moving the talks to the next phase, which was about Sanjeev's and my future.

'Mr Bora, Sanjeev and Indrani ought to get married if we can fix a date that is convenient for both families,' Uncle GM said sometime into the conversation.

He paused for a while, perhaps waiting for a response from Dad. Dad said nothing except for giving a thick smile.

Uncle GM looked at Sanjeev and me. 'Why don't both of you step out for a while so that we can talk?'

As commanded, we flocked out of the room, leaving our future to be decided by Uncle GM, Dad, Sanjeev's mother and Badi Maa. As we stepped out, I was filled with a prescience of something unpleasant looming before me. Sensing my nervousness, Sanjeev held me in a tight embrace once we were in his room. 'Poodle, don't you worry. Everything's going to be fine. I can hear wedding bells.'

Probably Sanjeev was right, I thought. Despite my father's reprehensible conduct in the past that no doubt deserved to be unreservedly condemned, I ought to stop worrying. He did come all the way to make amends by playing the role of the father of the bride, as desired by Uncle GM.

My throat was dry, and I quaffed down the glass of lemonade that Sanjeev brought me. We were called back into the living room after almost an hour.

Uncle GM's voice was grave. 'Sanjeev, Mr Bora and we have spoken at length. He needs time to get back to us.'

I could sense the tension in the air.

'Needs time to get back on dates?' Sanjeev asked, his brow creasing into a frown.

There was a moment of silence and then Uncle GM's voice sounded like a whiplash, 'Not dates, Sanjeev. Mr Bora will revert to us whether this wedding is possible or not.'

I could see the subtle rage in Sanjeev's mother's eyes and a confused look on Badi Maa's face. I quickly discerned that something was wrong.

Dad's face was sombre and he said, 'I should get going. I have a flight to catch early in the morning.'

'Binda, our driver, will drop you back to your hotel, Mr Bora,' announced Uncle GM, suddenly standing up to indicate that the evening was over.

'I'll drop you, Mr Bora. Indrani, you stay put here with Mom. I'll be back soon,' Sanjeev said unexpectedly.

Clearly, Sanjeev wanted to find out what could have gone wrong when the evening had started off so well.

Dad looked at me and smiled sheepishly. 'Pari, I hope you know what you want. You may feel differently about everything in a couple of years, or perhaps not. Give it some time and you may realize that this is not what you want. Give it time. That is my advice to you. Call your mother whenever you can.'

There was a moment of shocked silence. The tension in the room was palpable.

'Thank you, Mr Kapur, for your hospitality. Thank you, ladies,' Dad turned to Sanjeev's mother and Badi Maa, and bowed slightly. 'Sanjeev, I am ready to leave whenever you are.'

I watched my father's dispirited figure walk out of the room. I looked around me, at the cold faces of Uncle GM, Badi Maa and Sanjeev's mother and shuddered. My worst fears had come true, I thought; I was on the verge of losing Sanjeev, just like I had lost Vish. What could have gone so terribly wrong when the evening had started off on a fairly good note?

'Papu,' I said in a strangled voice, following him out to the driveway, hoping to get an answer. But before I could speak any further, Sanjeev looked at me and said with a firmness in his voice that he never used with me, 'Indrani, go inside. I'll be back soon.'

I looked at my father. He nodded as if to say, 'Do as he says.'

I stood on the driveway as Sanjeev and Dad disappeared through the gates in the car. I went back into the house looking for Sanjeev's mother, hoping that she would put me out of my misery and tell me what in the heavens was going on. I knocked and entered her room.

Her face looked grim. 'Indrani, he was evasive about everything that GM asked. I understand that he had no answers. He was edgy when he spoke about Sheena. I don't know how things are going to pan out.'

I was at a loss for words. I had no one to blame but myself for foolishly hoping for a normal, happy life with the man who I fell in love with and his family that I had warmed up to instantly, without considering that nothing about my life was normal. My life was full of dark secrets which would never allow me to have a life with a family that was normal.

Sanjeev was not his cheerful self when he walked into the room.

'Indrani, your father is a shitbag! The things that he said made me squirm. If he was not your father, I would have broken his face.'

Sanjeev sat down next to me. I shrank away from him. The walls were closing in on me again. I was gasping for air. I was crumbling. I closed my eyes tightly as if to shut the entire world out.

'Sanjeev, please drop me home. I need to be on my own.' I was almost pleading.

'Poodle, none of this is your fault. I'll take you home. But I am not leaving you alone.'

Sanjeev drove me back home. He spent the night with me, perhaps worried that I would be unable to handle the traumatic ending of a much-awaited evening. That night, Sanjeev and I barely spoke, and neither did we make love; we just lay in each other's arms, both lost in our own thoughts. What my father did was petty. He had a chance to correct his karma but he continued to be evil.

Before he headed back the next day, Sanjeev invited me to have lunch with his family as we did on most Sundays. I declined because I needed to be by myself and because I did not know whether his family would be keen to have me over after the previous evening.

Sanjeev met me at eight in the evening like always. Dad had apparently rung him in the afternoon to say that he could not give his consent as he thought I was not making the right choice and we needed to give it more time.

'Ridiculous,' I said. 'Dad just doesn't want me to be happy. A leopard does not change its spots. That's the crux of it all.'

'Poodle, we don't need him or your family in our lives. We are getting married. Mom, Badi Maa and Uncle GM are all of the same view. In a month, you will be my wife.' Sanjeev was in an expansive mood.

He continued, 'I'll go to the marriage registrar's office tomorrow. You make a list of everything that you need to make a pretty bride. Mom will sort it out for you.'

A month later, amidst much pomp and splendour, celebrations and fun fare, complexities and ambiguities in my own life, I tied the knot with the man I loved so dearly and became Indrani Khanna, with the belief that I had left behind the last vestiges of the past shrouded upon me by the Boras.

13

As I began to settle into the Khanna household, I couldn't help but notice the underlying complexities in the family dynamics. Uncle GM and Sanjeev shared a knotty relationship; Sanjeev very often felt undermined and unappreciated for his diligent efforts at work. His ideas seemed to resonate with many but seldom with Uncle GM. Sanjeev, I thought, perhaps, misconstrued the advice that stemmed from Uncle GM's experience as condescending towards him. No doubt, Uncle GM often lost his patience with Sanjeev and voiced his disagreements in a temperate tone, which Sanjeev found offensive and humiliating, leaving him faltering and floundering in the presence of his colleagues; but I, somehow, did not perceive Uncle GM's intentions as ill-meaning.

As a result, Sanjeev often took refuge in alcohol. On such days, Sanjeev would be in a foul mood, much to my dismay.

Mom, it appeared, almost lived for Sanjeev. But often he took out his frustrations on her, almost to the point of bullying her.

Vivek was troubled by the way Sanjeev treated Mom and was often at loggerheads with him because of that.

A couple of months after we were married, Vivek resigned from his job and moved to Bangalore to start his own recruitment company.

Thankfully, my own equation with each member of the family was fabulous. I left for work at eight in the morning and returned by six in the evening. Within six months' time, from the post of academic counsellor, I was promoted to centre manager with a satisfactory pay hike. I wasn't sure what prompted them to make a twenty-one-year-old replace a thirty-year-old but, perhaps, I exuded enough confidence to earn the additional responsibility of managing the centre. Understandably, it was a smart business move, as I came at half the pay package, and lapped up the opportunity with a gusto that would be rewarding for all parties, particularly me, as I was able to hone my managerial skills.

By then, the entry of cable television had taken the country by storm. *Santa Barbara* and *The Bold and the Beautiful* kept both genders of most households glued to the idiot box, almost to the point of addiction. The world was at your doorstep with news, movies, reality shows, serials, sports telecasts, music and the works from all over the world through a variety of channels at the click of a remote if you had a cable connection or a satellite dish the size of a UFO atop your roof.

Uncle GM had received a proposal from Jamshedpur, the Steel City, to provide satellite dishes and cable connections to a few hundred thousand homes. Sanjeev had a natural propensity towards electronics even though he was a commerce graduate. When Uncle GM discussed the proposal with Sanjeev one evening at dinner, his effulgent brown eyes lit up his face in a way that I had not seen in a long time.

The project was a game changer for Sanjeev. But it also required him to move to Jamshedpur for the next couple of years, which meant that I had to quit my job and move with him. It was undoubtedly a blow to my career prospects and plans, but I knew that Sanjeev needed me by his side and that was non-negotiable. Our marriage was not meant to tame my passions. But my love for Sanjeev did make me take steps to heal his dwindling confidence, reignite the fire in him and revive his belief in his own capabilities.

Sanjeev immersed himself at work, building his team, identifying vendors, carrying out site visits, and planning deadlines for delivery and smooth execution of the project. I was busy, on the other hand, with the domestic chores of setting up a home, finding house help, providing succour, hot meals for dinner, and hot sex in the bed, when Sanjeev arrived home at night after a long day's work and sometimes a few drinks with his colleagues in the late evenings, apparently as a bonding and motivating exercise. Sanjeev, at last, had the chance of a lifetime not just to do what he enjoyed doing immensely but to be away from his uncle's shadow to a large extent, if not fully.

The Steel City was a mid-sized town with a mixed breed of professionals, most of whom worked for the company. There were a couple of leisure clubs where the uppity crowd went. I, however, found a noticeable gap between the haves and the have-nots, the powerful and the weak.

Sanjeev and I often met the uppity denizens. Most of them were married, but oddly enough everyone seemed to be having trysts with everyone else's spouses or partners. In the initial days, advances were made towards me, only to be rebuffed with chilling responses and dismissals. Finally, they gave up and saddled me with the sobriquet 'Gone Girl'. I was a clear misfit in that crowd.

As days crawled into months and I stayed home fulfilling the requirements of domesticity, I started sensing an unrest stirring within me. I was no longer able to exist as just Sanjeev's wife. Whilst I loved Sanjeev generously with all my heart, I reflected in my moments of solitude and quietude that I could not live like that anymore and be inured solely to a life of domesticity.

'Sanjeev, I can't do this anymore,' I said one evening, feeling guilty on the one hand but unable to dissolve myself any longer into the mundane life that I was leading and was expected to embrace, on the other.

'Can't do what?' asked Sanjeev, absent-mindedly.

'Sanjeev, I am bored. Bored of everything, bored of watching TV. Bored of reading. Bored of housekeeping. I feel worthless. I am stagnating here. I want to go back to Calcutta. Everything in this town is getting on my nerves.'

'What's the matter with you, Poodle? Any woman would give her right arm to live the cushy life that you are leading! We can go home for the weekend if you like. Bring back Nikita with you. She'll keep you busy.' The finality in Sanjeev's voice was upsetting.

It was odd that Sanjeev, who I believed up until a few months ago to be my soulmate, who could read my mind and touch my heart effortlessly, failed to see the issues that were driving me up the wall.

'Fine. I could perhaps stay back for a few days, figure out if I could do something here and when I return, maybe start a business of some sort,' I replied, hoping that he would agree.

'Business!' he exclaimed. 'You are twenty-one. This is no playpen. It is a town of professionals and business tycoons!'

'Maybe I can take up a job somewhere here in that case,' I said, trying to hide my disappointment at his reaction.

'Do any of our friends' wives have a job here? The ones who are, are perhaps in the sack with their bosses. Indrani Khanna, get it out of your head!'

What he said was perhaps not entirely untrue—the town had a deeply entrenched patriarchal mindset. But it was Sanjeev's lack of confidence in me that I found disturbing. I was neither the wife of his friends nor the working women who slept with their bosses in the chic offices. I had a sharp mind, a fire in my belly and a desire to succeed professionally. At twenty-one, I was perhaps not the canniest and was rough around the edges, but I was willing to learn, and make good of whatever I did, whether on the job or in any new enterprise, without the danger of falling for the bait of ethical compromises. Unfortunately, Sanjeev was not at his receptive best, and getting him to see my point of view that evening would have been like pulling teeth.

'Sanju, please think about it,' I implored. 'Please don't be closed to the idea. I wouldn't, of course, do anything that would make you unhappy. We'll talk about it again when you have had a chance to mull over it.'

I was ashamed of my witless optimism that Sanjeev would understand my desire to do something meaningful and add value to my life and his, my need to be independent and build my own identity apart from being just the wife of Sanjeev Khanna. For the first time that night, my mind was elsewhere when Sanjeev made love to me and I faked an orgasm. I felt slighted, albeit unwittingly. I was sad and troubled.

Sanjeev and I went home to Calcutta over the weekend. Everybody was delighted to see us. Badi Maa, Mom and Aunt Uma were in the 'we are family' mode and did not squabble amongst themselves as usual. Nikhil was glad to have his older cousin and hero back home. Nikita clung to me. The dogs were excited. Uncle GM maintained a reserved front, as usual. We caught up with friends for dinner and drinks. The weekend had started off on a good note, rekindling my optimism and hope that something was going to work out for me, one way or the other. That night I did not fake the orgasm. As I clung to Sanjeev, I realized how much I loved him despite his male chauvinism and insensitive attitude at times. I felt a sense of peace flowing through my mind and body. I slept.

Two years passed after that. The project was nowhere close to completion. At the pace that things were moving, it seemed that Sanjeev was not in a position to meet the deadlines because the vendors from Chennai who were meant to deliver the cables and the dish antennas were not supplying the materials on time. This unplanned delay meant that we would be stuck in the Steel City for a few more years. I feared that I was in danger of getting stuck in the same rut for the rest of my life—of being 'the invaluable lodestone of support' to Sanjeev, as he often eulogized while speaking about me.

From a past for which I continued to carry guilt in the deep recesses of my mind, a story that I could not say aloud for the fear of ostracism, I was now in danger of erasing my real self and my dreams as well. Sanjeev would not hear about me returning to Calcutta to live with the rest of the family and take up a job. The conglomerate in the meanwhile ran out of patience with the delay in delivery and the slackness in troubleshooting. Uncle GM was rightfully or wrongfully irked by the fact that Sanjeev could not leverage the huge opportunity that had unfolded. Sanjeev felt as though he was cornered from all sides. Uncle GM's tone, while voicing his views and concerns, perhaps needed to be less patronizing—he did not cut Sanjeev any slack.

Sanjeev was struggling on the one hand to appease the conglomerate and on the other hand to regain Uncle GM's confidence in him. His activities became more frenetic than they had been already. He was always on the edge, which led to him quaffing down glasses of alcohol in an effort to calm his frayed nerves, though it worked adversely. A meaningful dialogue with him became a rarity. He became obsessively possessive about me, which he euphemistically called 'being protective'. There were some temper issues. Ironically, it was his good traits that were crumbling slowly. It pained me to see the man whom I loved and who loved me falling apart and there was nothing that I could do. Or was there?

Despite the state of affairs on Sanjeev's work front and his mood swings, my extreme love for Sanjeev drove me to put my best foot forward and make things work. I knew that Sanjeev's love for me too was extreme, even though in a different way.

I, too, had began to have outbursts, which I decided needed tempering down, to have peace within. After all, peace, I believed, could yield high dividends eventually for myself, Sanjeev and our relationship.

Sanjeev and I had been married for over two years by then. With mounting pressure, I could see the gradual change in Sanjeev. He became dejected rather than being outraged, as he was in the earlier months. He would often hold on to me at night in bed like a scared, bullied child clinging to his mother's bosom, looking for refuge.

One night, as he put his head on my chest, he said, 'Baby, promise me that you will never leave me.'

Stroking his curly jet-black hair, I whispered, 'Never, Sanju, never. I can't live without you. I have never thought of a life without you. Why would I leave you? I love you, Sanjeev.'

'Promise me,' I continued, 'that you are going to give your best shot to finish this project. You can do it, Sanjeev, if you put your mind to it. You can and you will!'

'I'll try. They have stopped the payments. They are squeezing us dry. But yes, I will give it my best shot. I promise,' he said in a strangled voice.

I could feel a tear drop on my neck as he nuzzled me. My heart went out to him. That night we made love passionately, lost in time and the bond that we shared. After all, a dollop of romance, particularly at a time when all else was bleak, was much needed and the best antidote to our woes.

Sanjeev, as promised, started putting in more effort, took hard decisions and set the bar high for his employees to achieve the best results and win enough brownie points with the conglomerate, to impress upon them that they need not look elsewhere; Sanjeev Khanna and team was their only option and would perform and deliver to their satisfaction.

I, in the meanwhile, missed my period a month later. After a fortnight, when my period was still absent, I got myself a test kit from the pharmacy while Sanjeev was at work. A drop of urine and a wait for the next ten minutes after that, to determine the future. The ten minutes seemed like ten hours, when I must have peeked at the strip at least a dozen times. The blue line finally appeared. I was pregnant!

A soft breeze blew into the bedroom through the window that looked on to the leafy trees outside. I sat on the blue couch near the bed and looked at the pink and blue flowers on the curtains that danced as the breeze made them quiver in an enchanting rhythm that I had not seen before. I was blessed with a man who loved me, who had pointy edges, no doubt, but was turning a new corner. And now I was blessed with motherhood that had eluded me for several years despite having given birth to Sheena and Mekhail, albeit not under the most congenial and ideal circumstances. Life had given me a second chance, I thought; not everyone is privileged to have that.

Sanjeev was over the moon when he heard the good news. The next few months for me were about eating healthy, doing up the nursery with pink frills and curtains and a crib, buying unisex clothing from size 0–10 months, long walks, voracious reading, laughter and spending time with family and friends almost every weekend. I travelled to Calcutta often, much to the delight of Badi Maa, Mom, Aunt Uma and young Nikita. We had all decided that the baby should be born in Calcutta, and I ought to return to the Steel City only once the baby was more than three months old. Sanjeev and I started looking for an apartment to buy in Calcutta, which we decided to move into once Sanjeev's project was completed.

I moved to the family home in Calcutta a fortnight before my due date. There was an air of excitement at home. The baby kept me awake at night with its never-ending movements, twists and turns inside my womb. A week later, the movements stopped. I gave birth to a baby girl—a stillborn child! I felt crushed by grief! Life tests you when you least expect it.

Relatives and friends showed up in the next few days to commiserate with me over the loss of my child. The family rallied around me. I felt a unique vacuum inside me. I was sinking in an abyss of deep, desperate loneliness. Even in a roomful of people, I was lonely. I never returned to Jamshedpur, to the nursery with the pink frills and curtains. I did not know what happened to the crib that I had bought. I never asked. I was numbed with pain. I felt listless and depressed. Along with the child, something inside me had died. All the joy was gone from my life.

The family tried hard to soothe my anguish, but I was inconsolable. It was Vivek who came up with the idea that I needed a change of scene to lift me out of the downward spiral. He invited me to spend a few weeks with him in Bangalore and, if I was up to it, to give him a helping hand in his recruitment firm that he had set up a couple of years ago. Sanjeev wasn't sure how I'd cope but I knew that was my best bet. I had to get away to get better.

Vivek was at the arrivals in the airport along with a tall, attractive dusky girl with short black silky hair, large black eyes, full lips and a pleasant smile. He welcomed me with his warm bear hug and then said, 'This is Mitra, my business partner. My sister-in-law, Indrani.'

Mitra extended her hand out saying, 'Indrani, pleasure to meet you. I've heard so much about you.'

As I shook her hand, her smile reached her eyes. 'Vivek, let's go. I hope you have told Indrani that she will be staying with me.'

Vivek led us to the car park. 'I have not as yet. Indrani, have a look at Mitra's place and mine. I am just a block away from Mitra. I think you will be more comfortable with her. She has a bigger place and it is not messy like mine. But it's your call, whatever you are comfortable with.'

As he had said, Vivek lived in a small one-bedroom apartment which had an equally small sitting room and a smaller kitchen. It was no doubt a bachelor's pad with clothes, shoes, smelly socks and unwashed coffee mugs all over the place. Mitra lived in a two-bedroom apartment which she had tastefully decorated with soft beige and blue shades of furnishings and pots of plants that brought life into the rooms. The walls were painted in pastel hues and the apartment was spotlessly clean.

So, Mitra's it was. In the next couple of days, Vivek confided in me that his relationship with Mitra was not just that of a business partner, but way more. He wished to marry her but there were a couple of hiccups. Mitra was five years older, a divorcee and had a son who was in a boarding school nearby. That was hiccups galore for the Kapur and Khanna family. It was baffling how the Khanna siblings gravitated towards women with baggage.

Ironically, Vivek said, 'Indrani, if there is anybody who can convince the family, it is you.'

I wondered, why and how?

I started attending work with Vivek and Mitra. Spending long hours at work took my mind off the recent loss to a large extent. Vivek and Mitra patiently and generously taught me the ropes of the recruitment business. The trick to success in the business was to be conscious of the differential needs of the clients, even if they were from the same industry.

In two weeks, I had made the first placement in a multinational FMCG company. While I was learning on the job, a sudden sense of clarity set in: I wanted to start a recruitment firm of my own in Calcutta. It's almost as if I had found my calling.

I started INX Services, from a desk in Uncle GM's office in Calcutta. Soon, the company became my focus and gradually with a growing list of clients, a robust data bank of suitable candidates and my determination to succeed, INX Services became a sought-after recruitment firm in the corporate world in Calcutta. As business grew, I moved with an all-women's team to a bigger office in one of Uncle GM's properties on Chittaranjan Avenue soon after.

Sanjeev, in the meanwhile, struggled with the job at hand in Jamshedpur. He shut shop and returned to Calcutta eventually. We moved from his family home to our own apartment that we had purchased nearby. It was a decent four-bedroom apartment with no view whatsoever, but that was pretty much the case with most apartments in the overcrowded city. Sanjeev tried his hand in the recruitment business, but lost interest shortly after. It was clearly not his cup of tea, he said. But I thought that Sanjeev was facing a confidence crisis.

While Sanjeev was unhappy with his work life, his personal life turned out to be the place where he found happiness. I conceived again. Despite my pregnancy, I worked hard and INX flourished. My team too worked hard alongside me—there was no stopping us.

Vidhie Khanna came crying and kicking out of my womb a month earlier than the due date. She had a head full of jet-black hair that stood up like the bristles of a porcupine, massively chubby cheeks, large brown eyes and pouty lips. She was the loudest baby in the hospital nursery. She clearly believed in making her presence felt from the day she was born; an attention seeker of the first degree.

Her arrival was celebrated by the family with gusto. After prayers and ceremonies, we finally stepped into our apartment and Vidhie was placed in the blue crib in her nursery, which had every shade of pink in it, right from the walls to the curtains and to the furniture, except the blue rug on the marble floor to match the crib. Vidhie sighed as she drifted off to sleep, looking angelic and peaceful, almost as if to say, 'I'm home, at last.'

That night when Sanjeev held me in his arms while we lay in bed, he whispered into my ears, 'Poodle, everything's going to be all right now!'

I loved Sanjeev but I knew that everything was not all right. We were drifting apart, the ruptures in our relationship staring at us in our faces. There was still love but no longer a meeting of the minds. It was neither his fault nor mine. It was just the way we both changed with the passage of time. Changing was risky, but not changing carried even bigger risks.

Sanjeev had his fingers in many pies but in my view was unable to articulate his ideas in a manner which made good business sense or were pragmatic and financially viable. I thought that he had a tendency to meander along in the most crucial moments instead of going full steam ahead cannily, which led to failures, frustrations and, in the end, drained morale, repeatedly. I also could not help but feel that the success of my enterprise added salt to his injuries, which led him to often say things to me that were provocative and undermining. He would make jibes. We started getting into nastier fights. This need to assert power was perhaps a case of him becoming increasingly insecure with my success and financial independence.

I started spending longer hours at work than I needed to, met friends whom I did not need to meet, just to stay out of his way and his jibes. The Sanjeev I had fallen in love with was lost somewhere and no matter how hard I tried, I could not find him anymore.

Vidhie started walking when she was ten months old. Her first birthday was a grand affair celebrated by the Khannas and the Kapurs, almost as though it were her wedding and not her birthday. In the eyes of the world, Sanjeev, Vidhie and I made the complete family picture. But, in my head, there were many missing parts. I loved Vidhie more than life itself and was fiercely protective about her. But the separation from Sheena and Mekhail and the loss of the baby after that, had created a vacuum inside me, which Vidhie's beautiful smile and words could not fill. I was captive to the demons in my head that were still scrambling about freely.

Gradually, Sanjeev and I started spending more and more time apart. To avoid unpleasant arguments that erupted at the drop of a hat if he was at the apartment, I would be at the family home, and when he was in the family home, I would take refuge in the safe harbour of the apartment with Vidhie.

Vidhie was almost three and had started going to kindergarten. She was a perceptive child even at that age and the tension between Sanjeev and me was almost tangible. As time passed, our crisis deepened in different ways and was increasing manifold. I knew that the end was nigh, and that it would be a wise move to cut loose to prevent any further rancour and pain for both of us.

Over time, our firm had built a name for itself, and we began to receive assignments for placements in other cities and for national positions. And so, my work often took me to different cities where my clients had their headquarters. The need of the hour was to set up more offices in those cities to provide speedy services and identify suitable candidates with an in-depth understanding of the requirements from a national perspective. After several discussions with my team, my colleague Sanjana and I decided to move to Bombay and set up shop there, for starters. Besides, it gave me the perfect reason to leave Calcutta without much fuss and loss of face for the Khannas and the Kapurs, which I would have otherwise felt troubled about.

Sanjeev was not surprised at my decision. He knew that it was coming for the last couple of years, just that he did not know when. My story with Sanjeev did not end well after all, despite best-laid plans and efforts.

As Sanjeev and I walked into the family home, my heart felt heavy with a sense of foreboding. The living room was silent as we asked to speak with Uncle GM and Mom alone. Aunt Uma was summoned, and the tension in the room became palpable.

I took a deep breath and began to speak. 'Sanjeev and I have been having issues,' I said, 'and I don't think we can be together any longer.'

I told them that Sanjeev has agreed to let me move to Bombay to set up my office, while our daughter stayed with them.

The accusing eyes of my in-laws bore into me, but I continued. 'We've been close to living apart for over a year now. It's not his fault, nor is it mine. We've simply drifted in different directions.'

Uncle GM's face reddened with anger. 'Marriage is not a joke!' he bellowed. 'What will people say?'

But Mom remained calm and collected. 'Indrani, we can find a solution to this,' she said.

As the conversation continued, I could sense the weight of my decision on the entire family. But when Aunt Uma spoke up, it was like a beacon of hope.

'Indrani, you must do what makes you happy,' she said. 'Whether or not things work out between Sanjeev and you, I will never cease to be your Aunt Uma.'

Her words were like a balm to my soul, and I felt a sense of relief wash over me. As we sat down for dinner, I knew it would be my last meal with the family for a while. But even as I prepared to leave, I felt their love and support in a way that gave me the strength to face whatever lay ahead.

I did not have a crystal ball to gaze into the future. Whatever was round the corner could be for the better or for the worse. I would only know once I reached the corner. But what I knew for sure was that I was moving on; I had already moved on, a long time ago.

14

I was three months shy of thirty when I arrived in Mumbai, the city along the blue depths of the Arabian Sea that never sleeps.

Vidhie was to stay at the family home in Calcutta till I settled in the new city. Sanjeev promised to bring Vidhie in a couple of weeks to meet me for a few days.

My leaving the comfort of home, family and friends behind in Calcutta to start a new life in the otherness of a new city on my own did not sit very well with several people. Understandably, women who do not conform to norms are labelled as witches or bitches. But no matter how kooky all of it appeared to others, I was entitled to my own beliefs. I was a fighter and survivor. Being hard-headed did not mean that I was hard-hearted. There were no guarantees in life. But I was determined to make good of the decision that I had made and the key to that was my unorthodox way of surviving.

I had been to Mumbai previously on several occasions, for work and leisure, and had a few friends in the city. So, I was not totally on my own in that sense. A couple, whom I knew, stepped in to help me; I stayed with them for a few months and used their office premises on a profit-sharing basis till I found myself a home and an office.

My trusted colleague Sanjana arrived a couple of days after me and was staying at her aunt's place. Mobile phones had made an entry into the Indian market about six years earlier. Thankfully, I did not need to run to a phone booth every time I wished to hear Vidhie's voice. My absence somehow did not seem to bother her when I spoke to her. At least, that's what I thought for the first three days.

'Vidhie, what are you doing?' I asked her in one of my calls after that.

'Wearing your shoes, Mamma,' she said and giggled. My heart missed a beat.

When Sanjeev came on the line, he said, 'I think Vidhie prefers to stay in the apartment. She seems happier when she sees your clothes and shoes. Whenever I bring her here, she runs into your closet instead of her room. She is perhaps missing you. Just doesn't know how to say it.'

'Sanju, I miss her. Is it possible that you bring her over for a few days? The sooner the better,' I said urgently, feeling a lump in my throat. Thankfully, Sanjeev agreed.

Mekhail and Sheena hovered at the back of my mind, but I had made my peace with the fact that I might never see them again. As the days went by, I got busy setting up shop, hiring staff, meeting clients as well as keeping a watchful eye and tab on the work at my office in Calcutta. Work took all my time and I couldn't find a moment to go house hunting.

Sanjeev arrived with Vidhie a week later.

Sanjeev and I greeted each other with a hug; but it was not the warm embrace that we were both accustomed to. Perhaps, it was not a good idea to have asked Sanjeev to come. Sanjeev easily got into a foul mood when he was hurting or his ego took a hit. Undoubtedly, he was hurting, and his confidence had taken a nosedive. And it hurt me to see him the way he was. But I had tried for several years to do everything that I could to help him, till I felt stifled with the struggle, till I could no longer breathe, even though I loved him and wanted to make the marriage work.

My friend, Balbinder Dhami aka Bittu, with whom I was staying, enjoyed guzzling down large amounts of alcohol every evening. That evening, Sanjeev joined him. Alcohol had always been a catalyst for Sanjeev's conduct, so after a few drinks he was sarcastic about everything. I was appalled at the look in his eyes, the same eyes that had once upon a time mesmerized me with love. A barrage of things were said till I flared up. I did not deserve it. That was the last straw. The writing was on the wall—Sanjeev and I were over for good. I had to end this tempestuous relationship that was now turning ugly, even though I loved him a lot, as I am sure he loved me too. There was not a glimmer of hope for a tomorrow with Sanjeev. Vidhie was troubled by the ugly turn of events. Sanjeev left with Vidhie two days later. Parting with both of them was heartbreaking for me.

The late Alyque Padamsee—or AP as I called him—the erstwhile Ad Guru of the Nation, then perhaps in his seventies, was a big support for me in the city. AP was tall, lanky, had curly matted hair, green eyes and a booming voice.

I had met him at a client's office a few years previously in Calcutta where he was an advisor on their board of directors. He took an instant fondness towards me. We became good friends and, true to his words, whenever I needed guidance from him in any matter, he was always available, heard me out patiently and advised me. Over time, AP became like a godfather to me in the city. He knew the nuances of the city like the back of his hand.

A couple of days after Vidhie had left, AP invited me to a fashion show at the Taj President hotel. This was my first evening out in Mumbai. It was refreshing to get out of the rigorous routine of 'all work no play' I had adopted since coming here.

Everyone knew AP, and most people in the room knew each other. AP convinced me to go to the Library Bar after the show. I reluctantly trailed behind AP, towards Library Bar.

The bar was packed with people, the air was thick with the smell of alcohol, perfumes and aftershaves mingled together, surrounded by loud music and louder voices. The sofas were all taken. The lights were just bright enough for the rich and famous gentry to be visible but not enough for the spots and scars on them to show.

As we walked in, I heard a shout over the loud music, 'AP, this way!'

AP waved at the man who had called him. 'Peter! Hey man, how are you?' AP replied loudly.

Dicky, a friend who was with us that evening, whispered into my ear, 'That's Peter Mukerjea, the CEO of Star India.'

Peter Mukerjea was heavily built, had a beer belly, thinning hair, black eyes, a broad nose and a bristly thick salt and pepper moustache covering his upper lip. He had a thin lower lip and dark skin. His eyes were large and red, almost popping out of the sockets. He looked exhausted.

'Peter, this is Indrani,' AP said, introducing us.

Peter smiled broadly as he turned to me. 'Indrani, aah are you a Bengali?'

'I'm not,' I replied. 'My married name is Khanna.'

I had no idea what prompted me to declare my marital status like that; perhaps an intuition of some sort.

I looked at his companion who was hanging onto his arm. An attractive woman, perhaps in her thirties, in a short dress. 'This is Sarla [name changed],' Peter said.

Sarla smiled at me, clinging closer to Peter. Then he turned to the dark, tall and hefty bespectacled man with massive lips and features slightly askew. 'This is my colleague, Sumantra.'

A short, fair man standing next to Peter loudly announced, 'Hello, I am Suhel Seth.'

Peter was checking me out, I could tell. He offered to get us a round of drinks just as AP was about to order my vodka with soda.

'Indrani has come from Kolkata to set up her office here. She runs a headhunting firm in Kolkata and is doing very well.' AP was effortlessly soliciting my cause, the good old soul that he was.

Peter Mukerjea quickly pulled out a visiting card from his wallet and jotted down his mobile number on it. 'Call me. I'll introduce you to our head of human resources.'

'Thank you,' I said and took out the last visiting card from my purse and gave it to Peter.

'Indrani,' he said, reading my visiting card out loud.

I studied Sarla's visiting card that she handed to me. It had her designation as the manager of human resources in an advertising agency.

'Indrani, do come and meet me. We may have some assignments for you,' she said with a nervous edge in her voice and a faux smile on her lips. 'Can I have one of your cards, please?'

'Thank you so much, Sarla. I'll call you and fix a meeting next week,' I said with a smile, trying to put her at ease. 'No more cards on me.'

'Where is your office, Indrani?' Peter asked me.

I was still eagerly waiting for the drink that had not arrived, 'In Kolkata. I have set up a make-shift office with a friend here till I can find a suitable place that fits our budget.'

'I'll return to Kolkata, once I have met my clients and have my team in place here,' I added quickly, though it was untrue. I had no plans to return to Kolkata. But for some strange reason, I did not want Peter Mukerjea to know the plans in my head.

'You must be joking!' he exclaimed. 'How can you leave this city and go back to Kolkata!'

'Tell me, do you want to be a big fish in a small pond or a small fish in a big pond?' he asked, looking straight into my eyes.

'I want to be a big fish in a big pond,' I answered looking back into his coal-black eyes.

His expression changed from being condescending; he was clearly taken aback.

'Call me,' he said, once again.

I was by then bored of the conversation and whispered into AP's ear, 'The drinks still haven't showed up. Let's leave.'

After much cajoling, I managed to drag AP and Dicky out of Library Bar. AP told Peter that we were going to another venue, to which Peter promptly responded that he would follow suit with his gang. Thankfully, we did not see Peter Mukerjea and gang anymore in the massive discotheque, which was a converted textile mill. I danced away to the funky music to my heart's content at last, sweating out all the anxieties of the past few months, feeling a sense of buoyancy that I had not felt in a long time. I was in high spirits; I was enjoying myself!

The next morning, I left for work, feeling rejuvenated by the previous night's uninhibited dancing. I handed over the visiting cards that I had collected at a fashion show and the Library Bar to my colleagues Sanjana and Kanishka, the new recruit, so they could call and fix meetings with prospective clients. Sanjana informed me a little later that Sarla had called and was keen on a meeting the next day. 'Nice of Sarla to initiate a meeting. Lots of vacancies perhaps,' I told Sanjana.

Sanjana and I met Sarla at her office. She was dressed in a pair of grey trousers and a blue shirt, her hair loosely falling on her shoulders.

'How wonderful to see you!' she said with enthusiasm.

I introduced Sanjana to her.

'Did you go to Athena that night?' Sarla asked, before she went on to volunteer information about her relationship with Peter Mukerjea.

'We did, but it was shut. So we went to Fire and Ice instead,' I answered.

'Oh, we were there too. Didn't see you. Peter is a member there. We were in the VIP lounge,' Sarla announced.

She continued, 'Peter and I prefer quiet dinners and movies to these noisy night clubs. But we had guests from out of town who were keen to go out. We didn't have much choice.' And then gave a small laugh.

Sanjana frowned and intervened, 'Sarla, can you please brief us on your corporate structure?'

'Oh, sure!' Sarla replied, her broad smile disappearing.

As Sarla spoke, I listened and Sanjana made copious notes. Just as I thought that Sarla was done with trying to impress me about her dates and evenings with Peter Mukerjea, she suddenly said, 'Peter and I are having friends over for dinner at home. Maybe we'll invite you one of these days.'

'Thank you, that's very kind of you. I'll surely come,' I said, knowing well by then that the last thing Sarla would do was invite me for dinner with Peter and her.

I wondered what made her so insecure when I was anything but even remotely interested in her Peter or their relationship, whatever it was.

'What was all that about?' Sanjana asked me as we exited Sarla's office.

I shrugged my shoulders. 'No clue, honestly! What a waste of time. A long drive for a cup of vending machine coffee, I suppose, and no assignment.'

Sanjana and I forgot all about Sarla and Peter Mukerjea for the next couple of weeks.

Sanjana agreed to come over for a sleepover that weekend.

My purse that very often burst at its seams with the world inside it was periodically spring-cleaned by Sanjana.

As Sanjana turned my purse upside down, the visiting card with Peter Mukerjea's name fell on my feet.

I picked it up. 'I thought I had given you this card!'

Sanjana took the card from me. 'You had his card all along and never bothered to tell me! Star TV is our client. It makes sense, common sense, to meet the CEO, doesn't it? Particularly when he has written his mobile number!'

Sanjana rolled her eyes, 'Call him tomorrow, Indrani. Let's get some business going here.'

'Not tomorrow. I'll call him on his landline on Monday,' I said meekly.

On Monday, I called the direct line of Peter Mukerjea instead of his mobile. His secretary Tina answered, 'Peter's not in town, I'm afraid. Can I please take down your name and number?'

'Indrani Khanna.'

Before I could say anymore, Tina said in an excited voice, 'Oh! He's been waiting for your call. Were you not supposed to call him two weeks ago? Now he's in Hong Kong. Please give me your number. I'll let him know. I will call you once he returns.'

I gave Tina my mobile number and hung up. Sanjana was disappointed that the meeting with the CEO of Star TV, which could have happened two weeks ago had I not carelessly shoved his visiting card to the bottom of my purse, was now going to have to wait till his return.

Two minutes later, my mobile phone rang. An 'Unknown Number' flashed on the screen.

When I answered, Peter Mukerjea spoke, 'Hello, Indrani, how are you? This is Peter Mukerjea.'

'I am good, thank you. How are you?' I asked, surprised that he was calling me from Hong Kong barely two minutes after I had given Tina my number.

'I didn't know how to reach you. I misplaced your card somewhere,' he said, sounding apologetic.

I didn't remind him that Sarla had promptly grabbed the card from him, deftly tucking it into her purse and called my office the next day for a meeting.

'I'll be back the day after. Why don't we meet at my office on Friday at 2 p.m.? Does that work for you?

'It sure does. Thank you. I'll be there,' I said hastily, without checking my diary.

Even though the very first encounter with Peter Mukerjea at Library Bar was not impressive, he was a client, and a busy one at that. Getting an appointment with him was surely worth rescheduling any other meetings that I had on Friday. It made good business sense and 'common sense' as Sanjana would term it.

'Look forward to seeing you, Indrani. Bye!'

'I'll be there. Bye,' I said, looking at my colleagues Sanjana and Kanishka who were by then wide-eyed with curiosity.

I chose a khaki-green skirt, work suit and a pair of black low-heeled formal sandals for my meeting with Peter Mukerjea.

Tina was sitting outside his office cabin. She asked me to take a seat on the sofa in front of her desk and walked into Peter's chamber.

She soon exited and showed me the way in. Peter was seated behind a big desk, his work jacket hanging on the chair where he sat. He rose and shook my hand with a warm smile under his bristly moustache; it was a firm handshake.

'Good to see you, Indrani! You are punctual. That's good.'

Despite his pot belly, he looked dapper in his white cotton shirt buttoned with cuff links at the wrists and a pair of grey pinstriped trousers.

He started talking about work, and asked Tina to get their head of human resources to his office and also beeped his colleagues in.

'Let's first meet Sumantra and the HR head. We can have a coffee after that,' Peter said.

Just then the HR head, Radley [name changed], entered.

'This is Indrani. She owns a headhunting firm and has done some work for us in Kolkata. Please see if we have any assignments for them. Take her to meet Sumo after that. I have told him to expect her,' Peter said, all in one breath and then he quickly added, 'Make sure after Sumo's meeting you bring her back here.'

'You're in good hands,' he said, turning to me. 'I'll see you in a bit.'

Radley diligently gave me a full low-down on their organizational structure, briefed me on a few vacancies that we could work on and promptly took me to Sumantra's office after that.

Sumantra, too, was dressed in formals like Peter. He was animated as he spoke about the radio business that he had set up. Sumo clearly was in love with his job. He spoke with such passion about his work, as one would about his lover. He was the chief operating officer (COO) of Radio City.

After that, I was escorted back to Peter's office. He asked Tina for the coffee to be brought in. We did not talk about business anymore.

'Are you still married, Indrani?' he asked.

'Yes, kind of,' I replied.

'Kind of?' he asked, raising his eyebrows.

'I am still legally married, but things have gone awry between my husband and I. We are separated.'

'I have a daughter, who's four. Vidhie.' I continued, 'She is with my mom-in-law at the moment.'

'I'm divorced. I have got two boys, Rabin and Rahul. Rabin is twenty-one and Rahul is eighteen. Rabin lives in London. He's working. Rahul lives with his mother, my ex-wife, in Hampstead. He is in senior school,' Peter said.

Peter spoke about his school days in India, college and work in England, his move back to India and how he joined Star TV and rose up the ladder to head the company in India. Our conversation was smooth and easy. He did most of the talking. He was no Clark Gable. But he had a charming presence and was a sprightly gent.

'Let's catch up for a beer soon,' he said.

'I'd like that,' I replied. 'I must get going now. I've already taken up a lot of your time.'

'That's absolutely fine. It's my pleasure,' he said, with a smile.

I rose to leave. He walked me to the door. My trip to Star TV was satisfying. I walked out with a few assignments and, in a strange way, a lighter heart, even though I barely spoke about myself or my life—Peter did all the talking.

He called me on Sunday night.

'How are you? Did you have a good weekend?'

I had barely met him two days ago for an official meeting; for him to take the liberty to call me on a Sunday night was indicative that he had already taken a step beyond a professional and business alliance. I was in a new city, making a new life for myself. I knew he had a crush on me, and if I am being honest, I didn't mind the attention.

'I'm very well. How about you?' I asked.

He answered my question with yet another question, 'What did you do yesterday?'

'Nothing much. Stayed at home,' I replied.

'How come you were home on a Saturday evening? The city rocks on Saturdays,' he said.

'AP is in Alibaug. I don't really have many other friends here,' I said, not intending to make an instant picture of loneliness and pathos, but just as a mere statement of no relevance.

'You have one now!' he replied with a slight laugh.

I was wrapping my head around the implication of his cheesy comment. I said nothing.

'There's a wine-tasting event at the Grand Maratha on Tuesday. I'd like you to join me. I'd be really happy if you would come with me.' This unexpected invitation was a fast move, I thought.

'I'm afraid I will not be able to do a late night. And it's midweek,' I replied.

'Don't worry,' he said. 'It's not a late-night affair. The wine-tasting starts at 6 p.m. and will be over at eight. You can be home for dinner, you see,' he insisted.

'All right, if you promise that it's an early night. What time would you like me to reach?'

'I'll pick you up at 5 p.m. We'll have to leave early just in case there's traffic.' I could visualize him smiling behind his bristly moustache.

Peter Mukerjea was a punctual man. Unlike most people I know, for whom 5 p.m. meant 7, Peter was at the porch at sharp 5. I went down when he buzzed me. He was behind the wheel. His chauffeur stood outside the big Land Cruiser and opened the door to the passenger seat in the front, with a smile and a nod. He jumped into the back seat quickly after that.

Peter introduced me to his chauffeur Prashant. Prashant was a slightly built man, perhaps in his thirties. He told me that Prashant was his man Friday, almost family and an old hand.

Peter was in his formal work clothes, a pink and white striped shirt with silver cuff links and a pair of cream trousers. He smelt of a strong aftershave that was musky.

I had worn a brown ankle-length skirt with cream embroidery on the slit and a short-sleeved beige blouse that fitted snugly. My hair was washed that morning and it fell neatly like silk threads with my pearl danglers peeping through them. I wore my favourite high-heeled brown Roman sandals. My brown leather purse completed the look along with the nude matt make-up that I wore that evening.

I had never been to a wine-tasting event before. Peter, I could tell, was rather pleased to guide me at every step on what one was meant to do. The host of that evening, oddly enough, looked like a younger version of Peter Mukerjea, with more hair on his head and no pot belly.

Barely two sips of red wine was served in the Riedel goblets that were placed in front of each guest.

'Just copy me,' Peter whispered into my ear.

I nodded. Peter took the goblet close to his face, tilted it slightly and sniffed with his broad nose, inhaling the headiness of the mature wine. I followed. Everybody else in the room did exactly the same, some even with their eyes shut, to perhaps accentuate their sense of smell. I almost felt drunk as I inhaled deeply, taking in the strong whiff of the wine.

Then everyone swirled the wine in their glasses deftly in a circular motion, as advised by the host. I did the same, but alas, the wine was on my skirt rather than the glass!

'Oops!' It was a faux pas.

Peter quickly picked up a piece of dry bread and rubbed it on the wine stain on my skirt.

'It'll soak the wine off the fabric. Wipe it with a bit of soda and salt after that. I always end up dropping wine or food on my shirt. I am an expert now at instant stain removal!' he whispered and chuckled.

The entire event lasted for a couple of hours, as Peter had said earlier, with the host showcasing several types of red, white and dessert wines of different vintage and the kinds of goblets and flutes that are to be used for them. It was no doubt a learning experience for me and despite my stained skirt I enjoyed myself.

Peter was in a cheerful mood. 'Let's go downstairs for a drink in the bar and then I'll drop you home.'

I agreed. I could do with a drink, I thought. And Peter, I realized, was easy company.

'What's your poison?' he asked when we perched ourselves on the bar stools.

'Stoli on the rocks!' I said.

He ordered a bourbon for himself and the vodka on the rocks for me. I was slightly surprised that he laced his bourbon with a coke.

'What a waste of a good bourbon,' Gramps would have said, I thought in my head.

'Salut,' Peter said, raising his glass

'Cheers,' I raised my glass and clinked his.

He opened the conversation by talking about his parents.

'My father was from Calcutta, eldest of seven siblings. His parents had passed away when he had just graduated to be a doctor. His siblings became his responsibility. He was of Bengali origin. He met my mother while he was practising in Delhi. She was Punjabi and fourteen years his junior. She had just graduated in medicine. Despite much resistance from both families, they eventually got married. They then moved to the UK for higher studies. That was where I was born. They returned to India when I was just a few months old. They joined the army after that.'

He gulped his bourbon, before continuing.

'My mother passed away when I was around twenty-seven. She was fifty-five. Died of a heart attack. I was on holiday in France. I didn't come for the funeral. I continued with my holiday. My sister hasn't forgiven me for it till date. But then again, she was already gone. What good was it going to be, if I cancelled my holiday and showed up here to mourn? Anyway, that's my way of looking at things.'

His gaze looked distant as though he was delving somewhere back to the day when he heard the news of his mother's death. 'She was a good soul. Always stood up for me.'

Peter signalled the barman for a second round of drinks.

'Dad passed away a few years ago at the age of eighty-four. He was a grouchy old man. But I wish he was alive. He would have been proud of me today.'

I could see the nostalgia in his eyes and hear it in his voice. He said that he had a brother who worked in Dubai but had quit his job and returned to India to give it a shot with his estranged wife, who lived in Delhi with their two young daughters.

He continued talking about himself. He told me about his ex-wife, who was his sister's classmate at school, and that they had married when he was barely twenty-two. Both his boys were born before he was twenty-six. He said that he hated having to change nappies whilst his friends were all still bachelors, having a good time, banging a different chick every night, as he put it. The inflection in his voice was noticeable, as though he regretted that time.

'All my salary was spent on buying nappies. And then I got hired by an advertising agency. I did well. I was enjoying my job at last.

And lo and behold, I was called to my boss's cabin one fine afternoon, and I was laid off. My differences with Shab, in the meanwhile, were becoming more distinct. She just didn't grow, didn't grow at all, mentally. After a while, I just didn't know what to talk to her about anymore. I couldn't stay in England any longer with a wife and two kids, and no job. So, I returned to Delhi and lived in Dad's apartment for a while till I found myself a job as a sales director in an advertising agency.'

It was clear that Peter was not going to stop, it didn't matter whether I wanted to know more about his life or not.

'Who's Shab?' I intervened, thinking it was a rather odd name, even though I guessed he was referring to his ex-wife.

'Sorry, Shab is my ex-wife, short for Shabnam. My brother is Goat, short for Gautam and sister is Pussy, short for Shangon. Goat's wife is Aarti. My name is actually Pratim, but in England they would make fun of me calling me Prat, meaning a stupid person, so I changed it to Peter.'

'Well, they sound like an odd bunch!' I thought. Fancy being called, 'Hey, Pussy!' or 'Hi, Goat!' Before I could stop myself, I had a smile on my face. I needed another drink! A double Stoli on the rocks.

'I met Sashwati in Delhi. She was fun. She brought colour to my otherwise insipid existence. She was like a breath of fresh air. Shab and I were divorced soon after. Shab went back to England with the boys. Sash and I were in a relationship for twelve years. In the meanwhile, I joined Star TV as the sales director. I made sure that the big bosses in the US and Hong Kong saw what was going on. And soon, I became the CEO of Star TV.' Peter looked pleased with himself as he spoke. Needless to say, Star TV network owned the number one entertainment channel and from what I had read, Peter Mukerjea changed things around in the company after he took charge.

There is no doubt that very often to get to the top, to get recognized, to look good, you have to be as hard as nails and trample others. Peter Mukerjea did exactly that to reach the top. That was my analysis and understanding after his conversation with me.

'I'd like another drink please,' I said.

'My apologies. I got carried away. I should have asked,' Peter said.

'Make it a double, please!' I told the bartender.

'You're sure?'

'Absolutely sure!' I had hoped to shock him into silence. But no such luck.

'Sash and I got engaged. But it just didn't last. She was the other extreme of Shab!' he said, whatever that meant.

'Is Sarla your girlfriend now?' I asked.

'You must be kidding. Of course, not,' he replied with a laugh.

There was no doubt that Peter Mukerjea was a colourful and complex man. But, strangely, I was enjoying his company that evening. Perhaps his life was not as complex as mine, but people tend to always gravitate towards likeminded people. Peter Mukerjea sounded like a ruthless man when he boasted about the conquests in his personal and professional life. But life had taught me invaluable lessons, one of them being that there's always a reason we do what we do. After all, as human beings we are all frail and flawed. Our weaknesses are accepted by those who love us, our vulnerabilities often nestled in their empathy, till they can endure it. Once it is beyond their endurance, they move on to a different plane and that is what life is all about for many, if not all.

'What about you, Indrani? You haven't said much about yourself,' Peter said suddenly.

'I didn't get a chance till now,' I replied.

'My parents live in Guwahati. They have a business of their own—they run a boutique hotel and are dabbling in other businesses of construction. That was what they were doing when I met them last. I have not seen or spoken to them for almost ten years. I have two siblings, Sheena and Mekhail. Haven't seen or met them for the last decade. I have a daughter with Sanjeev, my estranged husband, who's four years old now. I've already told you about Sanjeev and Vidhie when we met in your office. That's it, really. In my life, things often came together only to fall apart!' I concluded with a sigh.

Peter Mukerjea had shared a lot about himself that evening. I was, however, a bit more reticent about my personal life. I was definitely not going to share my deepest vulnerabilities with a man whom I had met for the third time in my life and barely knew.

It was past 1 a.m. I had spent almost eight hours that evening with Peter Mukerjea. My takeaway was that he didn't exactly have razor-sharp wit but he knew how to get what he wanted in life. There was something else about him that I could not lay a finger on.

We finally exited when the bartender announced that the last drinks needed to be ordered, permit time ending in five minutes.

Peter dropped me back at two in the morning. He walked me to the door and like a thorough gentleman, shook my hand and air-kissed me with cheeks barely touching.

'Goodnight. Sleep well. I'll call you tomorrow,' he said.

'Goodnight,' I said.

Peter waited till the door opened. The housemaid looked at me and then at Peter. I went in and rushed to the bedroom before I bumped into anyone else. As I lay in bed thinking about the really long evening with Peter Mukerjea, I knew what was bothering me—Peter Mukerjea was my alter-ego, he was my spirit doppelgänger! It freaked me out.

PART 5

Prison and Chargesheet

15

After my near-death experience in prison, my security was beefed up. The preciousness of the things you took for granted as a free person suddenly hits you when you start to acclimatize to a life behind bars. Like a one-foot-high foam mattress at home, for instance. In jail, I was sleeping on a blanket on the floor. The green sari that the prison guards made me wear despite being an undertrial accused scarred my confidence. Though nothing has been proved against me till date—and by law one is innocent till proven guilty—I was set apart and it disturbed me to no end. The fact that I was in prison was the biggest humiliation there could be. Forget about the crime per se, once you are in prison, it stays with you for life. It's not just the stigma of it all but also the emotional damage. Even someone as strong as me was reduced to a shambles.

Prison basically segregates you from the rest of the world. Imprisonment denotes that you are not fit to be a part of society. You are considered an outcast. That itself is traumatic, particularly when you know you are not guilty of the crime. In prison, I met people who were being tried for peddling narcotics, human trafficking, some for financial frauds, but none of them was as lost as I was. People who are guilty are mentally prepared for the consequences they may have to face. They know they might be behind bars one day. It is less traumatic for them because they are mentally prepared

233

for this eventuality. For someone who hasn't committed a crime, it is different. It is not about the financial status of the prisoner. Regardless of where one comes from, life during incarceration can be very difficult. I wasn't mentally prepared for this.

I was very badly off when I went into prison. Not in my wildest dreams did I imagine being there. I was accused of the most heinous crime that can exist—I was accused of murdering my own daughter.

I had to deal with three things. First, the uncertainty of whether my child was alive or not. The years from 2015 to 2019 were traumatic for me. The understanding was that she wasn't there anymore. There was a body, rather a skeleton, that matched my DNA, thus leading to the deduction that it was Sheena.

Second, what Peter did to me was unpardonable. I didn't care much for his family. But Peter's betrayal hit hard. I loved Peter. I did everything in my capacity to make him happy. I considered his family my own. It looked to me now like I had essentially lived a long phase of life with blinkers on; it was as if I didn't know what he was like. I never thought of a life without him. With him, I never thought that I needed to choose a career over our life together. He wanted to retire and I was happy to lead a retired life with him at a very young age. I was in my thirties when we decided to go live in England—I was thirty-seven years old. I gave up everything to make him happy. I lived my life to suit his desires and needs. I could've stayed back here and got a job at a corporate company with a package worth crores. I could have run a successful business of my own. I would have had a fancy life. But I chose to be a housewife in Bristol despite the energy I had within me. I did it only because I loved him that much. When Peter abandoned me, the shock didn't wear off. He dropped me like a hot potato and all marriage vows were forgotten. Even for a minute, if we assume I was guilty, I feel as my husband it was his moral duty to stand by me. He should've protected me. It was a grief I harboured for a long time. If Peter was arrested first, I would have turned the world upside down to protect him. He and his family went out to the press and maligned me, which was even more hurtful.

And third, I was left financially unstable and access to my funds was taken away. By then I had mustered the courage to fight my battles by myself. The big question playing on my mind during my initial days in prison was—why are you trying to cripple me?

Let's assume I am a terrible person. But why keep me away from my own funds? I wasn't running away with his money. From my account, ₹6 crore were moved to Peter's and his sons' accounts; I had no money! I started believing that he didn't want me to hire the best lawyers I could. I asked him these questions point blank and he kept quiet. I had asked him as to why jewellery worth crores was moved to a new locker which was under the joint ownership of his sons after my arrest without either my or Vidhie's knowledge or consent. He kept mum, he had no explanation, no answer whatsoever. I still don't have answers to these questions.

The instances did not just end with me, which made it even more distressing. The first time Vidhie came to visit me in prison alone, she said, 'Papa wants me to transfer the shares of our home in Marlow back to him or Rabin.'

I didn't know why this was an issue. Our Marlow property was worth several crores, and Peter and I were co-owners. It was bequeathed to Vidhie when she was a minor. The understanding was that on her eighteenth birthday the shares would get transferred to her and she would be the owner of the flat as an adult. One of the reasons why we were in Mumbai in August 2015, instead of the UK, was to transfer the shares of the property to Vidhie. Peter and I would have lifelong rights to live there, but the property would belong to her.

This was done with the intent of securing her future—all the children were provided for with a roof over their heads. Rabin was given a flat at Nottingham in London; Rahul was given a flat at Berkhamsted; the big two-storeyed house in Guwahati was given to Mekhail and Sheena, a floor to each of them and the land equally divided between the two.

When I got to know this property was being taken away from Vidhie, particularly at a time like this, I could not allow it. Eventually, Vidhie was coerced into transferring the property to Rabin Mukerjea. She finally did it because she couldn't deal with the pressure. This would all tie in later. When the building manager—Madhukar Kilje—came to depose in court, it created headlines. It shook the court. He said that when I was arrested, Peter had sent a letter asking to stop the transfer of the flat to Vidhie. Like me, Vidhie wasn't aware of this. I got to know of this much later.

After I was arrested, Vidhie, who till then had led a cocooned life, found herself alone and unprotected. Of course, I didn't know about this when I was inside, but later my friend Saveena Bedi told me how things were for my Vidhie. She informed me how once Vidhie had gone to meet her and didn't have money to pay the cab guy, or any money for her expenses. She was left out in the cold. Saveena, who had known Vidhie since she was five, couldn't bear to see her crying about how difficult things were for her then.

To be very honest, I was very hurt when Vidhie wrote a fairly slanderous book about me; the book was published in 2021. My lawyers wanted me to put a stop to it. They had an objection to a lot of it, including the title—*Devil's Daughter*. But, I let the book be published. As a mother, I didn't think I had the right to stop Vidhie from expressing what she felt. A lot of what she said wasn't factually correct. But it was important that I let her get everything she was feeling out of her system. My relationship with my children has been one where I have treated them as adults, letting them know that I am always there if anything goes wrong.

A month into my time in prison, the first chargesheet came. I was troubled when I read what was written in it. Gunjan, came to meet me in prison after the chargesheet came along. I asked Gunjan when she would file for bail.

She said hesitantly, 'With a chargesheet like this, we can't apply for bail.'

We had to wait. We eventually agreed that a bail on medical grounds would be filed. I was still recovering from the hospital trip, physically fragile and needed to be in a better place to recuperate.

Unlike the world over—with exceptions here and there in some countries—where you are innocent till you are proven guilty, in India, you are guilty till you are proven innocent even though the law stipulates otherwise. In my case, this left room for a lot of slander while I languished in prison.

When I started reading the details of my chargesheet, I was very disturbed. We agreed that a good trial lawyer must be hired. We hired Sudeep Pasbola. I met him in court and appointed him soon after. I also requested Gunjan to help me retrieve access to my finances. Once Peter was in prison, everything was left in his sister's custody. I was also under pressure to sell the assets that were in my name, like my flat in Covent Garden in London, and splitting the dividends. I took the court's permission to access my local accounts. Access to my overseas accounts was not possible even with court orders from India because the banks there were unwilling to provide any information to anybody till they had direct access to me. It took my team a long time to get me access to my funds. When the access finally came through for my local accounts, I felt a bit more secure. Mostly, I could start paying my lawyers again and was able to fight my case.

For the first three years, after we met in prison in October 2015, Vidhie vanished from my life. She was studying in England. Vidhie told me later that she was under a great deal of emotional pressure and Peter's family had categorically told her that she should not stay in touch with me. Vidhie wasn't in direct contact, but she would be in touch with my lawyer for money. I would try and help her out as much as I could.

The main thing that shook me about my chargesheet was the accusation of murder itself. The prosecution story was that on 24 April 2012, I killed Sheena. Prior to it, a conspiracy was hatched between Peter, Shyamvar, Sanjeev and myself. Peter stayed back in England because he didn't want to be in the thick of it. Then, Sanjeev, Shyamvar and I executed the said plan. The prosecution also admitted that I had not established contact with Sheena. She contacted me in March 2012 after a gap of over three years to make amends. The questions that cropped up immediately in my head were: How and for what reason would I want to kill my estranged daughter? By design, a conspiracy has to be triggered by the people who execute it. If one were to buy this theory, wouldn't it be easier for me to do something of this nature to her when we weren't in touch, as opposed to when things were better?

The chargesheet itself seemed ridiculous. Am I so stupid that I would keep two witnesses and commit a murder, I thought? They must really underestimate people's intelligence. I am not an Indian citizen. I don't live in India. I lived between our homes in England and Spain from 2010. After Sheena's alleged disappearance in April 2012, I came back to Mumbai about twenty times till my arrest. Also, it just didn't make sense to me how it was concluded that the three of us decided to park the car and strangle Sheena in the busy streets of Bandra at 6.30 p.m.

Every act of murder has to have a motive behind it, and my motive for killing Sheena is unclear. It is widely speculated that I was against Sheena's and Rahul's relationship. But they weren't in touch with me and had been dating since 2008. Then why suddenly would I decide to kill one of them to break them apart in 2012? As if there aren't less gory ways to split a couple! Though, let me put it on record. I wasn't really against the relationship. I was against the fact that my daughter was dating a man who wasn't settled. She was unhappy with him. The story that I was against the relationship came from Peter in the first interview he gave after my arrest to NewsX. Why would I murder my own daughter because I hate her boyfriend/partner? If it came to that, any sane man or woman would eliminate the partner, and not their own daughter or son!

The press tried to give a spin about some hidden money—₹900 crores—in some offshore account.[3] This theory suggested that Sheena refused to give me this money, thus I killed her. This wasn't in the chargesheet but I was later told this by my lawyers. Investigation showed that Sheena had only a lakh in her account. After much investigation, no such fabled account was found!

Two elements of the chargesheet stuck out—one, that I was an ambitious woman, and the other was that I remained on cordial terms with my ex-husband. I suspect K.K. Singh from Bihar (the CBI officer on the case) wouldn't understand the dynamics of a modern family. Estranged couples are often cordial, even friendly, for the sake of healthy co-parenting. It is possible to be friends with an ex. As for a woman being ambitious, it's an age-old story of how men perceive women who want to make it big.

More than men, women tried to pull me down. After the first chargesheet came out, people from all corners of our social life descended upon me with their claws out. In all my years in

Mumbai, I had never felt any animosity against me, maybe because I didn't ever focus on other people. I was always that hardworking girl who left her home early in life and knew going back wasn't an option. I had to hustle, work hard and make it on my own. I was working sixteen hours a day, some days even more. Peter was working equally hard. We had created our own comfortable life. I married Peter because I fell in love with him. And I left him when I felt our love had vanished.

Of course, we had a busy social life. There were several invites that arrived home every day but Peter and I wouldn't have the time to attend every party. We picked and chose the ones we wanted to attend. Our weekends were always just the two of us, catching up. Vidhie kept us busy and running. We were both homebodies, who would enjoy an evening with good food and good wine.

My work was always my focus, and after that it was my family. I reconnected with Sheena and Mekhail soon after I married Peter. I wanted to make up for lost time. My parents were ageing and it was a complex relationship to navigate. Peter's entire family was also my responsibility. They were to some extent financially dependent on us. Peter had two boys with whom I had to create an amicable relationship. I was focussing on building a stable family structure and also taking care of the extended families on both sides. I didn't care much for evenings with stupid conversations with floozy women. Often, at these get-togethers, I would be chatty, but my mind would be preoccupied with work. Yes, if Mukesh Ambani or Anand Mahindra or Indira Nooyi spoke, I'd listen, because every conversation with people like them was a meaningful one. I don't think anyone understood that in those evenings when I was out, I was mentally working or networking. I make no apologies for not having time for socialites.

After my arrest, Raveena Raj Kohli—the president of Star News for a brief while—had the nastiest things to say about me.[4] She said, 'Within six months of being on the horizon, she was married to Peter Mukerjea. She burst into the scene as an attractive single mother and found a man besotted with her. The man had corporate power and influence and that's how she dreamt of becoming a massive media tycoon.' Kohli in her interview even said that we wanted her to be a part of the INX team. Talk about a creative mind! The fact is that no one ever asked her to. She didn't even feature in the long list, leave alone the shortlist, that we had made for the final team. The only conclusion that I can derive after listening to her several interviews was that she was upset with Peter and me because we didn't hire her at INX. After she had to exit from Star News, she wasn't a great fit for us, we decided. That was the long and short of it!

I never understood Shobhaa Dé's rant against me.[5] She was a divorcee herself before she remarried so I don't get why she would write a spicy column on my 'quickie divorce'.

When I was getting married, or even for the years I was married to Peter, I never felt that I was in any way an outsider. I came to Mumbai to establish my HR firm in the city. I didn't come to the city because I was getting married to Peter. I met Peter after my firm had opened an office there. All the people Peter knew in the corporate world, I knew already. The self-established socialites came into my life only after Peter was in it. I inherited his world. Mumbai was his city. I am a confident person, so I didn't notice who was bitching behind my back.

For these socialites, it is necessary to be seen at events and then write columns about people they don't know. The people who inhabit this so-called social circuit didn't know me beyond a party—I had not met them for meals or gone out with them for a drink. Let's just say, I wouldn't be able to hold a conversation with most of these socialites. We had no common ground for conversation, because we were leading such different lives.

Wherever I went, I was always with Peter. His peers were easily two decades my seniors. Women who were his friends and I rarely had anything to talk about.

When I walked into a room, people noticed me. I am a good-looking, intelligent woman who can hold a conversation with an industrialist or a CEO. I wasn't a ditzy girl talking about fluff; I spoke business. The glitzy social circuit of Mumbai had issues with this newbie in town, walking in and inheriting a circle that they had been striving hard to get into. In the end, all I really wanted was to get home, curl up in bed and sleep.

The moment I was arrested, it seemed like people came out and said everything they had been feeling about me for a decade and more. It felt like they were waiting for me to fall. And what was really jarring was that most of these people didn't really know me, but aired their opinions freely about me, anyway.

Queenie Dhody gave an interview to *India Today* saying: 'She was never a part of Bombay society. She was too much of an outsider. Bombay society would not accept her, so she was creating a society that was clearly all in her head.'[6] But the fact is I didn't ever strive to even belong in that society. I lived in South Bombay because Peter had rented the Marlow apartment next to the sea and later bought it when we decided to get married. I loved the view from our home. That's it and that's all. I wouldn't mind if our house was in Alibaug. It was always about the terrace and the sea for me. Amitabh Bachchan, the supreme actor of our industry, lives in Juhu—is he any less classy than the socialites of South Bombay?

In the same chargesheet, three men stand as co-accused. But they were not branded as 'ambitious'. In a now much-aired interview, my former colleague Vir Sanghvi talked about how he thought I had 'delusions of grandeur and was obsessed with being a media baron'.[7]

Peter Mukerjea used to sell garments from the back of a car in a flea market in England. He worked hard and made his way up to the position of CEO of Star TV. But he isn't faulted for his ambition. Peter has had a failed marriage (with Shabnam). He lived with a girlfriend for twelve years. He met me well after that. But those twelve years with his girlfriend, or the next, did not appear in his chargesheet. The socialite columnists also didn't make much of any of that.

My relationships and exes have been scrutinized to great detail. I have kids with more than one man and that was packaged in a way to make me look like someone with loose morals. There is no way to substantiate it but the character assassination was subtly put in between the lines playing to the deep-seated misogyny of our system.

Every ridiculous thing about me was heard. I was an enchantress who does black magic. A lot was said about my crazy eyes. On Karan Thapar's *To the Point* on *India Today*, Tavleen Singh said, '[Indrani] comes across as the most heartless woman known to mankind.' She didn't quite substantiate why I am the worst woman alive. Actor Rishi Kapoor dedicated one whole tweet to me and called me a 'real weirdo'.[8] There was an article that read 'Sheena Bora murder case: Why Alpha men are putty in the hands of Alpha women.'[9] Someone called me a desi Don Draper and made a listicle about it citing that Don and I have similar pasts and affinity to the other sex. A *Times of India* article called me 'The Great Gatsby of Mumbai' and somehow knew 'how I had Peter under my thumb'.[10] A Twitter user even whipped up a conspiracy theory and wrote: 'Is Mukherjea couple's relationship the present & future of marriage as an institution

among porn loving elites in India?' It was like the sharks had smelt
the blood in the water and there was a frenzied feeding—anyone
and anything was game.

Journalists tracked down Mekhail's father, whose spouse had no
idea about me or Mekhail. She was Siddharth's childhood sweetheart.

At the time of my divorce, there was a lot of chatter about the
distribution of assets between Peter and me. Mean articles were
written about me taking back my rugs, paintings, etc. by the same
columnists. Everything I took in my settlement was earned by me
and has emotional value for me. I didn't understand why anyone
had to get their knickers in a twist about the number of rugs and
paintings I got. The division was mutually decided between Peter
and myself and to comment on that was simply in poor taste.

I was judged for getting a divorce in the middle of a case. But I
had my reasons. I had made up my mind to divorce Peter in 2017.
As things were unfolding, I knew I didn't want to stay married to
him. My lawyers were able to efficiently arrange a 'quickie' for me
because my advocate Edith Dey doesn't believe in dragging divorce
cases. Quickies are better, in more sense than one!

I read several articles about how Peter helped me further my
professional aspirations. It was also a widely spread misconception
that Peter helped me get an in with Star. But what fact-checkers
didn't clarify was that Star was my client since 1997. I had been
with their Kolkata office since then. I set up my office in Mumbai
because I had huge contracts already in place for recruitment for
Amex and Standard Chartered. I met Peter by fluke.

Once I came to terms with the chargesheet, I decided to take
charge of my case. There is no one who knows the details of my case
better than me. And so I started making copious notes. Reading
every bit of information thoroughly, refuting it with the truth. I
was obsessed with the chargesheet. I would wake up in the morning

and get going with it. And till the time I went to sleep, I was at it. Sometimes, I would wake up from sleep at night and revisit some parts of it and jot notes. I was breaking down the chargesheet pointwise. It was hundreds of pages long. I filed my bail on medical grounds in March 2016.

Three months later after his arrest, Peter was chargesheeted and the onus to a large extent was shifted to him. It didn't absolve me in any way but it suggested that Peter was a part of the devious designs from inception.

Several months later, another chargesheet appeared. This had Mekhail's version—of being abandoned by me as a baby. It ended with how he thought I had tried to kill him. The motive? None has been mentioned till date.

The more time went by and I immersed myself in my chargesheet, the more it dawned on me that I wasn't in contact with anyone from my family. I would go to the court and Peter's family would be there to see him. I knew this as our hearings were held together. I had no family. Both my parents had passed away. Vidhie was in the UK. Mekhail didn't come to see me, of course. Sheena was apparently not alive anymore.

When my father passed away in December 2016, I took court permission to go and perform the last rites. I found it odd that when I filed that application, the CBI objected despite the fact that I was willing to be escorted by them and be under their supervision during the entire process. The public prosecutor made some ridiculous argument that a priest could visit me at Byculla Jail where I could perform the last rites of my father. However, the court passed an order stating that I could perform his last rites either at my residence (18 Marlow) or at a venue of my choice outside of home but it had to be within the jurisdiction of Mumbai. I requested my advocate to make the arrangements at home which would give me an opportunity to perform the shradh ceremony in peace and also visit home—a place I hadn't seen in months. However, the custody of the keys and the house per se was with Shangon. At court, I spoke to Peter and told him that my advocate would make these arrangements at home and my team should be permitted to do the needful. The next thing I know, instructions were given for the house to be locked up. Even the house help was sent away so that I couldn't enter my home. My advocate organized the ceremony to be conducted at Brahmana Seva Samiti in Mulund.

That was the first time, on 27 December, that I stepped out of jail to go to a place that wasn't the hospital or the court. I was picked up at 7 a.m. by an escort team of Mumbai Police and CBI, and taken to the venue under high security. It is odd how when the venue was not disclosed to the press, there were hundreds of spectators outside, climbing over walls and trees to take video footage of me. It was a very emotional day. The priests performing the ceremony explained how the spirit who had left the mortal world and gone towards moksha would not find salvation if I didn't forgive him. I closed my eyes and thought of my father's face. 'I forgive you. Go well!' I said in my heart. I was brought back to Byculla in the evening after a visit to a Shiva temple close to the Brahmana Seva Samiti in Mulund.

The loneliness slowly made me turn towards spirituality. I was never a spiritual person before. Earlier back at home, I would light a couple of incense sticks every day and that was all in the name of prayer or spirituality. But during this phase, I started praying for long hours. I laid out a cardboard box and covered it with a red cotton dupatta—this became my altar. I cut out pictures of

Ganesha, Vishnu, Buddha and Radha–Krishna from newspapers
and stuck them to pieces of cardboard so that I could prop them
up on my altar. Gradually, as the months passed by, I knew I had
to pull myself together. I started doing yoga and meditation. That
helped, too.

Strangely, I wasn't the only woman in prison who faced such
loneliness. Families abandon women prisoners far more quickly than
they abandon men. Habitual criminals who are men are harboured
and protected by their families, but it is not the same for women.
This realization was compounded with the reality that as a woman it
doesn't matter which strata of society one is born into, the treatment
is the same. The mindset remains that if a man has committed a
mistake, the entire family is there to stand by him but, God forbid,
a woman does the same. She will lose it all—her dignity, her place
in the world, the people who are her own, her power … in the end,
love for a woman is conditional.

Everywhere I looked in the prison, there was someone feeling
slighted by their own. Being with them gave me strength. If they
could survive, so would I. Since the food poisoning incident, my
security had been beefed up and everything from food to medicines
was brought to me. I developed a bond with the cops and jailers.
Since I would spend more time with them than the prisoners, I
came to know them better. The jailers told me stories about their
hometowns, their lives, their pressures. One of them told me how
her parents couldn't afford oil to cook sabji at home so they would
make a geela sabji for dinner. Another told me a story of how when
she was a little girl their thatched roof leaked—the family would
stand in one corner all night to escape the rain—and they didn't
have enough money to fix it. Some didn't have electricity at home,
so studying was difficult. Another one told me how she would walk
for miles to get to school as a young girl of eight, carrying books

on one side, a 5-litre can of milk on the another and a tokri of vegetables on her head to sell. On her way to school, she would sell all of it and go. She had no shoes to spare, no extra sandals. And only one pair of school uniform. Her mother didn't have enough money to buy soap for the entire family's clothes so she would buy one bar of soap only to wash her uniform. Many of these constables told me how much they love their police uniforms now and how they were a source of great pride for them. Yet, despite their jobs, they struggled very often to get by each day. But what I found remarkable was that even through all these hardships they remained sincere at their jobs.

The privilege that I took for granted in my life didn't come easy for many others. And that realization was life-altering for me. Since I was kept apart from all the other prisoners, I was also regarded as the 'jail ki laadli (the spoilt one)' by other prisoners. Most authoritative figures at the prison were wonderful but there were some who had become brazen and rude over the years. It's almost as if power got to their heads. For the tiniest of things, they could be unusually harsh. Sometimes prisoners would get beaten up. Of course, often, the prisoners themselves were at fault but legally the authorities cannot touch prisoners. Corporal punishment is a violation of human rights. But the jailers also know there are other ways of punishing a prisoner—they can stop mulaqats, canteen access, letters. There is no need for physical violence to drive home a point. For, ultimately, Byculla Jail was a holding house for undertrials. While the cops at prison were very nice to me, every time there was an incident with another prisoner, it really bothered me.

Another thing I noticed was that the cops would never touch any foreign prisoner. There were many foreign nationals in Byculla Jail: from Africa, England, Australia, Finland and Spain. Some were being tried for passport scams or in drug-related cases. These foreign citizens are covered by consulate backing. Officials from the consulate office would come and check on them. Though a consulate can't interfere in legal matters of the case but as far as human rights go, especially the well-being of a prisoner, they can come down heavily in case of any violations.

During my years in jail, the authorities changed, and a lot transformed for the better. For my own part, I did try and educate prisoners about their rights and remind the authorities of their boundaries. Once I got over the shock of my situation, I sought solutions.

In April 2016 my bail was partially allowed. I was given access to private hospitalization, home food, medicines from home. By then, I had started being comfortable with prison life, so I used none of these privileges granted by the court. Human beings adapt quickly to circumstances.

PART 6

Marriage

16

After our initial few meetings, Peter and I spoke to each other often over the phone. The conversations flowed easily as though we had known each other forever.

One evening, I went with Peter to dinner at his colleague Raj Nayak's house, where I met several people from Star TV. Raj was the sales head of the company, and the dinner was apparently hosted for the sales team. It goes without saying that everyone in that terrace party was intrigued by the new woman that their boss, Peter Mukerjea, had shown up with.

On the way to Raj's house, Peter briefed me about a few of his colleagues to look out for.

Raj and his wife, Sagari, were good hosts, ensuring that everybody's glasses were topped up at all times, nobody was out of sorts and everybody was having a good time. It was easy to identify the colleagues Peter had described earlier. Despite having walked in with pre-conceived notions about each one of them, I saw qualities in them which were endearing. Of course, I sensed undercurrents, like between the sales and content head. But then, content and sales were the two arms of the media business that could neither live with each other nor without. The sales guys believed that the television business should be advertisement driven, while the programming lot thought it needed to be content driven.

As the head of the company, what I noticed that evening was that Peter Mukerjea controlled the show well, with an apt balance of 'divide and rule' as well as 'let's work as a team and make Star TV a success and the most coveted place to work in'. I had an interesting evening getting to know a whole new set of people, a set of people that Peter Mukerjea spent more than ten hours everyday, from Monday to Friday, a set of people who were responsible for not just making Star TV the most popular network in the country but one that gave Peter Mukerjea every reason to thank his stars for making him who he was in his professional life. Peter Mukerjea owed every bit of his success to this set of people. That was clear to me, even then.

Peter left for Hong Kong the next day with a promise to ring me every day which he did without fail. When Peter returned, we met the next couple of evenings and went for dinners to homes of his business acquaintances. All this time, Peter never made any physical advances towards me even though he showered me with attention, affection, flattery and compliments.

One of those evenings, Peter said, 'I have never met anyone like you. I have never felt so close to anyone ever. We are perhaps soulmates.'

His deeply seductive and romantic behaviour was overwhelming. His grand gestures and constant contact and attention were overwhelming. I was so overcome that I didn't see the danger lying ahead.

My fourth date with Peter was at his residence. He hosted a dinner for a small group of friends that evening. Peter lived in a penthouse which was spacious, with a large terrace and a spectacular view of the Arabian Sea. The apartment was untidy and lacked aesthetic coherence with furniture of all sorts thrown in here and there to make it liveable, with curtains of all sizes and colours.

That evening after the guests had left, Peter and I sat on his terrace for a night cap. As usual he spoke, spoke a lot. He talked about his extended family, uncles, aunts and cousins.

'I have never talked about this to anyone, not my parents, not Shab, not Sash, not to any of my friends. I do not know why I am telling you all of this, but I feel better now that I have,' he said at one point.

He took a deep puff of his cigarette and looked up at the sky that was dark, except for Sirius, the brightest star that twinkles in the night sky.

'This apartment is rented. But I have two homes of my own in England. My divorce settlement was done several years ago. I've given Shab the house that we used to live in as a part of the settlement and also give her four hundred pounds every month for her maintenance. Rabin is now working in a company that belongs to Elizabeth Murdoch in London. I pay Rahul separately for his education and his expenses, and have to do that till he graduates. I've been alone for years now. I do want to settle down,' he said and stopped to take a long drag of his cigarette which was now almost a stub.

'Indrani, I like your spirit. You are young but your soul is not. We could be really happy together. Marry me. Baby, will you marry me?' he said most unexpectedly. I thought for a moment that he was joking but then looking into his eyes I knew he was not.

Peter was a man intriguingly different from anyone else I had known or met in my life. I liked him, even though I was not as yet in love with him. I believed that my life had not ended with just one true love or one heart break. It was possible to fall in love again.

In that moment of fragility, I answered, 'Peter, my life has been a roller coaster. I have a past, not just with Sanjeev, but a past that goes way back, a past that has scarred me, a past that I find hard to talk about, a past that you may find hard to deal with.'

I knew that tears were streaming down my face. I sipped my drink, feeling the coolness of it trickle down my gullet.

'I have fought battles in my life that I have survived and some I have won. My intentions were always pure and unadulterated. But perhaps not everyone understood that,' I said, wiping my tears.

Peter hushed me with his finger on my lips.

'Baby, I don't want to know about your past. I don't care about your past. Let us agree today that you will never ask me about my past and I will not ask you about yours. Let us agree that our life together begins today. Let us agree that we will only ever talk about today and the future. I love you. Say yes.'

In his words, there was a promise of ambrosia.

'Yes,' I said, without considering that I was in danger of putting both Vidhie and myself in a situation where the purple pleasure of the moment could be replaced by implications and consequences.

'I have a condition though,' I continued. 'Before I agree, Vidhie has to like you. Vidhie will stay with us if she likes you. If she does not, then the answer is, "no".'

'She will not like me. She will love me. I have a way with women. Your answer will be yes, as will be hers. And, of course, she will live with us. I will adopt her and raise her as my own,' he said, taking my hand in his.

My tears continued to pour out. Peter was a good man, I thought. I was not swept off my feet, but I would learn to love him, I knew. There was a feeling of bliss that travelled down my being; bliss that is always an attribute of the soul. There was surely a soul connection with Peter that I felt. I did not know whether it was a quest for a deeper meaning in life, but I knew that I wanted Peter to be a part of my journey ahead in life along with young Vidhie, the real love of my life. I wanted to be lost in the promise of a meaningful journey ahead because I knew that only by losing myself, I could find myself.

I looked into Peter's eyes and nodded, my lips quivering. He moved closer to me, took me in his arms and I felt his lips on mine, the kiss that erased the hesitation in my mind, the kiss that gave me the strength to brave the odds against tradition and go beyond social sanctions … the kiss of a new journey ahead …

17

That night I stayed back at Peter's. We slept on the same bed but didn't have sex. I suppose neither of us was ready for it. At least, I for sure wasn't, not until I had a conversation with Sanjeev that I was not just moving on in life but moving on with someone else in life. Besides, there was Vidhie. I was unsure how she would react or settle with the changes and the shift from her familiar comfort zone to a new territory. I had no change of clothes, so I slept in the dress that I had worn that evening even though Peter generously offered me a pair of his oversized airline pyjamas.

Peter changed into a pair of shorts and a T-shirt and with my head cradled in his arm, he fell asleep shortly after. He snored. I moved out of his embrace to the pillow next to his, ruminating over the evening's conversation.

My phone beeped, 'Where are you?' It was Sanjeev.

I turned the phone off and shut my eyes, not wanting to deal with any melodrama at 2 a.m.

Peter and I met every evening after that for the whole of next week. Friends were pleased to know about the proposal, though they warned me about the 'skirt chaser' reputation of Peter Mukerjea.

Peter introduced me to an estate agent who helped me find an office space closer to Peter's home that I could take up on rent. I moved with my bags to Peter's place over the weekend. I slept in Peter's bedroom every night, but celibacy was still maintained.

Peter rang both his sons, Rahul and Rabin, and informed them that he had proposed to me. I had not spoken to them, but Peter said that they were both happy for him. I, of course, had no reason to think otherwise, considering that he had been divorced for years before I met him. I believed without batting an eyelid that his boys had no chip on their shoulders about his divorce with their mother and were perhaps genuinely happy to see their father wanting to settle into domesticity once again. Peter had an hour-long conversation with his ex-wife, Shab, on the terrace out of my earshot. I didn't bother to ask how it went.

And then I told Peter about Sheena and Mekhail. It was on the terrace of our home that evening. Peter's response had the sort of kindness that made me believe that he will stand by my side regardless of what my past had been or what our future holds.

Meanwhile, unbeknownst to me, Sanjeev had somehow heard from the grapevine about my increasing intimacy with Peter Mukerjea in the last couple of weeks, even though he was perhaps still unaware that I had already moved into Peter's house a week before. Sanjeev did ask me if what he had heard was true. I said 'yes'. I told him that I would be going to Kolkata in a week or so to bring Vidhie. He was infuriated.

Diwali was around the corner. Having always celebrated the festival at home in Kolkata the last few years, I felt nostalgic, and missed my friends and family back in Kolkata. Peter said that he had never celebrated Diwali but would invite a couple of his cousins and friends home for the festival.

'It would be the right occasion to introduce you to everyone,' he said.

Physically, Peter was far from my admired ideal, but I was drawn to him. Peter declared that he was head over heels in love with me, that he was smitten, that he would always have my back no matter what, that he would never forsake me and, above all, that being with me made him extremely happy. And, undoubtedly, he pursued me with dogged determination. Does love inspire you to become a different person? I had been in love, madly in love before, but there was no easy answer to the question that I posed to myself now, with Peter.

Peter perhaps sensed the burning desire in me to be close to him physically. That night, slipping into the sheets after me, he kissed me and slowly caressed me exploring the knolls and dells of my body. We had not seen each other in the nude before. The lights were off. He pulled down my shorts. Peter and I had never indulged in any sexual activity apart from kissing up until that night. My hands slowly began to caress and feel the flesh of his back and chest. By then I was quaking with passion as was Peter, moaning and groaning as he touched me. I was ready for the final act of intimacy, wanting to know and feel Peter like I had not done before. I did not stop my hand from going down his chest towards his manhood. My eyes opened wide; my body froze!

'Baby, I had too much to drink tonight. Please don't be disappointed. This doesn't happen every day. Trust me. It's just an effect of binge drinking,' Peter said sounding apologetic and embarrassed.

'It's all right,' I said, hoping to put him at ease, though, at the peak of my excitement, this was like a splash of cold water.

Peter held me in his arms and fell asleep instantly. As always, he snored loudly immediately after he dozed off. I was, of course, by then used to his snores and mild whistling noises in between his snores. They almost worked like a lullaby on me. I moved to my pillow and slept wondering what I was getting into, but then I knew I'd cope and things were going to be all right.

The next morning when I woke up, Peter was not in bed, and I had a hangover. My head was throbbing. I got up to quickly grab an aspirin from the medicine cabinet in the bathroom. Still in the nude, I walked into the bathroom without realizing that Peter was inside. Peter stood there brushing his teeth in his grey nightshirt and no shorts.

He looked at me and stared at my breasts. 'You've got small boobs. But your nipples make up for it.'

I always had a complex about not being well endowed. But I surely didn't need to hear it early in the morning, when I had a throbbing headache, that too after being deprived of sexual satisfaction the night before.

My gaze travelled down to the bottom of Peter's nightshirt.

'You've got a small willy. And your jewels don't make up for it. But I'll get by,' I said before I could stop myself.

His black eyes blackened further, his expression dark. My nipples perked up in excitement. I knew I had made a score with Peter Mukerjea. I made it loud and clear that I was not a doormat to be walked upon, that he ought to watch his mouth with me. He refrained after that from asking any questions on the caesarean scars on my belly.

Peter suddenly laughed out loud, pulled me into his arms and said, 'Baby, I love your spirit. I love you.'

The next day Peter and I drove down to Manori Beach to look at the orange sun set slowly and disappear into the ocean. It was spectacular!

Peter was a romantic at heart. On the way back home, he played 'Love is in the air ...' on the CD player of his car and squeezed my hand as the music overwhelmed me, the lyrics touching a chord in my heart. He wooed me to the fullest and with sincerity and I was, I must admit, totally carried away. It was not like he was laying the flattery on with a trowel; it appeared genuine, and I was convinced that he was in love, truly in love, with me.

I slowly began to open the door to my heart to Peter, ever so slowly, ever so cautiously, not quite as I had done completely with Sanjeev when I had met him. Peter regaled me with tales of his days as a youngster, some of which were funny, some bizarre. It was apparent that he was doing everything that he could to draw me into the relationship that I was treading into with caution. He was, no doubt, going the whole hog to bond with me. On the love-making front, though, the magic still continued to collapse between my desire and its fulfilment.

Peter's birthday was two days away. He was going to be all of forty-six.

'I'd like to bring in my birthday with you alone, baby. We'll go for dinner to the Zodiac. It's a place best designed for such special intimate occasions. French food. You'll like it. I'll get Tina to book a table for 9 p.m. It's fine dining. Put on your best,' he said before leaving for work.

I had moved into Peter's home barely a fortnight ago. But he organized a full-time chauffeur for me and most generously gave his second car for my use. Love, I suppose, has the capacity to exceed boundaries and Peter Mukerjea had made up his mind that we were going to be together, come hell or high water.

The dinner was lovely, with a four-course meal and all the wine we could have. At midnight, the waiters brought a cake with sparkling candles lit on it. The pianist played 'Happy Birthday'. The waiters sang. Peter blew the candles and turned forty-six. The guests in the room clapped. Peter bowed politely and nodded at the guests, most of whom he knew. He stood up, leaned over to me, and kissed me on my lips. I fished out the present I had bought for him earlier in the day from my purse and handed it over to the birthday boy. He unwrapped the gift, a Swarovski table clock, like an excited child opening his present on his fifth birthday.

'Wow! I love it. How thoughtful of you, baby!' he said 'Thank you so much for being with me and making this day so special for me. I love you and will always be with you, till death part us.'

He leaned over and kissed me once again. Peter was happy, very happy. I made him happy. I had no clue what it was in me that Peter was so much in love with. But it was all over his face, the happiness, the kind of happiness one seldom sees on anyone to that degree. That night Peter was in full element in bed. I felt connected and closer to him at that moment both emotionally and physically.

The next evening, Peter hosted a party at a restaurant close to his home called Mela. He had invited a few of his friends, some of whom I had met previously. Peter had invited a couple of his journalist friends too. The next morning our mugshots were splashed all over the newspapers declaring that Indrani Bora was the new love in the life of Peter Mukerjea. Clearly, our relationship was no longer a furtive, hidden adventure. I had love and had also found something beyond it, a connection with Peter which was lurking in between ecstasy and danger, with all the vagaries in his character—his flamboyance and fine etiquette on the one hand, his belches, burps, wind-breaking and nose-picking without inhibition on the other; his tenderness on one side and ruthlessness if he sensed danger on the other. It goes without saying that life had taught me some vital lessons, one of them being that nothing was permanent. But with Peter I learnt yet another lesson: faith and hope can be permanent. He had faith in his love for me even though I was confused. He had hope that he was going to win me over. And Peter Mukerjea was not wrong.

I flew to Kolkata three days later to call it quits with Sanjeev and bring Vidhie back with me. My conversation with Sanjeev about my future plans was not a walk in the park. His reactions oscillated between anger, regret and dissent, till, at last, he accepted that there was no point in trying any more.

The four days that I spent in Kolkata with Sanjeev's unpredictable behaviour—at times flying off the handle, then accusing me of adultery and then snivelling—took a toll on my mental equilibrium. I was relieved when I finally sat down in the airplane seat with Vidhie next to me. Vidhie and I came to Mumbai, to Peter, to a new life, a more promising future for Vidhie, a more meaningful life.

Perhaps it was all too good to be true. 'Can women have it all?' I asked myself as I looked out of the window, as we soared above the clouds, and I gazed into the blue expanse of nothingness. I had no answer. It was the trickiest question, one without an answer.

I had run the whole gamut from joy to despair with Sanjeev. But then I believed that good times followed bad times and good times were just round the bend.

I was pleased to see Peter standing at arrivals, waiting for a new beginning with the feisty me whom he had fallen in love with and the equally spirited little Vidhie, whose tiny heart he was determined to work his way into.

Peter held out his hand to Vidhie, 'Hello, I am Peter. You must be Vidhie.'

Vidhie extended her tiny paw-like hand into Peter's with a dazzling smile, 'I am Vidhie!'

Peter's eyes visibly warmed up to Vidhie's smile and response. 'We've got a room ready for you at home. I hope you like it.'

Vidhie smiled, looking up at Peter, perhaps unable to get a sense of what the 'room ready for you at home' really implied. In her head, she perhaps thought we had come somewhere for a holiday.

Vidhie looked at the streets of Mumbai with large eyes as we drove home from the airport. When we reached home, Peter looked at Vidhie, who by now was a bit daunted by the two over-enthusiastic dogs Sophia and Laila jumping at us the moment the front door opened.

'Don't be scared, Vidhie. You'll be friends with Sophia and Laila soon. Let's go to your room.'

Vidhie, still clinging on to me and looking doubtfully at the dogs, who had calmed down by then, bobbed her head in agreement. Vidhie was thrilled once she entered the room at the thought that was going to be her space for many years to come.

'Wow, I like it, Mamma! This is bigger than my room. Is this piano also mine?' Her eyes were wide with amazement.

'Indeed, it's yours, sweetheart. Everything in this room is yours,' Peter replied.

Vidhie was pleased as punch, no doubt.

'Thank you,' she said coyly.

Peter was impressed.

'You have raised her well. Very polite for a four-year-old.'

Vidhie followed us as we went to our room with a teddy that she picked up from the bed. By the look of it, she was not taken in by the rest of the house that lacked aesthetics.

'Is this your room?' she asked, looking around the master bedroom, which needed a complete overhaul.

'Oh yes, Mamma's and mine,' Peter replied.

'Mamma will be sleeping with you in this room, not in that nice one?' Vidhie looked at me with confusion apparent in her large brown eyes.

'Darling, let's get changed. It's really late, way past your bedtime. Let's all sleep together in this not so nice room tonight. What do you say?' I answered.

I carried Vidhie back to her room with the yellow rat curtains and changed her into her pyjamas, washed and cleaned her up, all ready for bed.

Peter too had changed when I returned with Vidhie to our bedroom.

'Let's look around and make friends with Sophia and Laila while Mom changes.' Peter held out his hand that Vidhie took without hesitation.

There was no doubt an instant chemistry between Peter and Vidhie. I could tell that even having met Peter for barely a couple of hours, she was warming up to him. It was a good sign. Despite being an extrovert, Vidhie usually took her own time with anybody she met for the first time. But she was at ease with Peter. The two disappeared while I showered and got into my jammies.

Peter and Vidhie were sitting on the terrace having a chat. Vidhie was tired and said that she was ready for bed. It was past 10 p.m. She had barely nibbled on the flight but declined any dinner.

'Baby, put Vidhie to bed, while I pour us a glass of wine. I am peckish. How about you?' Peter asked.

He looked at Vidhie, 'Nightie night, sweetheart. Sleep well. Can I please get a goodnight kiss?'

'Goodnight,' Vidhie replied and quickly hid behind me. It was clear that Peter was not going to get the goodnight kiss he had asked her for.

Vidhie dozed off in no time, the moment I turned off the bedroom lights and lay down next to her. I looked at her tiny frame under the duvet, sleeping peacefully without a care in the world. I hoped at that moment that the decision to bring Vidhie with me was the right one.

When I returned to the terrace, Peter had poured us some wine, which he had left to breathe till I arrived. I could see even from a distance that he was in deep thought, while taking drags of his cigarette.

'Salut, baby,' he said raising his glass. 'To us, Vidhie, you and me!'

'To us!' I said, clinking his glass.

Peter and I retired after dinner. That night, and the next few nights, till we arranged a nanny for Vidhie, she slept in between Peter and me every night.

I had not explained anything to Vidhie as yet about either my relationship or plans with Peter. It was odd, I thought, that she had not addressed Peter by his name or as anything else, even though she conversed with him like family.

One fine day, perhaps after about a week of moving into Peter's, Vidhie yelled out with joy when he returned from work, 'Papa!', and leapt into his arms.

And that was it. Children have their own way of figuring out equations in life. Peter Mukerjea undoubtedly had succeeded in charming little Vidhie enough for me to say, 'I do', just as he had promised. In my mind, there was no looking back. Strangely, Vidhie had not asked after the family back in Kolkata even once.

A few weeks later, Peter started the paperwork for Vidhie Khanna to become Vidhie Mukerjea, even though we were yet to be married—I was still Indrani Bora.

Christmas was round the corner. Peter thought that it would be a good occasion to invite his sons Rabin and Rahul, so that we could all spend some time together and get to know each other. After speaking with his sons, Peter said that they would arrive just before Christmas, spend a few days with us and then go to Dehradun to meet Shabnam's family. He said that Shabnam wanted to travel to India with the boys, but would go to Delhi instead of staying back here, now that things were not the same anymore in the home front with me having moved in.

'I don't have a problem. She can stay with us for a couple of days if she wants to,' I said.

From whatever Peter had told me, I gathered that their relationship was long over several years ago, and Shabnam couldn't possibly have an axe to grind with me.

'Let's see. I'll suggest. But I doubt that she'd want to come,' he said dismissively.

Holiday plans were made: travel to Goa with the boys and Vidhie for Christmas. The boys would head off to Dehradun after that. Peter, Vidhie and I would go camping in Ranthambore to ring in the New Year. In preparation, Peter bought crisps, beer, Coke and cartons of Marlboro cigarettes. He then went with Pronto to the airport to collect the boys whose flight was scheduled to arrive at midnight. The guest bedroom that had a rickety cane bed with a lumpy mattress was spruced up to enable the boys to get a good night's sleep before leaving for Goa the next evening. The house needed serious overhauling if I was to spend the next few years here, I thought.

Vidhie was in bed by 7 p.m., as always. I wondered what it would be like to meet two grown-up boys of the man I was planning to get married to—the boys who were closer to my age than the man I was going to marry. I'd find out in the next few days, I thought. I drifted off to sleep with the TV on.

The entire week leading up to the arrival of the boys, I had tried explaining to Vidhie about Rahul's and Rabin's relationship with Peter, and that soon they would be her brothers.

The boys rose at midday and stepped out of their room, still looking tired and jet-lagged. Rahul was tall, almost six feet three and had a small head, not proportionate to his body. He had large charcoal-black eyes, a sharp nose and thin lips that broke into a smile when we were introduced by Peter. He had turned nineteen just a couple of weeks ago. Vidhie acted shy when she saw him.

He quickly lit a cigarette as he sat down at the breakfast table next to Vidhie.

'Don't smoke in front of Vidhie. And no smoking indoors, please,' Peter said.

'Aw, Pop, come off it now. You never had those house rules earlier,' he said with a woebegone expression, his smile disappearing. Just then, Rabin walked in.

Rabin was twenty-two, about Peter's height, had full lips, a rather big backside for a male, flab around his waist, and a noticeable belly. The brothers almost looked like Laurel and Hardy.

Rabin was an introvert, one could tell even at the first meeting. He was shy and almost deferential. He spoke very little but when he did, he was polite, his eyes had honesty and his smile reached his eyes. He was confident and opened his mouth only when he knew his beans.

Rahul, on the other hand, was like a porcupine. He was a nervous wreck, talked too much, mostly nonsense, often out of turn and with impudence. He was a chain-smoker and Peter's advice clearly had no effect on him. His comments were perhaps not meant to titillate or provoke anyone in particular; but it was more than visible even in the first couple of hours that I spent with him that he had damaged bits which made him abrasive. Or perhaps he was a teenager who wandered in an air of dreamy abstractions and shot off his mouth unwarranted.

It was time for us to head off to the airport for our Christmas holiday. I did, I must admit, wonder at that moment if balancing matrimonial bliss, with two adult stepsons, perhaps still aggrieved for being almost abandoned by their father at a young age, would mean walking a tightrope for me.

Time would tell, I suppose.

18

We had a great vacation in Goa. The return to Mumbai meant a lot more activities than our routine lives of work and play. We decided to buy the apartment that we were living in as tenants. The legal proceedings for my divorce decree needed to be completed. The apartment needed a complete overhaul for which we hired a designer, while we moved to an apartment on the floor below. We let go of the temp nanny and brought Shikha to take care of Vidhie. Shikha came along with her husband, Bhola, and her sister Maya, who was an experienced cook. Bhola was going to do the odd jobs along with Sushant who was an existing house-help at Marlow. Vidhie was delighted to have Shikha and Maya in her life.

Oddly enough, the frequency of Shabnam's calls to Peter increased as did the length of time he spent on those calls. In the first few weeks, I didn't pay much heed, thinking that it was perhaps a passing phase or they were discussing issues that needed to be addressed, which would be resolved soon. There was no point in being hung up on such trivial stuff.

That week, I met Peter's brother Gautam in Mumbai. Peter and I then travelled to Bangalore where we met Shangon and her husband Sanjoy Dasgupta for a night out. Peter also took me to the house where his father spent his last years. He had died at least six years ago but all his belongings were there, and clothes still neatly folded on the shelves or hung inside the wardrobe in the bedroom. The house was in a prime location around which there were a lot of business activities and new offices emerging.

'Mumu, you wanted to set up a branch of your office here. Why don't you use this place? You can easily convert it to an office. I know a designer here whom you could perhaps use,' Peter said as he opened the wardrobe and looked nostalgically at his father's belongings.

Peter and I spent the entire day sifting through the belongings of his father—moth-eaten letters that he had sent to and received from Peter's mother, diaries, medals, photo albums, even toys that his three children had played with as toddlers. Even though I had never met Peter's father, it almost felt like I knew him after that trip. I walked down the memory lane that day of a person whom I had never met and would never meet. When I looked at Peter, all I could see was a vacant look in his eyes as he gazed back at the past.

Returning to Mumbai meant more work activities and social gatherings where I met all the people whom Peter rubbed shoulders with, the rich and the famous.

Soon, Peter and I travelled to Hong Kong to meet his boss, James Murdoch, the son of Rupert Murdoch, the man who made news, controlled politicians, controlled lives of numerous rich and famous people, moulded public opinion—globally! Apart from his drop-dead gorgeous looks, he was as bright as a button; he was hardworking, had pet liberal causes, some philosophical musings and an equally drop-dead gorgeous wife.

Peter surprised me with a diamond ring at a store in Hong Kong. Peter's bosses in Hong Kong had most generously arranged a dinner for Peter and me sans my knowledge with a handful of his colleagues for us to celebrate the engagement.

'Mumu, be my wife till death do us part. I love you now and will always do till death parts us. I will be by your side in good times and bad times, in happiness and in sorrow, in sickness and in good health. I love you now and shall love you forever,' Peter said as he slipped the ring onto my finger while at dinner with his friends.

Come March, Vidhie, Peter and I travelled to England. Peter wanted me to meet Shab and the boys, and some of his old mates from university and work. I was unsure why Peter wished for me to meet his ex-wife, but I knew that there was a decent enough reason for that, which I would understand in good time. He had said that Shabnam was keen on the meeting.

We went and stayed at Sloan Club in London. Peter rented an Audi for our time there. He had a thing for fast cars. Vidhie was four at that time, just over with being a toddler. Rahul and Rabin had also come to London. On one of the days we didn't have a stroller and had to walk a lot. We went to Hyde Park to eat.

We were walking on Oxford Street when Vidhie gestured to Peter and said, '*Godi*, I want to be carried!'

Peter looked at the boys and said, 'I can't carry her around.'

So I picked her up and carried her all the way. This memory kept coming back to me later.

Over the next two days, I met Peter's friends Ken and Anna, Russel and Sandra, and a couple of his colleagues from Star London. It was all going well until Peter told me Shabnam wanted to meet me.

Shabnam lived in a semi-detached house in a hamlet called Berkhamsted. She lived there with Rahul. By then, Rabin was living in a studio apartment that Peter had purchased for him in Notting Hill. Shabnam's house was about a 40 minute tube ride away from London but we drove. Several years ago, after Doon School, Peter had moved to Berkhamsted for his A levels and stayed there with his erstwhile Doon School headmaster. Shabnam was his childhood sweetheart and after they got married in Dehradun in their very early twenties, she moved to Berkhamsted with Peter. She was the classmate of Peter's siblings who were twins, Gautam and Shangon, at school in Dehradun.

Before we went to the house where Shabnam lived, Peter showed me an apartment he owned in the vicinity by the lake which he had put on rent. The house that Shabnam lived in was apparently the family home that went to her after their divorce.

Shabnam opened the door when we knocked. Rahul didn't come down from his room upstairs immediately. I felt Shabnam suss me out, inspecting me up and down, before looking at Vidhie who was in two pigtails and a mauve jacket over jeans and a T-shirt. Rahul came down a few minutes later. He was very warm and said, 'Welcome home.'

I don't think he or Shabnam thought of our relationship as a serious one. They were used to seeing Peter with girlfriends on holidays. Peter was engaged to Sashwati before me.

Vidhie was happy to see Rahul. When Shabnam asked Vidhie her name, she replied, 'Vidhie Mukerjea.' Shabnam and Rahul exchanged a look at that. By then Peter had already given her his name even though we were still not married. Vidhie knew Rahul as her elder brother. When Rahul went up to his room, Vidhie followed him.

Peter had told me prior to coming that he wanted some time alone with Shabnam so he could tell her that he and I were getting married. They were already divorced for several years at this point. I wasn't breaking up a family, but somehow this was the final nail in the coffin. Shabnam, Peter and I sat for a bit and chatted. When she went into the kitchen to make coffee, I followed her in to help her.

I still remember her words from that day and often replay them in my head. 'Always remember this about Peter. He thinks something, tells you something else, and goes and does something entirely different.' I had brushed it off as sour grapes. Peter and she had obviously spoken about me before. It was insensitive of Peter to make us meet. It was very apparent that she had not moved on from Peter and he was marrying someone years his junior. I felt she was insecure.

She kept the coffee in the kitchen. I picked up my mug, she picked up hers and yelled out to Peter, 'Pete your coffee is ready.' When we sat down, it felt like she was taking us on a trip down memory lane, almost like sending across a message. I frankly didn't care about it at that time. I was happy with Peter, our love and how life was coming along. I had no idea she was trying to cling on to Peter.

Once we decided on lunch, Peter and Shabnam went to pick up the food. It was my cue to stay back so Peter could have the chat. I wanted to let them talk it out while I prepared Vidhie's lunch— butter rice and veggie mash. Vidhie came down for lunch and went sprinting back upstairs.

When Peter and Shabnam returned, something was not right. Their vibe had changed. We were in the garden. They laid out roast chicken, baguette, salmon and potatoes. We had lunch but everyone was quiet. Peter and I had a habit of giving each other a peck on the lips before we ate our meals. Shabnam was organizing lunch as I leaned forward. He said no.

I looked at him and asked, 'Are you worried?' It was tough for him. He shouldn't have put himself or anyone else in that situation.

At that moment, I realized Peter had a full family in England. At that table outside in their garden, on one side was Peter's past— Shabnam and Rahul. And on the other was his present—Vidhie and me. He was still in the middle, playing the balancing act in the best way he could. Everyone except Vidhie was eating in silence. I think Peter did it because he needed closure. As a woman, I was feeling horrible for Shabnam. I almost felt guilty though I really had no reason to.

When it was time for us to leave, it felt more emotional. Rahul was supposed to go back with us to Oxford where Peter owned a home that he had bought when Rabin was studying in Oxford Brooks. When we were leaving, Rahul did not join us.

We were at the door when Vidhie asked him, 'Why aren't you coming with us?'

Shabnam responded saying, 'He doesn't want to leave his mother alone. His mother is alone.'

I felt no negativity from Peter's sons till that day, but at that moment I sensed that there was a switch that had flipped, in Rahul at least.

We said our goodbyes. Shabnam gave Peter a warm hug. The hug she gave me wasn't warm anymore. She opened her arms to hug Vidhie but Vidhie didn't reciprocate. Children have the innate ability to sense positive and negative energies way more than adults do. She came and stood behind me.

When we got into the car, I looked outside the window and tears just rolled down my eyes. That moment was overwhelming for me.

Peter asked me, 'Are you crying?'

I nodded. I didn't even want to face him. I wanted to cry it out of my system.

Just then Vidhie saw an ice cream truck in the downs and we stopped for it.

Peter said while eating his ice cream, 'I had to do this. I had to end it with her. I could never do this till date.'

Later on, once we were at the house in Oxford, Peter and I got ourselves a glass of wine. We were both lost in thought.

He said to me, 'I hope you understand why I did this. I had to end it. She had to see me with you to know it was over.'

'But it was over. It was over a long time ago!' I replied, my eyes brimming with tears.

While sipping my wine, I raised the Vidhie incident with him. 'Yesterday when Vidhie wanted you to carry her and you refused, I regretted leaving Kolkata and bringing Vidhie with me. Even if Vidhie was twenty-one and wasn't in a position to walk, Sanju or anyone in his family would have readily carried her. I don't want Vidhie to be deprived of a father who will go all the way for her.'

In that instant, Peter held both my hands in his and promised me, 'I give my word to you. I will never do anything to compromise Vidhie. You will never have that regret. She is my own. And you are my own. I will love you both like mine forever.'

I believed him. Peter can be an incredibly charming man, even today.

Life carried on. We went back to meet Rahul again a few days later. By then, his body language had changed. He was cold. Peter had to buy him a car and we had come to pick him up for that. Shabnam stood there cribbing about the lack of space in the sports car that Peter and I were using, She wondered how Rahul would fit in it with all three of us already in the car.

Then she looked at Peter and said, 'Now I am going to go and pay your credit card bills.'

Peter didn't appear to take it kindly.

He said, 'I have transferred that money into your account. Haven't I?'

Shabnam taunted him saying, 'Where are you spending so much money?'

Peter made it known that he would change the address.

Then she asked again, 'What did you buy from Hong Kong that's so expensive?'

I butted in saying, while looking at Peter, 'It must be the engagement ring you bought me.'

Shabnam said snarkily, 'You better be careful where you spend your money.'

It was evident that she was keeping a track of our expenses. Thirteen years after their separation, their domestic set-up was still strange.

I pointed it out to Peter later, when we were in the car, 'Why does she care where we spend our money?'

Apart from Shabnam's strange comments and behaviour that day I could also sense Rahul's hostility towards me. It was just so obvious that he was angry with me. He was acting out, banging car doors. Eventually Rahul chose a car, Peter paid for it and we called it a day.

In a few days we returned to India. I got busy with the increasing workload at my headhunting firm. I started setting up offices in Bangalore and Delhi.

One day, the same week, Peter got a call from Shabnam.

She told him, 'I have done some homework on the girl. The reviews aren't good!'

She was on the speaker phone. I was reading on the bed. She claimed that she had found out from her sister-in-law that I am hugely 'infamous' in certain circles in Kolkata.

'You shouldn't marry her,' she announced.

Peter didn't react. He was embarrassed by her snooping.

I told Peter right away. 'I don't like this. I think you need to cut off all contact with her.'

Peter had told me that as per their divorce settlement, he was to pay a monthly allowance of £400 to Shabnam. But Peter wasn't being honest with me about the money he was giving her—it was £4,000 that he was paying her and not 400.

He had conveniently left out a zero for reasons best known to him. I wouldn't have loved him any less if he was just honest about it. Shabnam's interference in our lives and Peter's not-so-transparent admissions regarding his ongoing financial arrangements with Shabnam were getting on my nerves. I suggested he do a one-time settlement with her and get over with it once and for all. She would keep calling every other day, it was just becoming a nuisance.

It was a long battle dissociating from Shabnam. It was decided eventually that he would give everything to her. Rabin had been given a flat in London. Rahul got the lakeside apartment in Berkhamsted. Shabnam asked for more money as settlement along with the house that Peter owned in Oxford while she continued living in the family home in Berkhamsted. After this alimony arrangement, Peter was left with nothing in his name. But the peace was worth it. The apartment in Marlow was a rented one. He continued to get a handsome salary from Star, of course, but had no assets or savings. He had nothing. Peter Mukerjea was definitely not anywhere near being financially at his best at that point

My divorce proceedings with Sanjeev were on as well. Our four-bedroom place in Kolkata was given to him. The deal that I signed with him was that the flat would go to him and his mother, and he would give me full custody of Vidhie. I had my jewellery. My company money was intact, but my personal savings were nil.

Peter took a loan from Star which he would pay with his salary eventually. We bought 18 Marlow. This was bought in Peter's name alone. The initial discussion was that we would jointly own a place. Peter had insisted that I give everything that Sanjeev asked for. The home in Kolkata was the only roof over my head. I had a little child with me. Sanju had a family home, but I did not. Peter had assured me that we will be financially secure. I had understood that we were both buying the Marlow property jointly in our names. But when we went to the registration office, it was in his name alone. He did not tell me about it prior to our visit to the registration office. I let it pass.

After the home was purchased, Peter got an opportunity to do an executive programme course in the US at Kellogg School of Management, all paid for by Star. Peter and I spoke about a possible scenario if something were to happen between then and the day of our marriage. It was a precarious situation. We were not married yet. My divorce was yet to get finalized. Vidhie and I had no safety net. When I voiced my concern to Peter, he volunteered to make a will wherein if anything were to happen to him before we were married, 18 Marlow would be the roof over Vidhie's and my head. And then he went to Kellogg.

In the meantime, I started focusing on securing my own finances by working hard and building a robust client list for my HR firm. The arrangement was that a week before Peter finished his course, I would join him in Illinois. While Peter was at Kellogg, one morning, out of the blue, I received a call from a mutual friend. He used to treat me like a younger sister and was evidently fond of me.

He told me, 'Indrani, I have something to tell you. Peter has signed a will and gone. I have to go and get it notarized.' I was aware of it and told him so.

'Yes, I know of it. My divorce could take longer. The wedding is tentatively in November but I wanted to not be without a crutch in the gap of next three months.'

'He hasn't willed the place in your name. It's being willed to both his sons.'

I was shell-shocked. I asked him to hold on to it. It was another initial sign of dishonesty in our relationship.

I called up Peter and he said, 'It must be an old format. This is a mistake.' He asked me to calm down and said he will get it corrected.

The friend called me back a few days later to tell me that now the apartment had three parties—Rahul, Rabin and I.

I called Peter again. He said, 'No, but what if you throw them out of the house in case I am not around?'

I reminded him that very recently four properties in the UK got divided between three of them—Shabnam, Rahul and Rabin. His reasoning did not make sense to me. They had four other homes and could have never be homeless. I put my foot down. I asked him to hold it until our wedding, after which he would transfer 50 per cent of the flat to me. This was agreed upon earlier and I stuck to it.

That will didn't happen. 'I don't believe you will die in the next three months, so I can take that chance,' I told him.

It was a question of the security of my child and so I insisted on it. But, eventually, I relented.

In October, my divorce went through. With Sanjeev, it was love at the first sight. With Peter, it was a love I grew into.

I still loved Sanjeev but I was not in love with him anymore—we never had a 'closure' conversation. The call to divorce was because Peter was a catalyst. I wouldn't have leaped into the paperwork had I not met Peter.

Sanjeev was angry and bitter till the point of divorce—he believed that I had left him for Peter.

In October 2002, Peter and I travelled to Kolkata for my final divorce date. I was meeting Sanju after a long time. It was incredibly difficult for me when Sanju and I met at court. We mutually agreed in front of the judge to call off the marriage. It was raining heavily that day.

Peter and I were staying at the Oberoi. When I went back to the hotel, I felt emotionally relieved. I wasn't troubled. My wedding prep was done. The invitation cards were ready. The moment the divorce was through, we texted our close friends that the wedding would be in November, as per schedule. Through October, our apartment was getting done up. We briefly moved to an apartment a floor below in Marlow.

Nitin Desai, one of the most renowned set designers decided to gift us the *Devdas* set for the wedding ceremony. The set was erected on our terrace at 18 Marlow with a crane. I felt lucky to have the most well-designed set propped up at our home for us to get married in. In hindsight, I feel that it wasn't lucky. *Devdas* was a sad love story.

On 8 November 2002, Peter and I signed the papers for the registration of our marriage under the Special Marriage Act. I was leaving for office when the registrar came over. I wasn't aware that the registered marriage was scheduled for that day. Peter slipped on the wedding ring on my finger and we signed the marriage documents. We had some champagne before I left for office. All my colleagues from across the country had come over to Mumbai for our annual meeting.

In the evening, we had a get-together at the Taj. On 8 November, we had our individual bachelor's party and hen's night. My hen's night was a quiet dinner with my friends Ghazala and Mahua at Trishna, a seafood restaurant in Kala Ghoda. We weren't drinking for the last few months because Peter wanted to lose weight, and I wanted to give him company. So it was butter garlic crab, pepper rawas, garlic naan sans alcohol for me on my hen's night.

On 9 November, I had brought out a few sets of jewellery from the bank locker and laid them on my bed to decide on what would go well with the outfits that I would wear for the upcoming wedding functions. There were almost twenty sets of gold jewellery studded with a variety of gems and diamonds.

Shangon walked into the room and exclaimed, 'O my poor brother. He has had to spend so much money on all this jewellery.'

I corrected her, pointing out that it was my family jewellery. I found it odd because everyone was making me sound like a gold digger. I owned crores of jewellery at this point which belonged to me as family heirloom.

Shabnam and Shangon were friends, and it seemed like they had exchanged notes about me. I didn't appreciate that but I did not want to make a big deal of it ahead of my happy day. Rahul came to the wedding. He was very upset and in tears. He had to be consoled during the wedding. Peter and he had a long chat, the details of which I still have no idea about.

Peter told me that very same day that a few hours earlier Shabnam had called him and asked him if he wanted to come back to Dehradun.

I found it outrageous.

Peter apparently said, 'No Shab. I got married yesterday.'

I was hellbent on not spoiling my mood a day before my wedding. I asked Peter to handle it. But today I realize that there was more to Shabnam's story than Peter let out that day. She wasn't a desperate mad woman chasing a man. Peter had led her on.

When we came back from our honeymoon in Italy, my reality was nothing like the bliss I had experienced while on vacation. Gautam and Aarti by then were living in Mumbai, trying to make their marriage work. They lived in Bandra. I was carried away by the family bullshit. While coming back from the airport, I suggested we meet Goat and Aarti.

Peter snapped at me and said, 'Just because you have no family, you shouldn't pile on to mine.'

I was in a happy haze and him snapping at me reduced me to tears. Pronto was in the car and I didn't want to pick up a fight in front of him.

As luck would have it, I had to travel to Delhi for a work trip. I called up Peter's secretary Tina to get my booking done.

Suddenly, she said, 'Hey! Could you check with Peter when Shabnam wants to leave Mumbai for London?'

I fell from the sky. I had no idea Shabnam was in Mumbai. Peter had arranged for tickets for her to come to the city two days prior to our wedding and she was staying with Goat and Aarti all along. Shabnam was in the city when we got married. While we were in Italy, she went to Dehradun. Two days before we returned from Italy, she came back to Mumbai. That's when the penny dropped as to why Peter was so hostile to me when I mentioned going to Goat's and Aarti's. They had been hosting Shabnam since before we got married. Gautam, Shangon and Shabnam were school friends. Aarti was Shabnam's friend from college. It is through Shabnam that Aarti and Gautam met. This bunch goes back a long way. I don't blame Shabnam for picking up the wrong signal from Peter. He paid for her to come to Mumbai when he was marrying me. No wonder, she made that call to him. Shabnam perhaps assumed she was an escape route from the marriage.

That day I was raging. I was really angry. I told him, 'You have to take a call now. You can't have anything to do with Shabnam. Don't think that my love for you is my weakness. I will walk out on you. I have a thriving business. I will file for divorce if this happens again.'

He had done everything to settle her down. There were too many lies told by him and I didn't want to start our marriage on this shaky foundation. This rift left me with the feeling that I couldn't trust Peter. I wasn't a crazy woman who was jealous. I think Peter was playing with us. I went back to the words that I heard in Berkhamsted about Peter saying something and doing something different. It's a pattern with him. He wanted everyone to remain emotionally dependent on him. He liked it like that. I was not the bimbette Peter thought he married. I started asking too many questions. Peter told me about how Sashwati was fine with Shabnam. But I am not them. I am Indrani and I wasn't okay with it. He continued to be in touch with Shabnam, often without my knowledge.

On Christmas Day that year, Peter was gone from the house for a while. I saw him on the terrace for a long time on a call. I confronted him and he made up some story about a work call. I asked him to show his phone and my doubts were affirmed. He was talking to Shabnam. That day, I was at my wit's end. I was angry. I was deeply hurt. I had trusted him and he betrayed me. I was standing on the terrace alone, contemplating if I should jump off. I couldn't deal with him anymore. I was so much in love with him that I couldn't bring myself to leave him. That year, he drove me to a point where I felt weak. I had forgotten my own strength. But Peter drove me to the point that I felt only death could rescue me. I was drunk, I stood on the parapet, looking down.

Somewhere, I heard Vidhie call out, 'Mumma, don't jump.'

She could see me get up on the ledge. She had heard our fight. Her voice brought me back to sanity. I went back to sleep. In the morning, Peter promised me it wouldn't happen again. He kissed me. He hugged me. But I made sure not to let him get under my skin and pulled myself together. Barely a month after getting married, I realized I needed to grow a thick skin.

When I was in jail, Peter went to the press and said in an *Indian Express* interview that I was going to jump off the terrace to get the Marlow property in my name.[11]

I continued being in love with Peter after the terrace episode but I became cautious not to get to that point again.

At the start of 2003, Peter had received a letter in his Star office. It was a letter from my parents and was addressed to him. Our wedding photographs were covered in the newspapers *Telegraph* and *Statesman*. Aveek Sarkar was a friend of ours and he gave it a massive spread. I hadn't spoken to my parents since Sanjeev and I got married in 1993. When Peter came back home from work that evening, he took me out for coffee. We went to a small Cafe Coffee Day in Shivaji Park. The letter said that Sheena and Mekhail had now grown up—fifteen years and thirteen years old, respectively. When I left Guwahati in 1990, my parents were fairly wealthy. But things had happened in between. The letter said that they found it hard to sustain the kids' expenses.

They wanted financial help from me. Peter asked me what I wanted to do. At that moment, I had no idea what I wanted to do. I decided to write back to them. I sent them my cell number and asked them to call me back. I saw this as an opportunity to reconnect with my Sheena and Mekhail. I wanted to help them financially. And, more than anything, I wanted to meet my two children from whom I had been away for so long.

My mother called me soon after. Their businesses had declined. Dad wasn't doing well healthwise. I told her not to worry about the finances—that would be taken care of. But I wanted to see my children again. I didn't want to go to Guwahati, so I asked Mom to send Sheena and Mekhail to Kolkata.

This situation made Peter very uncomfortable. No one knew the truth about Sheena and Mekhail, till then. Peter took me out for dinner to Indigo that night and discussed how this secret coming out would impact his public image.

'Mumu, let sleeping dogs lie. Let's not unnecessarily upset their lives and our lives with all this,' Peter said.

He suggested that we send money and handle it. Peter and I came to an agreement that we would maintain to the world that they were my siblings, as on paper, and we would stick to that story. He didn't quite get the point of getting them back with me. But I held my ground. I wanted my children back.

I landed in Kolkata a day before them. I went to pick them up. Sheena and Mekhail were there. They waved at me while collecting their bags. Sheena was a spitting image of me but she was almost milky white. She was wearing jeans and a T-shirt and Mekhail was in a checked shirt and jeans. I recognized them instantly. They remembered me from my pictures. I hugged them from across the barrier and asked them to come out. It was very emotional for me. They didn't know how to talk to me.

Mekhail sat in the car in the front. He looked outside, awestruck. Sheena sat at the back with me. I held out my hand and she held my hand back. I wasn't crying but I felt a combination of joy and sadness.

We checked in. I asked them if they remembered me at all. They didn't.

Sheena asked, 'Did you once call home and disconnect?'

Maybe I had. She thought it was me. It felt as if Sheena had waited for a call from me.

I caught up with them about school. I had a conversation with them about what they wanted to call me. Their school documents had them as children of Durga Rani Bora and Upendra Kumar Bora. I couldn't change everything in their life out of the blue. Peter was right that I couldn't upset their lives. But I wanted to spend time with them, be there with them. I explained Peter's position, how he felt it was a big deal for him. I was completely honest about balancing relationships. I loved Peter and didn't want to upset him.

We spent a few wonderful days in Kolkata. We ate a lot, shopped a lot. I told them they didn't have to worry at all. Sheena insisted I come to Guwahati and see the house. It was falling apart.

After I returned to Mumbai, I decided to go back to Guwahati. Peter asked me if I was sure, but I wanted to make up for lost time. I didn't stay at home. I stayed at a hotel in the city. The house was in a bad shape. My parents had aged beyond years. They were struggling financially. They had rented out a part of the house. I decided to let bygones be bygones. I decided to get the house redone for my mother.

I spent ₹50 lakh getting the massive, almost 6000 sq. ft property done up. I got them cars and chauffeurs. I got air-conditioning installed in every single room. The eight-bedroom house was brand new. I got the house up and running, and hired new staff. I asked Sheena and Mekhail where they wanted to study. Sheena wanted to study in Mumbai after her twelfth-standard board exams. Mekhail decided he wanted to go to Bangalore International School after his tenth.

After I came back to Mumbai, I wanted Vidhie to know her siblings, albeit who she thought were my 'siblings'. I didn't want to go back to Guwahati, the memories still haunted me, but I knew the only way Vidhie could get to know her siblings was to go there. Once there, I told Sheena that Vidhie was her responsibility. Vidhie was enchanted by the small-town life. She came back with a love for cycle rickshaws. She wanted to go everywhere in a rickshaw, including the airport and was willing to ditch the fancy cars for it.

I wanted to make up for the years I wasn't around. Sheena and I started taking vacations together. I went to Goa with her. My family started coming to Mumbai. I sent my parents, Mekhail and Sheena, for a vacation to Europe and the UK. They had a wonderful month. I was actively making a bridge with my family.

Sheena was in Guwahati, studying and dating a good guy who loved her, and was in a more settled space. Everyone was more or less happy.

The next year Mekhail joined Bangalore International School for his A levels. In the first year itself, Mekhail ran into some substance-abuse related trouble. He was becoming aggressive as a teenager. There was an incident too which took place.

Peter called the security chief of Star, Suhail Buddha. He was a former cop with Mumbai Police. Mekhail clearly needed help. Buddha suggested that we put him under treatment with Dr Yusuf Matcheswalla at Masina Hospital.

Mekhail's drug abuse and violent stints were intense. I wasn't aware of this state of affairs with him before this. Dr Yusuf Matcheswalla, realizing the seriousness of the situation, decided to send Mekhail to rehab for four months. He privately sat for his twelfth-standard exams. Once he cleared his boards, I asked him where he wanted to go.

He decided to go to Delhi. I swung into action. My regional manager in Delhi was Vivek Mittal, who had earlier worked with me in my Kolkata office. I suggested he take up a bigger place and Mekhail could stay with him, with Vivek as his local guardian. Mekhail cracked the entrance for IHM, Gurgaon. Vivek moved to a new apartment in Gurgaon and the two of them started living together. I got them a car and a chauffeur and ensured Mekhail was well settled.

19

By 2003, I opened another firm called INX Global Pvt. Ltd to start global recruitments. I became a part of IMD Global, which partners with boutique headhunting firms globally. Shortly after, I was appointed as director, Asia Pacific, based on my performance. On my own merit, I was flourishing.

In 2006, Sheena moved to Mumbai to study economics in St. Xavier's College. Initially she wanted to study English. But after a few lessons, she found English boring and eventually shifted to economics. She wanted to go to Delhi but I wanted her to be close to me. Mekhail was already away from me in Gurgaon.

My parents, along with Sheena and Mekhail, were vacationing around the globe a lot in those years, trips that I had arranged for them. I couldn't compensate emotionally for the lost time but I wanted my children to have all the experiences they had missed.

Life on the domestic front looked relatively settled. I was thriving in my career, too. But it wasn't as hunky dory for Peter. He was facing issues at Star.

One day he came home and said, 'Either I can resign or they will take away my current responsibilities while I retain some of the benefits of my portfolio.'

Sameer Nair was going to become the CEO of Star. Only the administration and legal departments would report to Peter while all the other key functions would thereon report to Sameer. Peter had one year of his contract left with Star still when this decision was taken. Peter was really upset about this shift in power.

My view of Peter at that time was that he had evidently lost his appetite for hustling. When James Murdoch moved away from Hong Kong in 2005, I suppose Peter assumed he was the obvious choice to head Star Asia. But, during this time, the Murdochs decided to let go of Peter to bring in new blood.

In my understanding, Sameer Nair rightfully deserved the CEO post because he had created a great product in *KBC* (*Kaun Banega Crorepati*). Peter was in charge of sales and he spoke better, was more charming. But Sameer was the one who turned Star into the media giant it is when he and his content team made *KBC*. I would always tell Peter this too. Peter was able to make Star profitable because of the programming genius of Siddharth Basu and Sameer Nair, as well as the regional programming head Steve Askew who was based in Hong Kong. And then, of course, the host of *KBC*, the one and only Mr Amitabh Bachchan, did the magic.

A few things were happening at Star.

The second layer of people at Star—Sumantra Dutta, Raj Nayak and Sameer Nair—were all pushing their way up in the organization. Peter could've perhaps sustained the team had he continued to be their leader and chosen one of them to head Star News. But Peter's choice of who would head it wasn't the best one. This unhappiness in Star's corridors started percolating, and this unhappiness travelled home to me. He would come back and discuss the details of his work with me. These conversations became a constant at our dinner table.

Sameer Nair started having discussions with NDTV. Raj Nayak started having chats with Network18. It was around that time that Peter bumped into Uday Kotak of Kotak Mahindra Finances on a flight from Delhi to Mumbai. The finance market was on a boom and Uday suggested that he could arrange a group of investors to fund a green venture in the television industry. Peter came home and told me about it and told me that, as he was still employed with Star, I had to front all meetings with investors. It was the time when everyone was sussing out the market and widening the room for newer television channels. Sameer by then had become the CEO of Star and Peter was sidelined and given the responsibility to head only legal and administration.

As discussed, Uday started the conversations with the prospective investors for the new proposed project. The core strength of INX Services was media and banking hirings because I had a reasonably in-depth understanding of the media industry. To hire in a particular industry it is important to first understand how that industry functions and the skill sets that are required for the executives to be a right fit in that industry. I think I did a good job of getting investors on board. I sold the professional strengths of Peter and the core team well to the investors.

The money came in quicker than expected. Investors believed Peter could make a Star happen again and that INX Media Pvt. Ltd and INX News Pvt. Ltd could be sold at a premium a few years down the line when the investors would make a killing.

But the key team that made Star happen was missing. We ended up hiring a lot of ex-Star people in the hopes of replicating the success. But most of those who were hired for the core team were past their prime and lacked ambition; most of them were above fifty and didn't have the appetite that was needed to make a new venture succeed.

I had been an entrepreneur all my life. But Peter was used to getting a pay cheque. There is a difference in approach. I saw INX as my baby, Peter looked at it as someone else's child he had been asked to care for and nurture. Peter, who was used to the salaried life, lacked the zeal needed to be a successful businessman.

Looking back now, I feel a lot of our hires were incorrect. For example, the person we hired as the programming head had never worked in television before. For the distribution role, Peter hired someone who had been asked to leave Star TV. Maybe he, too, had lost his appetite for the beast that was TV—it had to be fed all the time. The consumer had to be kept happy every minute, every day. The new team didn't have the ability to churn out as much.

For INX News, Peter brought in Vir Sanghvi. He is undoubtedly a great writer. He would have had great presence as a TV anchor. In 2006, he was fifty plus. I felt he lacked the drive. It is one thing to write a food column from your office and another ball game all-together to perform your duties as the CEO of a start-up news company in the real sense where people had to work really hard.

Neither INX Media nor INX News were established companies. It could have never had the routine of a corporate organization. This start-up needed blood, sweat and tears and none of these men in the core team were geared up for the work it would take. After all, it was Peter who had hired the core team, and their energy was similar to his, not mine.

I had hired the 9XM (the company's music channel) team. I focussed on getting younger people. 9XM's head Vikas Varma was a friend. I had placed him in UTV prior to this gig. He was the only head I hired and the property did exceedingly well. We gave him the brief of discarding VJs and using animation characters instead. He stuck to my brief all along.

There was a massive shift in Star at that time. Raj Nayak joined Colors. Sameer Nair, along with Shailja Kejriwal, joined NDTV. Both Raj and Sameer left Star lock, stock and barrel with their teams.

But the mindset with which Peter went into INX was different. Peter and the gang that he hired at INX were living in the past glory of Star. The idea wasn't to create a great property. We had investors putting in heaps of money. So if it worked out, great. But if not, we would still walk away richer because we had no skin in the game. The investors misjudged the appetite because I had gone for all the seed money procuring meetings. It wasn't a question of right or wrong. It was an approach mismatch between Peter and I. For the investors, my passion and Peter's experience equalled to a great team.

I was thirty-six at that time. I didn't want to undervalue Peter's judgement of hiring the core team. But the more I worked with the team, the more I realized why Star let go of these people. They were hired at exponential costs. In addition, he hired a whole bunch of ex-pat people as consultants who had no understanding of the Indian market to supervise sales, marketing and content.

I had serious disagreements with Peter about many things. As we inched closer to the launch, I started working overtime. Peter was absent for the first six months of INX's inception because he was on gardening leave. After that Peter decided to go on a trek to the Himalayas. He didn't have the mindset to get a new company up and running any longer.

The few people whom Peter hired to join INX who were passionate about the company were the Star legal counsel, Ajay Sharma, and the head of operations, Vynsley Fernandes.

In the first phase of INX things moved along all right. But the deadlines weren't being met. I hired a couple of girls, Kumud Choudhury (senior VP) and Sharmishtha Ghosh (programming), to expedite the process, both ex-Star. Peter ended up hiring Ashok Bhushan for movies, who was his ex-wife Shabnam's relative. He was seventy and again lacked appetite for work. They didn't get the young viewers and what that viewership liked to watch. We were acquiring Dev Anand movies and positioning ourselves saying we'd touch young hearts.

Peter and my roles were divided unevenly. All the main functions reported to Peter. But he wasn't around. He was spending a lot of time holidaying in those days. He was in France with his kids, including Vidhie. I had to step up from being the group director to CEO because someone had to take charge. Finance, sales and distribution at INX always reported to Peter. By the time content was moved to me, the money had dried up. Peter didn't bargain with anyone because his philosophy was to give more than the market price to get a better product. But I feel, for what we paid, we didn't get the kind of content we should have.

The market had immense competition at this time—from Colors, Sony, Star, Zee, Imagine, and so many more. In 2008–2009, the demand had multiplied and the suppliers were fewer. Peter's mindset hadn't evolved. He didn't listen to me either. The male pride and ego triumphed. My expertise was recruitment and so I knew we had a bunch of bad eggs. There's a saying: Content is King, distribution is God. Neither did we have great content nor was the distribution top-notch. I executed Peter's instructions but somewhere along the road I realized everyone in the company was in it only till the time that things were going good.

INX launched in 2008. Personally, Peter and I were frequently fighting over company issues. I was working sixteen hours a day while my husband was vacationing incessantly. Something he said in jest once stayed with me.

We were watching a heist movie and I turned to him and said, 'Let's do a bank heist.'

It is one of those silly things we say when we watch a film.

And he turned around and said, 'We are doing a bank heist, legally!'

I thought he was joking and we both laughed it off. Much later, in prison, I understood what he meant.

We had great investors. They believed that Peter was going to put in his 100 per cent but he didn't.

I had to take some tough calls when I saw things going south. We were being run by a bunch of people who were all past their prime. The media business is a lot like modelling. At fifty, you can't walk on the ramp like an eighteen-year-old. As bodies age, so do our minds. People are often unable to accept retirement gracefully.

Peter's mindset was we should make as much money as we could through this. I couldn't take hard calls with Peter, the way perhaps I did with other people, like Vir Sanghvi, for example.

Vir and I got into a major situation, after which we parted ways. However, what I felt terrible about was letting go of Avirook Sen, who was Vir's deputy at INX News. He was Vir's hire and I must credit him this—it was a good decision to get him. After Vir was let go, we went to Delhi to decide how to proceed. Avirook was an upbeat team leader. He was becoming the face of the channel. I had a chat with him when he was appointed as the editor.

I told him, 'You have to step up to the role. You are a fresh face.'

Avirook is very articulate and a great speaker. He was very happy about the big responsibility.

That evening Peter and I had a tiff over making him the face of the channel. Peter felt he was a print guy with a print mindset. And so, Peter wanted a known face and he had his ex-classmate Karan Thapar in mind. But, for me, Avirook mirrored my excitement about work. The team he had dreamt of made a great channel. After Avirook left, the team was shaken up. At that point, it became a choice between Peter and him. What was my choice?

There was no scope of debating this out. Peter had made up his mind that INX News was to be under the guidance of Karan Thapar. He wanted to purge the system of Vir's hirings. I couldn't reason with Peter that if their loyalties lay with Vir, they would've put in their papers soon after. No one wanted to protest Vir's exit internally, everyone anyhow knew what really happened. It was a stupid decision on our part to let Avirook go. Peter didn't let me answer Avirook's calls.

After my trial started, I met Avirook again. He understood why I couldn't stand up for him. We damaged our own channel.

After the channel was set up, it didn't thrive. Everything on the news side became murky. The sales team wasn't doing their job up to the mark. In the news channel, the prime investor was Mukesh Ambani. He decided to let go of it and it was sold to an Indore-based businessman in December 2009. We effectively exited the news business with that move, two years after we set up and a year after we started functioning.

On the home front, it was all calm and peaceful. At the beginning of the college year, Sheena first moved to our home at Marlow. Her college was quite a distance from where we stayed. Travel to and from college ate into a lot of her time everyday.

Unlike Mekhail, Sheena had always stayed at home in Guwahati till she completed her twelfth. Now she wanted to live more independently. It was decided that she would stay somewhere close to her college and visit us over the weekend. This would reduce her commute time everyday leaving her with enough energy in the evenings to pursue interests that she enjoyed. She got a place at a hostel on Marine Drive but she didn't like it. She didn't like the food there and, within two days, she was back at Marlow. It so happened that I was discussing this at work in INX one day. My colleague Radhika Radia suggested that Sheena stay with them. She lived in a three-bedroom apartment in Chuchgate with her mother and they had a third room vacant. She said they would be pleased to have Sheena and another student as paying guests. Sheena and her classmate Vibhuti ended up sharing a room there.

Every weekend Sheena would come home. She would frequently go on holidays with us. Sheena settled in comfortably both at Radhika's and at Marlow, as she did in St. Xavier's.

Vidhie and Sheena would have some sibling issues on and off but the love between them made up for it. I wanted to tell Vidhie who Sheena was once she turned eighteen. Vidhie was about nine years old, and Sheena was nineteen.

During that time, I was devoting all my time to work. I was completely invested in INX. The HR firms were on auto-pilot and I would look into them only every now and then. I continued to hold my post as Asia-Pacific head for IMD Global. Every three months, I attended IMD Global conferences. Because the company was functional from 1996, it was running smoothly without me having to be hawk-eyed about details.

At the end of 2007, issues on the home front started popping up again. Peter's ex-wife was still in their English country home. Rahul was yet to get a job and earn his own money. He was living in with his then girlfriend. We were still funding Rahul, which was a sharp contrast with Rabin, who had a job and lived in the flat in Notting Hill that Peter had bought for him.

That year, Shabnam decided to move back to Dehradun where she originally belonged and where her parents lived. According to Peter, her parents had given her a plot of land in Dehradun and she had built a house there so that she could live close to her ageing parents. She had given out the house in Oxford and her home in Berkhamsted where Rahul and she lived on rent. In the meantime, Rahul's then girlfriend Sarah also split paths with him and moved on with another gentleman of her choice.

Rahul came to visit us in Mumbai. I tried to score him a job on one of his earlier visits with ITC Maratha because he was studying hospitality. He went to ITC for two days and decided it wasn't for him. He was twenty-one years old then and all he wanted was to drink beer and chill. On this trip he was twenty-five years old and all he still wanted to do was drink beer and chill. He went back to the UK after a month. By then Shabnam had packed up their home, all ready to head back to Dehradun. Peter brought Rahul back to Mumbai in early 2008.

20

Sheena first met Rahul in 2007. At that time, she found him to be lazy, untidy and unkempt. She was busy with college and didn't pay him much attention. In 2008, when he came back, something happened between them. I was unaware of it for a long time. They did a good job of hiding it too. One evening in early 2008, Peter and I took Sheena and Rahul out for dinner. The next day Rahul was going back to the UK. After dinner, Peter and I were catching a flight for a work trip somewhere. I think that night, the two of them got intimate. Rahul had broken up with his girlfriend and was on a rebound. Sheena was away from Kaustav, her boyfriend from Guwahati. They had probably had too much to drink. After that day, things changed between them. They stayed in touch during the time they were apart. Sheena was young. She was twenty-one. This was the reason probably that Rahul showed up with bags and baggage in 2008. I sensed something was up but I ignored it for a long time thinking that the children were probably just fooling around. It is natural to be young and reckless in your twenties. I must admit that I was so busy with INX that my focus was not on any of the children at all.

Vidhie was really young and needed more attention which, too, I could not give. She was in standard six and studying at the German International School. This was also the year of the Mumbai terror attacks in 2008. We had all freaked out because her school was in Breach Candy by the sea, very close to the area where Ajmal Kasab and the other terrorists had entered Mumbai via sea. It could've been her school. After those attacks, the kids in the German International School and the adjoining school at the American consulate were trained in drills on how to flee in case there was a terrorist attack. The kids were shown how to get to the American consulate from where they would be taken to undisclosed locations which would later be intimated to parents. It was overwhelming for us, and more so for the kids. Commandos in black uniforms were guarding the German International School at Breach Candy. The security was scary. To drop or pick up the kids, you needed to show IDs. Some parents started to pull the kids out of the school. Peter and I decided that Vidhie would be moved to Clifton College in Bristol, where she would have gone anyway the year after. I didn't want to put my child through this. Vidhie was a bright child and cleared the entrance interview to Clifton smoothly. The principal of Clifton College, John Milne, took a liking to her. There was no transit in terms of syllabus change, just a shift of location. She was anyway following the same curriculum at her Mumbai school.

Vidhie moved to the UK in 2009 as a full-time boarder in year seven at Clifton College when she was twelve years old. Strangely enough she was the only brown kid who was a boarder. Initially, she might've done things to fit in but eventually she settled into her ways.

In February 2009, I was swamped with work. I had organized a whole do for Sheena on her birthday but I had forgotten to wish her. I called her late in the night to have a chat. It was a trying time at work. There was a global recession that year. Our monies were finishing and we were nowhere close to raising the second round of investment. The plan was that once our channels were established, we would raise more money. But that didn't happen.

In February, my friends Radhika Radia and Pritul Sanghvi (regional head, West, of my HR firm) came to meet me in my cabin at work. Sheena was staying at Radhika's home. Radhika was really worried for Sheena. In my head, Sheena was settled, so I was a little surprised hearing this. Radhika had assumed that Sheena was staying with me in Marlow, since she hadn't gone to the Radia home in months. During that time, Rahul had started staying in Bandra at a place Peter arranged for him after I got him a job at Prime Focus. Radhika was panicking more because she knew Sheena had her final undergrad exams in a month and Vibhuti had also told her that Sheena wasn't attending college. It was even more disturbing to hear that somebody had seen Sheena do cocaine at a nightclub in the suburbs. All these things alarmed me to no end. Yet, I had to keep INX afloat so my focus was elsewhere. I didn't even realize that Sheena and Rahul were timing their weekend trips to Marlow together.

I took Radhika and Pritul to Peter's cabin. They narrated the story to him, too. Peter and I decided to take matters into our hands. I didn't condone this and neither did he. We somehow just knew Sheena was at Rahul's place. It wasn't hard to figure out once all the details were with us.

Once back in the privacy of our home, I sat Sheena down.

I asked her point blank, 'Are you seeing Rahul?'

'No, I am not.' She denied it.

Maybe it was a fling. Maybe it was casual. I frankly wasn't even interested in that bit of information. All I wanted to know was why she was bunking college. She had been a bright student all her life.

I took serious issue on two counts—drugs and bunking college. Sheena had always been honest about her relationships with me. She was seeing a guy called Aneesh before Kaustav and all I told her was to have safe sex, if she did. I am not someone who would pass moral judgements on people. I even told her what contraception to use. Our relationship was rather frank. And yet, Sheena felt the need to lie to me.

I told her, 'I have been a mother who has been really open to you about everything. All I am saying right now is that you are a good student. Don't fuck up your career. And you know the amount of trouble we went through with Mekhail. We finally brought him back on track. You have to kick off the drugs. I don't want to go through that again.'

It was decided that she would either stay at Marlow, Radhika's or in Guwahati, for the next few days till she finished her exams. The colleges were beginning to shut down for final exams. I wanted her to go to Guwahati for study leave. She seemed happy that I had rescued her, at least that is what she had portrayed to me at that time. She obeyed whatever I said.

That evening, Peter took Rahul to Olive for drinks and dinner. Peter later told me that he told Rahul to give Sheena some space. Rahul admitted that he and Sheena were in a relationship. I still don't know why Sheena lied to me. But I didn't push her. Sheena agreed to whatever I told her to do. But she had no answers to the many questions I was asking her.

At one point, I asked her, 'What do you do at home all day? Rahul is at work.'

She looked up at me and said, 'No, Rahul never goes to work.'

Later we came to know that Rahul went to work for four months. Once he moved to Bandra, he stopped going to the office. At that time Prime Focus was doing a lot of work with 9XM and they were embarrassed to inform us.

We had to be careful at home to ensure that none of this percolated to Vidhie. She was eleven—all of this happened before her shift to Bristol. She was so innocent back then.

I remember this conversation she had with Peter and I that year. 'Do you guys have sex?' She was sitting in the car's backseat, while Peter drove and I sat next to him.

We looked at each other and said 'yes'. She had follow up questions about whether we had sex standing up or sitting down! Peter was so shocked that he brought the car to a screeching halt. Vidhie made a distasteful face at us.

She thought kissing someone on the mouth was disgusting. She was in that phase of life where drugs, sex and relationships were taboos and sickening. I wanted nothing to taint her innocence.

Next morning, I was obviously cheesed off with Peter. It wasn't his fault but it naturally came out on him. He really could've raised Rahul better. Rabin wasn't like this. He always had his head on his shoulders, was hardworking and focussed. Rabin worked at good places, and he and I sort of got along, at least that's what I had believed. We could be in the same space in a civil fashion and could hold a conversation. I was angry with Rahul about many things.

In the mornings, we usually sat outside to have tea on the terrace. That morning, too, Maya came to serve us tea. She informed us that Rahul had come over at 2 a.m., and had spent the night in Sheena's room. Now, even Peter was angry. I asked for Rahul and Sheena to come meet us. We told them how unhappy we were about how things were going.

'You guys get your lives sorted out. I will get you guys married on this terrace. This is where I got married to Peter. But before that I need you to settle down,' I told Rahul.

I also rebuked Rahul for bunking work. He gave some ridiculous explanation, all of which translated to him being lazy. He didn't like his boss. But then again, no one likes their bosses. Peter backed me this time and made him call his boss and apologize. The moment Rahul called him up, his boss thanked him for calling. Soon, Rahul wasn't working at the company, his pending salary was processed duly. There's only that many exceptions that can be made even for Peter Mukerjea's son.

Peter decided to take Rahul to Amby Valley while Sheena stayed on at Marlow before she went back to Guwahati. Rahul stopped coming to Marlow after that for the next few months. Sheena told me that Rahul kept calling her from Amby Valley, and I told Sheena not to answer if she didn't want to.

In April 2009, Sheena moved to Delhi. I fixed up meetings with various contacts so she could find work. I wanted her to have a job, and she was to join ADA Reliance Group as a management trainee. It was a mistake on my part to let it happen. I wanted her to start having a career. But I didn't realize how bad things would get there afterwards.

In June, Vivek Mittal called me to say Sheena had been hospitalized. She had become incoherent before fainting. The doctors called for me. In prison, I met drug peddlers. Through conversations with them, I realized that if a serial drug abuser suffered from dire withdrawal symptoms and wanted to score drugs, they would find a way even in an unknown city.

Vivek and Mekhail thought it was a heat stroke. But when she was admitted in the hospital, she was treated for hysteria and hallucinations. She was apparently breathless and also had a stiff hand. Every time I spoke to her over the phone, she seemed all right. But two days later when I met her in the hospital, she was moody. She was not herself. When the food came, she threw it away. It seemed she was disturbed about something. She wasn't a child who had anger issues even in her teenage years, so this was confusing behaviour.

But it so happened that after I came back to Mumbai from Delhi, I couldn't get through to Sheena. Her phones were not reachable. She didn't reply to texts. I panicked. Did I make her feel abandoned?

My mother called me that week and said, 'Sheena has contacted us. She is all right but doesn't want to tell us where she is. She wants space from us.'

The next week her appointment letter from Reliance reached Guwahati and we again started trying her numbers. She picked up my mother's call finally. I got the sense that Sheena was upset with me about something. I couldn't figure out why. I learnt much later that she was in Dehradun during this period.

On Holi that year, Peter decided that he needed to let go of INX Media. His decision to quit INX caught even the investors by surprise. I decided to follow him. But I was asked to hold off for two months till May that year while the investors reached out to Pradeep Guha to take over the reins.

By the end of June, we moved to Bristol to be close to Vidhie who was studying at Clifton College. Peter also wanted to spend more time with his older son Rabin who worked and lived in London. We got a house in Bristol and divided our time between the UK and India. We were still deciding if we wanted to live in Bristol or in London.

All this while, ever since she moved to Guwahati after her hospital stint, Sheena had not contacted me.

Around the time I was moving to England, I found out from the then ADA Reliance HR Head, Rajeev Bhaduria, that Sheena upon joining Reliance would be put up at management trainee quarters. My driver and help went and set up her house—from AC to kitchen gadgets to washing machine, I provided for everything so she could live comfortably. Even though Sheena didn't want to stay in touch with me, for reasons known only to her, as a mother I could not help but ensure she was taken care of. I would check on her well-being through friends.

In the summer of 2009, Peter and I went to Egypt. While we were travelling, Peter got a call that informed us that Rahul had emptied out his Bandra flat. It was then that it dawned on me that Sheena cutting me out had something to do with Rahul. I kept enquiring about her from my mother and Mekhail. But, by then, she apparently had an estranged relationship with Mekhail and Mom too. I knew through my friend Rajeev Bhaduria that she was going to work.

In August, Rajeev called to tell me that Sheena hadn't been to work for fifteen days. That was when I got really worried.

In a way, whatever happened after this was in equal measures unbelievable and disheartening. We received a call from Rahul in September; he said that Vidhie had sent a nasty email to Sheena. When we asked Vidhie, she said she hadn't done it. Rahul was quick to say if Vidhie hadn't then I must have. This escalated to a huge fight between them and us. Sheena and Rahul sent Peter and me nasty messages. The kind of language used was unbelievable. The messages were filled with profanity and venom. Rahul sent messages that vilified both Peter and me. Sheena never spoke like that so I assumed it was all Rahul. I texted them back saying: 'I can't deal with this. You both feel free to do what you want to do.' It was the end of all communication between us thereon.

I texted Sheena saying, 'I don't care what you do. But I want you to get back to work.' I stopped checking on Sheena after that. She did go back to work, as I got to know later, but I didn't want to be accused of interfering again so I didn't actively seek her out. Rahul had slammed me in really coarse language for interfering in their lives. Sheena was almost twenty-three. I could only do so much, even for my own daughter. I trusted her to see the light and do whatever was best for her.

PART 7

Betrayal

21

⁘

Gradually, after my arrest, as the years passed by, I got to know how Peter and his family had been spreading rumours about me. They had all gone out of their way to give nasty interviews about me over the years. Locked away inside, it was heartbreaking for me to hear the elaborate lies they had woven about me. But it was the fact that Peter was an active party to it all that shattered me.

It was sometime in 2017 after Peter's arrest, that I knew I was going to leave him.

The process for it started when I found out that Peter and the family were treating Vidhie shabbily. After all, as a mother, even in prison, I constantly worried about my children. The day I got arrested, the transfer of shares to Vidhie for the Marlow house was stalled by Peter. During this period she was pressured into adhering to the Mukerjeas' whims. They arm-twisted her into transferring the property to Rabin. My child was at their mercy completely.

I knew she had no choice but to succumb to the pressures. When I spoke to her in prison later, she told me that the day I was arrested, she knew that from then on she would be on her own.

Rabin was entrusted with the responsibility of sending her money when she moved to London for university immediately after my arrest. He was handling my NatWest account into which the rental that I received from my Covent Garden property in London would be deposited every month. He was handling my money. It was only a matter of a mere wire transfer but at a point Rabin did not send any money to Vidhie. For a whole month Vidhie had no bed, no wardrobe, no duvet or blanket. She inhabited an empty apartment through the cold month of September in London. She showed me a photograph of her empty room when she met me in prison without the knowledge of the Mukerjeas. It broke my heart to hear and see Vidhie in that state. I was sad, very sad, but could not cry that day. My tears had dried up by then.

The letters I would send to her from prison weren't passed on to her directly.

Shangon would ask her, 'Do you want your mother's letters?'

She told me later that she felt coerced into saying 'no'—they'd be happy whenever she said no.

Vidhie told me that Shangon told her, 'You shouldn't call your mother "Mom" anymore. You should call her Lucy.' Lucy is short for Lucifer.

The hardest part for Vidhie was coming to terms with the fact that she wasn't in touch with Peter or me during the time we were in prison. There was an emotional void in her. She would make up stories for her friends in college every time they'd talk about their parents and homes.

Peter had promised to love Vidhie as his own but he didn't keep his word. And Vidhie, for the longest time, was under Peter's spell. She worshipped the ground he walked on.

Small incidents pushed me closer to divorce. In May 2016, Peter sent me a letter on my birthday saying how much he loved me. There were analogies drawn to Romeo and Juliet. He said he knew I was going to prove my innocence. A copy of the letter somehow reached the press. And just two days later he filed for bail in the sessions court saying that I had lied to him. He said he didn't know if I had murdered Sheena. And in his bail application he stated that his wife was highly ambitious and willing to sacrifice and give up her children to achieve her ambitions. His hypocrisy was out in public and it slowly made me realize how fake and shallow he is.[12]

For a long time, I believed Peter was innocent. But there was a feeling of betrayal. I kept asking myself what I saw in this guy. From day one, I had the niggling feeling that I couldn't trust him. I kept questioning myself—how could I? It's human nature that when you are hurt, and you see the one who hurt you suffering, you feel vindicated. Despite the love, I felt, 'You didn't get away from karma, did you?' The universe has its own way of meting out justice. I felt I got the raw end of the stick but I made it an opportunity to make peace with my life.

There's some twisted reason behind people staying in abusive relationships. It took me a long time to see things clearly. What I was going through with Peter was emotional abuse at this point. I had loved him so much that it superseded logic. I would blindly justify every wrong action of his. It took me almost two years in prison to come to terms with my expectations from him. Of course, I knew in the first year itself that I would leave him, but the love hadn't left my system.

For me, divorce was a practical decision. We were both in prison. We weren't seeing anyone, obviously. But it became important for me to provide Vidhie with security, financially. I needed to give her a roof that the Mukerjeas had snatched away from her. I had to do it in a legal way. A court had to order that division of finances be done in a proper and equitable manner.

Marriage vows are emotional, about sticking together through sickness and health, but dissolving a marriage is about legally separating everything that you had jointly acquired as a unit. The latter isn't a pleasant task at all. A lot of our inner ugliness crops up when money comes into play. His family went out of their way to tell people to not talk to me or acknowledge me. And, by now, I wanted to have nothing to do with them either.

Peter had married a smart and beautiful woman whom he liked having by his side. He was attracted to her beauty and brains but, over the years, he started grudging the same qualities. I turned out to be way smarter than he expected me to be. Men like him get attracted to women like me but when they start living with us, they begin to get insecure. Some men believe that women are their property. There's a strange ownership some male spouses feel. He hated the male attention that I got. He wasn't comfortable with the fact that I made more than enough money by virtue of having a thriving business and the appetite to moonlight effortlessly. What appealed to Peter about me was that I was a ballsy woman but when I became his wife and continued to hold on to my ballsy nature, he wasn't able to handle it.

Prior to my decision on the divorce, Gunjan had already told Peter that I won't have an issue letting him go. I received a letter from Peter after that, and the sentence, 'I had never thought of a divorce!' struck me. I took my time to make up my mind, as I knew it's a big step. But once I did, there was no looking back from me.

This is when Edith Dey came into my life. She handles the family court matters from Mahesh Jethmalani's chamber. She had slowly become an elder sister to me. Edith was incredibly warm from the first time she came to meet me. When the divorce conversation was initiated, Peter's lawyer sent an intimation to my legal team saying that we should not discuss divorce right away. Instead, the teams should begin by separating properties and finances. The first proposed split that his team sent over was really skewed: it suggested that I keep my London apartment and my Phoenix office space and Peter gets everything else. Edith shut it down right there.

From there began the process that took almost two years. We slowly started to verbally agree on things and how they could be split. The first few proposals we sent over didn't materialize into anything meaningful. I had to take some tough calls. I put a stay on all the bank accounts I accessed with Peter, so that he couldn't access them. Even though he had siphoned off some money earlier from these accounts, I believe this wasn't enough cash to sustain him as he had a battery of expensive lawyers and the legal costs were very high. But the final thing that prompted me to go forward with the divorce was the INX Media case.

22

In May 2017, I read in the papers that the CBI had filed a case on INX Media and Karti Chidambaram. My name wasn't mentioned in the article but it alarmed me. This bribery case from 2009 was out in the open now.

Peter and I had gone to meet P. Chidambaram, who was the then finance minister, and a deal had been struck. Some 'I scratch your back, you scratch mine' money was given to Karti's—Chidambaram's son—company. Even when Peter and I were in Bristol, I would bring this up again and again because I was afraid that it would come to bite us someday. When the government changed in 2014, a lot of past cases were pulled out for reinvestigation. I had suggested multiple times that we report this based on a premonition.

But, the ever-confident Peter just said, 'Let sleeping dogs lie.'

All of us have those lies that bother us until we come out with them. This was one of them. Even two months prior to my arrest, I had brought this up with Peter. I had always been straight with my financial dealings. Peter had sensed even then that I was beginning to crack.

And so, in July, after seeing the news, I wrote a letter to the late Arun Jaitley, the finance minister (2014–19), from prison. Until then, P. Chidambaram's name was not in the FIR. The case was directed solely at Karti. But I knew I wanted to testify in the case.

It was something that was on my conscience for a long time. Of course, I never heard back in writing from Mr Jaitley. But one day when I was in court, two people came to meet me. Usually guards are on high alert with me. That particular day, these guys were allowed in to see me and chat with me.

'Your letter to the finance minister has been received. You have made a brave move and the matter will be taken up seriously. We want you to cooperate and be honest with us,' one of the burly men said to me.

They looked intimidating. I still don't know who those men were. I never saw them again. Were they cops or people from the CBI, or just informers? I have no idea. My guards didn't stop them, so I knew powerful people were involved in the matter by this time. I didn't tell Peter about this because he and I were in a bad space with each other. We were writing to each other rather regularly at the time but all we spoke about were settlement terms and past grouses.

In October 2017, the Enforcement Directorate (ED) team showed up in court and requested to interview Peter and then me. The ED had filed an Enforcement Case Information Report (ECIR) based on an FIR by the CBI. Peter and I met at the court meeting room. He asked me to deny any knowledge of things. After Peter said that, I went back and thought about it. Did I need any more mess around me?

There was only one man who came to meet me. He came to prison to discuss the case. I gave him a full, blow-by-blow narration of the chain of events at INX. He wasn't expecting the details I gave him. I wrote him a full account.

Now the difference between Peter and me was simply that I had the courage to take the onus for decisions that were made, but he didn't. The CBI and senior officials from the ED came to meet me again in December 2017. The CBI officer, R. Parthasarathy, came to interrogate me. I instinctively felt I could trust him. I told him about the letter I had sent to Mr Jaitley earlier in the year. The team trusted me because I was nothing but honest with them all along. I wasn't afraid to own up to the truth.

The ED guys too came down to take a detailed statement. I never got chargesheeted either by the CBI or the ED in the INX cases. P. Chidambaram had been Peter's contact from many years ago, even before I came into his life.

The CBI asked me if I would repeat my statement in court. There was no question of going back on this; I knew I could get punished for it. The finance team at INX reported to Peter. It was definitely his call and decision. But there's no getting away from the fact that I was a party to it, too. In February 2018, the CBI returned to take me to Delhi. In the CBI case I was an accused. When I was presented in court, they requested I be given judicial custody for four days. There were voluminous documents to go through with me. I was taken to the CBI guest house and they told me to reiterate my statements. I was well cared for and I remember it was bitterly cold in Delhi.

I requested to meet the head of CBI at that time. Alok Verma was the CBI director and Rakesh Asthana was the special CBI director. There were things in the case which I was yet to say that could have dire consequences. The case was under Mr Asthana. Permission was secured to arrange a meeting with me.

I was taken upstairs by the CBI superintendent of police (SP), the investigation officer (IO) and some lady inspectors to Mr Asthana's cabin. I wanted to understand the consequences of my testimony. He suggested I could ask to be pardoned. If allowed by the court,

I'd become an approver in the case. But if the court decided that I shouldn't be pardoned, I would be tried for the charges. He assured me that the CBI would back it in case I decided to ask for a pardon, because I was helping them crack the case. I was the one ratifying the details found by the CBI.

On the third day, I was taken back to court to inform the court that I had cooperated and that all points had been recorded. I was brought back to Mumbai the next day by a different team. The court asked me if I was treated well—which is a mandatory question they ask.

The CBI team treated me with respect and I felt comfortable in their presence. My IO, Mr Parthasarathy, was a thorough gentleman and I so wish we had more male officers in the police service like him who know how not to rob a woman of her dignity even when she is accused of a crime!

In mid February, I wrote a letter requesting that I be allowed to record my statement in front of the magistrate. The judge allowed it and the CBI came to take me to record the statement. Days after my statement was recorded, Karti Chidambaram was arrested. In April, Karti was brought to Byculla Jail to confront me. I confronted him. And everything I had said, I repeated in front of him. There was a camera placed in front of us, along with two independent witnesses. I recounted everything on camera, the details of where we had met and the deal that was cracked.

A few months later, the CBI asked for Peter's police custody. He had earlier asked me over video calls about what happened in Delhi. He didn't cooperate when he was taken to Delhi and was questioned day in and day out. Later Peter told me that apparently Parthasarathy even had a man-to-man talk with him and warned him that this stand of his would antagonize me and deepen the rift between us. There was already marital discord.

Parthasarathy came to drop Peter to Mumbai. In front of him, Peter and I had an argument in court the next day. I told him that we were already stuck in one case. To come out honestly would absolve us of the second one at least. But Peter got very angry at this suggestion. That day I made up my mind that I had to leave him, for good.

23

We got around to agreeing to the divorce settlement terms verbally but he wasn't okay with the divorce at all. In fact, he was utterly embarrassed when my advocate Edith Dey sent the first legal letter to him in Arthur Road Jail in April 2018. We were both already in jail, being tried for murder and even in a situation like this, he was thinking about his image and 'What will people say?' It then dawned on me that this wasn't about love at all, it was about protecting his image.

The notice was out in the media. While he was livid, I made him understand that we had nothing to lose anymore. We were both accused of murder. This paper was merely the verbalization of the fact that we should agree on the financial split and separate legally.

We were anyway separated physically, and otherwise. 'Where is the question of loss of reputation when we are standing naked in public ...'

I don't think he understood what I meant when I said this to him.

During this time, Vidhie completely vanished from my life. But she remained in touch with Peter. He would sometimes show me those emails in court and I noticed how she referred to me as 'IM' and not Mom, like she usually did. Later, as I mentioned before, I got to know from Vidhie that Peter's sister Shangon had told her to call me Indrani or Lucy, and not Mum. She was being fed a different narrative: how I was a vile, manipulative person who was bereft of motherly emotions—I didn't even deserve to be called Mom. In May 2017, Peter showed me a copy of the *Savvy* magazine that had Vidhie on the cover. She didn't have nice things to say about me. I was very hurt. It was a slam piece on me. It was very disturbing for me. I was helpless. While I knew she was all over the place, there was no way I could reach out to her. I could see her emotional turmoil, hurt and anger in being stamped as the child of three murder accused.

In 2018, I saw Vidhie in court one day. Peter's lawyer had requested time for Peter to meet her. The judge didn't realize that it wasn't for me and allowed Vidhie to meet both Peter and me. I had no idea she was coming to see us. That day, I distinctly remember feeling that Vidhie wasn't warm. While she was sugar and honey with Peter, she was cold towards me. It made me very sad. And I had no idea what was causing this.

It was during our last goodbyes that she said to me, 'You are not giving me money to finish my education …'

I was confused, I must admit. Firstly, I have no context as to why she had no access to her education fund. Vidhie was sent to Regent's College for her post-graduation. Because of our arrests she was very disturbed and went astray. She partied non-stop, went backpacking all over the place and did not focus on her studies. Naturally, she flunked. But, she pinned it all on me.

I knew that the Mukerjea men had additionally siphoned off ₹6 crores from an account that Peter and I jointly held, soon after my arrest. After she blurted out that I was holding back her education fund, I asked her where she got that from. That day, in 2018, when Vidhie went back home after talking to me and getting my version of the story, she realized that her paradise had its problems. Her bubble was broken. That evening, she went overboard with alcohol and medicines. A few weeks after the incident, one of my lawyers informed me about it. Vidhie had to be hospitalized. After Vidhie came out of the hospital, she came to meet me in prison. The moment she saw me, she burst into tears and broke down completely. My priority after I heard about the overdose incident was getting Vidhie back on track.

Finally, in September 2018, we filed the divorce petition at the Bandra Family Court. There was a huge media ruckus outside the court. It was the first time since my arrest that I was out in a public forum where the media would have full access to me. I remember I wore sindoor that day and I wore it till the day my divorce got finalized. This was the last phase of my marriage with Peter and wearing sindoor was symbolic for me. I wanted to give some dignity to what we shared, no matter how it all turned out eventually. Finally, in October 2019, the family court granted us divorce.

In March 2019, Peter had a heart problem. He had a blocked artery issue. I guess all those pastries and sheekh kebabs that his sister brought to him in court meetings didn't help. I had told him multiple times to curb his gluttony.

But he always brushed it aside saying, 'I am already in prison, it can't get worse.'

While he ate, I sat there alone. Every time Sanjeev's family came to visit him, they brought me meals too. It was very emotional for me. The starkness of how the respective families treated me helped me see my relationships with greater clarity. Peter and my love was conditional. We had a good run. It has been slow learning for me. Like bad times, good times don't last very long either … Peter and I ran our course but the damage that was done is yet to heal.

PART 8

Jail ki Laadli

24

While I was a high-profile prisoner and no one dared to misbehave with me, I had noticed how other prisoners were treated. The jail authorities insisted that discipline be maintained at all times. In early 2017, the granddaughter of a prominent diamond businessman and a producer was hit by a cop in jail. She was twenty-one years old and was in jail for possession of drugs. She was a well-spoken girl, and the cops hit her for something as trivial as sneaking in a letter. It was a petty offence, at best. Everyone came out from their quarters and saw her getting beaten up, but no one intervened. I stood there alone, even after others left, all the while telling people around me that the cops couldn't touch her. She later reported the incident in the sessions court in Thane where her matter was being heard.

However, my image of being a 'jail ki laadli' changed with one incident that shook the whole prison and the nation.

There were numerous things that could land a prisoner in trouble. The prison rule of jharti was one such. Jharti was a system of conducting surprise checks on prisoners. This process is followed so that prisoners don't peddle drugs inside the prison. In the six years I was in Byculla, there wasn't ever a thing found on a prisoner. It definitely meant either all prisoners were great at hiding things or they weren't doing anything unlawful at all. It was a futile exercise that was a part of the jail manual. It rarely happened with me because I had constant security. There was no scope for me to sneak anything in. And they were always lenient with me.

I had made friends with many women, those whom I would happen to interact with—it was difficult though, due to the high security around me. The Byculla Jail also has a number of international prisoners who were mostly being tried for drug cases. Some of them became friendly with me.

One inmate was a thirty-two-year-old girl who was convicted for the murder of her sister-in-law. Manjula Shetty had been in prison for fourteen years and was due for release. All her pardons had come through and she moved from Pune to Mumbai as a warden in Byculla Jail, because her brothers were here. Now, for those who don't know, wardens are convicts who are paid by the prison authorities to shoulder management responsibilities. They take care of barracks, supervise distribution of food, and other such responsibilities.

She had told us that she was arrested when she was in college. Manjula had a boyfriend then, who was still waiting for her and whom she planned to marry soon after. She was fairly popular with everyone for her good behaviour and also taught yoga in prison. We would talk sometimes. Manjula was a nice middle-class girl. The murder she was accused of was the result of an accident, a case in which both she and her mother were convicted. Her mother died of cancer in prison.

On 23 July 2017, I heard screaming and shouting reverberating through the prison. We all went outside and saw this other warden from Yerwada Jail who had come to Byculla striding away. She was in half-wardi, a yellow saree.

That day, when I went out, I heard screams from the office. I walked towards the office, my jail guards following me. I peeped through the flap. I was horrified to see that it was Manjula's screams I was hearing, she was being beaten up very badly. Immediately, my guards realized what's happening, and hurriedly took me back to my barrack. Frankly, I was in shock. I asked a guard what had happened. The guard let it out that Manjula had sneaked in some leftover eggs and bread rolls. I just sat there in my cell, very perturbed by what was happening. In the next twenty minutes, she was brought out and I saw her as she passed by my cell.

I saw that one cop had a lathi in her hand. Another cop was holding Manjula by her hair and she was being taken upstairs to Barack No. 5. Her saree had unspooled and she was still getting beaten on her leg while she was being dragged outside. I didn't go up, but I heard the commotion on the first floor; she was given a thrashing that lasted over an hour. The Circle jailer herself and five other constables beat her black and blue. Manjula was unable to get up after that.

Later, when they came down I overheard that the jailer and constables had threatened any prisoner who wanted to help Manjula. Many wanted to go and help her but they knew they would meet with the same fate if they dared.

Despite these warnings, people wanted to help. That's how prison is, unlike the portrayals on TV you see—everyone wants to help. There was this young girl Uma—who'd keep coming back to the prison for some petty crime or the other—who tried convincing a constable to allow her to take Manjula to the dispensary. But the cops didn't even allow anyone to put a basic pain relief balm on her.

Manjula was very unwell by now. She couldn't drink water, she was urinating and defecating on her clothes so she had to be changed into a fresh pair. Maryam, another inmate who was in for human trafficking, saw the pain Manjula was in and took her to the bathroom to clean her. It was there that Manjula started frothing. Alarmed, the prisoners started creating a hue and cry, trying to get the attention of the jail cops.

I could hear the noise from my cell. Manjula was covered in bedsheets and rushed to the hospital. Her BP was zero by then. By the time she reached JJ Hospital, she was declared dead. Perhaps Manjula knew she wouldn't live, so she kept asking to see her mother's photo while she was lying all beaten up and injured in Barrack No. 5.

The next morning, when I enquired about her, I was told she was better and in a stable condition. We knew she was really sick but we were told a story about how her blood pressure had fallen. We all breathed easy when we were told that she was better.

But later into the morning, another prisoner who was at JJ the same night Manjula was taken in, returned to jail. She told us that Manjula was taken to the hospital dead.

Around 10 a.m., I saw a whole mass of prisoners coming down. Circle 2 had been shut for construction. All the female prisoners in Byculla Jail were housed in Circle 1. There were 330 prisoners and the barracks were packed with undertrials in those days. I went out and asked my guard on duty, Bindu, what was going on. I had asked Manisha Pokharkar, the Circle jailer, in the morning about Manjula and she'd told me she was okay. I had thought of it as a '*raat gayi baat gayi* (a passing)' incident.

And so, I was clueless as to why a swarm of prisoners had gathered in the courtyard. Bindu and her associate Surekha left me in the dark that day. The women, 330 of them, were walking and I joined them, curious to understand what was happening.

First the foreigners raised their voice: 'Where's Manjula?' The question echoed across the courtyard.

Jailer Manisha Pokharkar said, 'She is in the hospital.'

Everyone lashed out at them saying. 'She is dead! And you all killed her!'

I was stunned. Manjula's face appeared in front of me. I looked for Bindu and Surekha, but they were nowhere to be found. I was standing there with the other prisoners in the courtyard and feeling lost. Everyone was suspicious of me, unsure how to gauge which side I was on.

Some of them started hurling shoes at the jailer's office door. Everyone was very angry. The prisoners wanted them to call the prison superintendent so an official complaint could be lodged on the matter. One of the prisoners with us was a former cop, and knew what to do.

Since no one responded, the prisoners started shouting. The superintendent wasn't there so the senior jailer came. Officials from the prison who were liked by prisoners were sent to pacify the crowd.

I stood there as a silent spectator. I caught hold of one of the girls in Barack No. 5 and asked her what happened. She gave me a detailed account. People didn't want to tell me anything because they felt I might side with the cops.

'Why would she support us? She is looked after by cops. She gets privileges from them! She is on their side,' one of them said.

There was gross apathy and anger towards me.

A prisoner who was there, told me angrily, 'If you wish to stand by us with honour, please do so. Or else go and support the cops. We will let you go into their office. We are fine with that. We will not stop you. But before you cross that door and walk into their side of the fence, we just want you to remember that today if you allow this to happen to one Manjula and you are afraid to raise your voice, there will be many more Manjulas who will be beaten to death like this in the future.'

It was a call I had to take. The cops would sue us back. I was being taken care of by them. This would have consequences and it was a battle we might lose. But I thought of Manjula's screams and realized it's high time inmates exercised their rights. Keeping quiet was something my conscience wouldn't allow.

25

B indu and Surekha, who had abandoned me and their duty as my
guards to save themselves from the wrath of the angry prisoners,
were allegedly a part of the gang that bashed Manjula brutally in
Barrack No. 5. I was, until then, considered an alien by prisoners.
Now I recollect that when I saw Manjula being taken upstairs after
she was beaten at the office she didn't have fatal injuries. It was the
ruthless bashing upstairs that killed her. When the medical report
came later, we found out that she had multiple serious injuries that
caused her death. On the first day, before I heard about Manjula's
death, I was under the impression that the women from Barack No.
5 were exaggerating about Manjula's situation. I didn't believe that
cops could hit anyone that much. They were usually an amiable
bunch. But this incident made me see my own privilege. They
wouldn't dare do it to me because the press would get a whiff of it,
landing them in trouble. But with Manjula, they felt they could get
away. They probably didn't want to kill her but they went too far; it
was a strange ego trip they were on that caused it.

After lunch, Jailer Manisha Pokharkar, was confronted. This
wasn't the first time this had happened in her presence. It had
happened twice before with other prisoners but they had survived
the physical abuse. She had a habit of beating up prisoners and
would encourage constables to do the same. A prisoner would be

lying helpless and a group of cops would be attacking her with lathis, punches and kicks. It had happened with two other girls prior to Manjula during my time. They had probably survived because they were just undertrials. Manjula had been in prison for fourteen years and thus she couldn't take it physically. After Manisha Pokharkar took over, the inmates felt terrorized. She would also conduct the beatings in public viewing to cause fear amongst other inmates. When a young girl had sneaked in keema pav, a few months ago, Manisha and the gang had beaten her like an animal. The girl had a black eye, which later popped out. When her family came to meet her a few days later, she had guards around her so she couldn't tell them what had happened.

So now we refused to get silenced without recording our statements. All the prisoners demanded that we be allowed to lodge a complaint.

The inmates from Barack No. 5 wrote a detailed account of what had occurred. But we all knew it would never reach the authorities. We insisted that someone from Nagpada Police Station be sent to record the FIR as Byculla Jail was in its jurisdiction. One of the senior jailers asked me to intervene to calm down the inmates.

The inmates were looking to me because they knew the power I wielded in the outside world. I could have made it happen. I had money and the right legal aid by my side. I was educated. The prison guards brought out the microphone for me to speak in order to calm down the crowd. I got up and stood atop a table, a makeshift podium and said that we will definitely file a complaint and get an FIR lodged under Section 302 of the Indian Penal Code, but no matter what we do, we had to remain calm. I spoke in Hindi, even though I wasn't fluent in the language. At that time, I did believe that the administration would do the right thing!

However, the authorities pulled out the wire and disconnected the microphone that I was using. The prison guards expected me to stand with them and douse the rage but I couldn't have done that.

I didn't back down. I continued without a mic, 'We will also demand that the Nagpada police or a magistrate be called, failing which the media should be called and this incident be reported ...'

Everyone started clapping and cheering. There were over 300 witnesses and we weren't willing to let it go! I reminded everyone that as per the prison manual the authorities had no right to touch a prisoner. I told them to go and speak in court about it if it ever happened with them.

This was the first time in my life I was doing a selfless, good deed at the cost of putting my neck on the line. No matter how this turned out, I could face myself in the mirror knowing that I did the right thing. Suddenly, the prisoners saw me as a different person. I was no longer the 'jail ki laadli' prisoner they envied. I stood there without guards, batting for them, promising that I will bring Manjula justice.

We weren't giving up. Pandemonium descended on the barracks. There was naarabaazi (sloganeering). Because Byculla is in the heart of the city, everyone around could hear what was happening inside. The mulaqats were stopped that day. Someone had informed the media so they showed up by about 4 p.m. The officials disconnected the TVs so we couldn't see what was being said.

I requested the jail officers to call Sudeep Pasbola, my trial lawyer. Initially, they avoided having to make this call for a long time. And then late in the afternoon the jail superintendent Indulkar showed up. I put my foot down when he arrived and got him to call Sudeep Pasbola.

In the evening, the Nagpada cops came but instead of registering an FIR on the jail cops who had taken Manjula's life, they pinned the FIR on the prisoners for inciting a riot. I realized that it wasn't a myth that wherever you go, the cops are always hand in glove.

By then Advocate Bhavesh, Pasbola's junior, came inside the prison. Through him, the prison authorities tried to negotiate with us. We were allowed to meet the director general (DG) of prisons, Dr Upadhyay. As a first solution, Dr Upadhyay pronounced that Manisha and her gang of constables be suspended for six months. We didn't agree. Was that really enough for killing someone so brutally? We were insistent that an FIR be lodged—it was non-negotiable that a complaint be officially registered.

No one ate food that day. Everyone was upset. The jailer and her gang were moved to a secure place, perhaps fearing that the inmates would attack them in a fit of rage. The other cops continued to negotiate with 300 of us but no one was in the mood to budge. And finally, in the presence of Advocate Bhavesh, we lodged the FIR against Manisha Pokharkar and her gang of constables who had beaten Manjula Shetty to death a day earlier in the presence of over 300 female prisoners and children.

When we returned to the prison circle after meeting the DG and lodging the FIR, all the lights were off. It was night. We saw the prison police standing there with meshes and helmets. Prison police, both male and female from across Mumbai and the suburbs were summoned to Byculla Jail.

A lathi charge on a woman by male officers was by no means a legal act. A lathi charge anyway cannot be inflicted on anyone without prior announcement. Usually, a magistrate has to be present to announce and warn the onset of a planned lathi charge.

In Byculla that night, though, there was no magistrate nor any warning. Suddenly the torchlights of the cops' mobile phones came on and they started beating up everyone they found and saw. The prison authorities were angry because, with my lawyer's help, we had managed to lodge the FIR. My lawyer spoke to the media and gave them a lowdown of what had happened.

In the lathi charge, one of the cops on duty hit me on my hands, legs and head. When that happened, everyone reacted. We all were shoved back into our barracks and locked up.

The next morning, Gunjan came to meet me. She saw me and realized what had happened. She told me that the prison authorities had filed a rioting case on us. They had shot themselves in the foot by hitting me. Gunjan decided to charge them back when I showed her my injuries, and filed a complaint. The rioting news led people from the British Consulate to come and meet me—this was a case of human rights violation and the matter was made worse by the lathi charge.

An FIR was lodged but the six cops responsible were absconding. I went to court the next day, showed my injuries and narrated the entire incident to the Hon'ble Judge Jagdale. Since it was an open court, the media recorded the proceedings as well. The court ordered that I be taken to JJ Hospital and if I wanted to file a separate complaint about what had happened that night with the SP, I was to be taken to Nagpada Police Station next.

Efforts were made to try and influence the doctor to state that my injuries were old. But the hospital gave the correct report and I went and filed the complaint at Nagpada Police Station, naming Indulkar as the officer who hit me. What set me off was that even after assaulting us, the jail authorities had the audacity to threaten us.

I could still hear what Indulkar had said to another inmate, 'You women have done what you had to do! Now you watch out what we will do!'

I got out and spoke about it because I realized there was no remorse. A woman was beaten to death and no one was taking responsibility. Justice had to be served!

Within a week, the jailer and the five constables were arrested. A thorough investigation ensued. As of today, the accused in the Manjula Shetty murder case are in prison. But this incident changed my bond with the women in prison. I started sitting down with prisoners and even chatting with them frequently. Prisoners started coming to me proactively after this incident. Even though there were guards around, they wanted to discuss their cases with me. A lot of people started coming to me to take legal advice. They sometimes needed financial help. Even though bails were granted, many of them didn't have money to pay the bond money. Everyone realized I was not a cold-blooded monster who had killed her daughter. I was in a shell till Manjula died. But that incident made my humane side visible to everyone. They saw my strength and realized I could make things happen. Over the next few months, human rights activists and women's commissions visited the prison—something that continues till date. After that no prisoner was hit again. I would continuously remind everyone of their rights. If they stuck to the rules, nothing untoward would ever happen to them again.

After the Manjula case, the entire administration was changed. It was a big victory for those who fought for justice at Byculla Undertrial Jail.

PART 9

Reunion

26

In 2010, we bought a house in Bristol. We had moved on from INX completely. I started wrapping up my own companies in India too. We were starting to move bag and baggage.

Somehow, I started liking living in Bristol. We retained apartment No. 19 Marlow on the fifth floor for our own use when we visited Mumbai and rented out No. 18 on the fourth floor. We had a home in Goa too. Peter's brother stayed with his family not very far from our home in Goa.

After the receipt of the nasty messages from Rahul's phone allegedly sent by Sheena to Peter and my numbers, I consciously stopped discussing Rahul and Sheena at home. It was all just too painful.

One of the days, when we were back in Mumbai that year, Rahul called Peter. He had had a motorbike accident and had hit a pregnant woman. The police were involved. Peter took care of it. But that incident was enough to make me paranoid. For me, he was the one who had caused the rift between Sheena and I.

We were happier in Bristol as a family. Vidhie moved from being a boarder to being a day scholar. I would drop her to school in my Land Cruiser. I had gifted Peter a Maserati on his fifty-fifth birthday. I wanted to let go of the negativity of Sheena and Rahul, and really move on with the life we had created in Bristol. We also bought a new place in London and a holiday home in Spain. We had decided that our lives were in Europe and we would come to Mumbai every now and then.

In December 2010, we celebrated Christmas in Goa. Sriparna, Peter's niece—his brother Gautam's daughter—was getting married in March 2011. It was a happy end to the year for the family. I visited my parents in Guwahati and stayed at home for a few days. I had forgiven my parents by then. They were ageing and ailing now. I told my sister-in-law Aarti to send an invitation card to my parents, which was never sent. My parents had no connection with the Mukerjeas, but I wanted them to meet finally.

I came back to Mumbai about ten days before the wedding. It was then that Aarti told me that Shabnam was going to attend the wedding. She had asked Peter to check with me before inviting Shabnam.

And Peter had told her, 'Indrani is okay with it.'

Peter hadn't informed me and that was enough to get me seething.

We had three drivers: Prashant, Shyamvar Rai and Mario. After Mario got older, Agnelo was brought in to replace him. Shyamvar was Vidhie's and Sheena's driver. When we visited India, Maya, our cook, would come to work for us. Prashant was our driver. Prashant was like family for us. He called me when I landed in Mumbai. He was very upset that he wasn't invited for Sriparna's wedding. He was an old family-hand. In fact, he had seen Sriparna from the time she was a baby. I was upset too that day about the Shabnam information that Aarti gave me. I vaguely mentioned it to him.

Prashant told me that Peter had been meeting Shabnam, Rahul and Sheena when I was in Guwahati. I found out that Peter had hosted Rahul and Sheena at home while I was gone. I also learnt later that Peter had met Shabnam at the airport and then at Leela.

Prior to Goa, he had met the whole bunch and I wasn't told about it. Even Vidhie was there and she never mentioned it either.

I called up Peter that evening. He was boarding from Heathrow with Vidhie. I didn't ask him anything else.

I just said, 'Aarti told me Shabnam is coming for the wedding.'

He acted surprised.

He animatedly said, 'Oh my God! How could she do this? This is not done!'

I asked him, maintaining my composure, 'You really didn't know about it?'

Peter swore, 'Of course not. This is the first time I am hearing of it.'

When they reached home, Vidhie immediately went off to sleep. I told Peter I needed to speak to him, so I took him to Four Seasons for a drink.

When we were seated by the purser that evening, the vibe was tense.

I called him out, 'You are lying to me!'

Peter swore Aarti was lying. So I put her on a speakerphone and when she heard what Peter was saying, she blew her head off. Aarti and Shabnam are friends from college. It was a fair thing to call her. But why go behind my back? I was also under the assumption that there was no contact between Peter and Shabnam in the last nine years after the initial marital discord their conversations had caused.

I told Peter I wouldn't go to the wedding if Shabnam was going to attend it. I wouldn't have said no had I been asked properly. I wasn't even told that he was in touch with her. My decision was final.

Despite my best-laid plans, there was an SOS call made to us the next morning. Aarti had started bleeding and had to be hospitalized.

There was a uterine surgery needed and I rushed to Goa to take care of her. She was so unwell that she couldn't even stand up. Peter and Vidhie came five days later for the wedding celebrations. And a few days later, Shabnam came to Goa with Rahul and Sheena.

It was too late to back out then. Aarti needed help and post-surgery care and I couldn't leave her alone. I just told them to make sure that I didn't have to cross paths with Shabnam. I didn't want to attend the same functions as her. To be fair, Gautam put his foot down. He didn't want an unpleasant situation with me. The choice was made and it was decided that I would be there for all events.

Shabnam was staying close to the house. The atmosphere was tense but everyone ensured our presence never overlapped. I couldn't stand the fact that things were hidden from me. Another thing that bothered me was the fact that Peter made it look like Sheena was a bad influence on Rahul. I felt that Rahul had spoiled my daughter. It was always a bone of contention between us. We couldn't talk about it without fighting.

The wedding experience was strange. Rahul and Sheena were there but they didn't speak to us. I saw Sheena but she didn't make any effort to meet me.

We left Goa once the wedding got over. A few days later, we went back to England. But from that time onwards, something changed within me. In all these years, I hadn't contacted Sanjeev because Peter was uncomfortable. We had a fight once early on in our marriage because Peter heard that Sanjeev was in Mumbai and he didn't want Sanjeev and me to meet. I kept Vidhie away from Sanjeev too. I really wanted our marriage to work and was nothing short of honest and faithful to Peter. I didn't want him to be uncomfortable.

But in 2011, I decided Vidhie should get to know the Khannas— her biological family. I decided to reconnect with Sanjeev. Vidhie was a tough teenager and I felt a bit of family grounding would help her. She should at least know her biological father. And I didn't want to hide it from Peter. It is not in my nature to hide anything. At this point, Peter didn't have a leg to stand on. I did a Skype call with Sanjeev in Peter's presence and told him that I want him and Vidhie to reconnect. Vidhie and Sanjeev started talking on Skype that year.

27

In November 2011, we received an email on the family mailing group. It was from Rahul and he announced that he and Sheena had got engaged in November. Peter and I stayed out of it while others congratulated them on the mail chain.

In January 2012, we spent New Years in Spain. Rabin visited with his then girlfriend, Jess. We had a good year end. We returned to Bristol in February.

On 8 March that year, I received an email from Sheena.[13] She started with apologizing about everything that she had done including the messages. She judged me for something that wasn't my mistake. She had found out why I left them and never returned home when she was a little girl. I initially didn't understand what she meant. But I figured that my uncle told her about my rape and her parentage. I am not sure if I would have mustered up the courage to tell her the truth.

After 2008, Rahul isolated her from everyone so there was no opportunity to have the conversation. I don't think I felt it was necessary to have this chat either. My father was old by then. It is very difficult to explain how I could forgive someone like him but as time passed I did end up forgiving him for the pain, hurt and trauma he had caused me. If I had told Sheena, it would have upset everything in her life. The only people who knew the truth outside the family at that time were Siddharth, Sanjeev and Peter. I would have had no issue referring to Sheena and Mekhail as my kids. But Peter was so paranoid about his social status that we mutually agreed—let sleeping dogs lie.

My parents had apparently told Sheena that they were disinheriting her because of her relationship with Rahul. They were completely against this relationship because Rahul wasn't doing anything in life and it was all very awkward anyway with both of them being step siblings.

That email made me so sad. She signed off saying, 'If you don't want to respond, I will understand. But don't send me an angry response.' She wanted to clean up her karma, she said.

I wrote back to her warmly. I was just glad she reached out to me. Parents love their kids unconditionally. We can forgive anything. She was ecstatic that I had responded. I gave her my numbers and she texted me her number. After three years, Sheena was back in my life. I was over the moon!

Sheena wanted to meet me. I told her I will be back in India in April. We called each other a few times. She told me that she was going through a very bad patch with Rahul and yet his mother was insistent they get married. She had secured an admission at Oxford Brooks and needed money to pay her tuition fee for the course and living expenses.

I came down to India in April. I went to Goa first and started looking at properties in Goa. We were keen to set up a boutique hotel in a place like Goa, Alibaug, Panchgani or Lonavla. We had been on the hunt for a good plot of land.

I met Sheena on 7 April at China House in Hyatt. She broke down when she met me. Among other things that were bothering her, the main reason she met me was that she found out the truth about who her father was and why I had left home and Guwahati.

My maternal uncle had told her about my rape. And that shook her. She questioned my mother about the picture painted to her about how I was this heartless person who left her children and ran away. She had apparently also told Rahul about this once she learnt the truth.

Sheena told me about another guy she had met. She said that he lived in the US but his parents lived in Nagpur. She wanted me to meet him and his family. During our long conversation, there were many things she told me about her relationship with Rahul that got me concerned.

She said that she wanted to leave him but was unable to do so as he wasn't letting her go. So the only way to leave him was to cut off all contact and move base without telling him the details.

'At this rate, I will end up killing myself someday. You don't know what I am going through.' She was in tears by now.

There was pressure from the Dehradun side of the family for them to marry at the earliest and she was in a helpless situation.

I told Peter that I met Sheena and she wanted me to go to Nagpur. He did not let me go to Nagpur—he reasoned with me that everyone involved was an adult and that it was Sheena's decision, not something I should interfere in. I wrote back to her making an excuse to get myself out of the situation.

At home, Vidhie was being very difficult. We were thinking about moving her to Kolkata for a year. During the trip that I made to Goa and Mumbai in the first week of April, Peter and Vidhie were to go to Kolkata to meet Sanjeev. But Peter cancelled that trip in the last minute. Vidhie and Sanju were in contact for a year then.

I hadn't met Sanjeev in ten years. We were still deliberating on whether to send Vidhie to Kolkata for a year or so, perhaps to do her A levels at the Kolkata International School after she finished her GCSEs at Clifton College. Peter said that I should go meet the family before we took a call on moving Vidhie to Kolkata.

Peter booked me a ticket for 23 April through his Emirates miles to go to Kolkata. On 21 April, he changed his mind. He cancelled my Kolkata ticket, changed it for me to travel to Mumbai. Sanjeev was annoyed that Peter had cancelled the plan of bringing Vidhie in the first week of April.

On the 23rd, I landed in Mumbai. Sheena was busy that day, so we decided to meet later.

I know a lot of you still have that one question on your mind—so what really happened on 24 April 2012. That fabled day has been the subject of much speculation and rumours. While I am not at the liberty to lay out the details of what happened that day due to legal restrictions, I will simply say what Vasily Grossman wrote in his book *Life and Fate*, 'There is only one truth. There cannot be two truths. It is hard to live with no truth, with scraps of truth, with a half-truth. A partial truth is no truth at all.'

PART 10

Devil's Daughter

28

Over the years, during my time in prison, my lawyers would come frequently to visit me. But in February 2019, for the first time in a long while, my daughter came to see me. Vidhie was twenty-one and looked so different from the eighteen-year-old girl etched in my memory.

'I have missed you,' she told me while sobbing. She needed me. I knew it for a long time but this is the first time she verbalized it to me.

All her friends had graduated and moved on. She had wasted a lot of time and she was still where she was before. 'Now I understand the value of education. And I want to make this right and do you proud,' she said.

My child needed the emotional support that had gone missing from her life in my absence. I told her, 'You are a rockstar! Just do it!'

I decided to pay for the new course she had decided on and help her out. The prison authorities were kind enough to give us extra time that day. I had always felt that it was a matter of time before she came around. Reconnecting with her anchored me just as much.

She was all over the place in the years after my arrest. Her home was no longer her home.

She told me one time, right before I was leaving prison, 'Home stopped being home after you were arrested. It was then that I realized Marlow was probably never my home.'

The family had moved out all my things within days of my arrest. Rabin was staying in our room with his then girlfriend Francessca and the whole house was otherwise emptied out. Whenever Vidhie would visit from the UK, they'd take out a cot and set it up for her. This is where Vidhie had grown up, had all her big and small moments, since she was four.

From an education perspective, by 2019, Vidhie had wasted a lot of time. She left college, went backpacking, tried her hand at a journalism course which she flunked. Then she came and stayed in Mumbai for a year which I didn't know about because she never came to meet me.

She finally decided to do a three-year degree course in Spain. She promised to work extra hard to fast track the three-year course in two years. I made sure that the rent of our Bristol house would go to Vidhie, and I made Peter sign documents to that effect, to make her financially secure as far as possible. As for the course fees, I paid €20,000 upfront.

But in those days, Vidhie was playing both ways. She would be really warm and wonderful to me. But everything we would discuss, would be reported back to Peter and his family. In the meantime, she also told me that she had started seeing a guy called Nid. However, apparently his family was apprehensive about him dating her because of the case. She also told me about a book she started writing about her backpacking experiences. Vidhie and I had attained the kind of peace which was probably going to make up for our lost years.

29

The second time I sought bail was in September 2018 at the sessions court, again on medical grounds, as my health was deteriorating. It was rejected again. By then the witnesses were beginning to fall.

Right after that I had what perhaps was a brain stroke. As per the JJ Hospital medical reports, all symptoms were there, sweatiness, bouts of losing consciousness, low blood pressure, facial paralysis. I reapplied for bail, but this time I argued it myself in front of the judge. That, too, was rejected.

Peter's bail applications were also getting rejected. Two of them were rejected in sessions court, one was rejected in the high court; one medical bail was rejected in sessions court, another in high court. Funnily, now when I look back, his bail rejections never became a topic of discussion like mine.

In June 2019, I had written a letter to the Delhi CBI court requesting to be pardoned in the INX case. I copied the letter to Parthasarathy, who, as the investing officer of the case, requested the judge to convert me into a prosecution witness. I was flown to Delhi that year for a decision to be taken on the matter. By then both Alok Verma and Rakesh Asthana had left the CBI. They had both made headlines themselves with the ugly mud-slinging fight that they had got into, accusing one another of corruption, bribery, and so on and so forth … 'CBI vs CBI' as some of the newspaper headlines read.

The judge at the CBI court in Delhi asked me if I was being coerced to give a statement.

He asked me, 'Did anyone tell you that you'll be pardoned if you gave the statement?'

I replied that I was aware it's the discretion of the court.

In July, I was converted to a witness in the INX Media case. My statement was a voluntary confession statement. The judge took cognisance of the fact that I proactively took the onus of telling the truth. The next month, P. Chidambaram was arrested.

On 3 October 2019, my divorce with Peter officially came through.

After the Maharashtra government changed, Peter filed for a bail in the high court. Peter had had five bail rejections before that. Peter's erstwhile cellmate in Arthur Road Jail, Chhagan Bhujbal, took up an important portfolio in the new government.

In December 2019, I decided that enough evidence had come on record. I filed for a bail on merit for the first time at the sessions court. Usually, trial court doesn't grant bail for a murder charge but it is protocol to file it in a lower court before moving to a higher court.

On 6 February 2020, Peter was granted bail by the Bombay High Court. But the CBI put a stay on the bail saying they would appeal in the Supreme Court.

I decided to argue my bail again. I knew it wouldn't go through at the sessions court but I was bound to get a good order where the merits of the case would be captured. In that application, I brought up Rahul's messages. Another date was fixed in March for CBI's surrejoinder. I argued, they argued and then they were to give me a surrejoinder. The next date was 16 March, but that day I wasn't taken to court because COVID-19 was becoming a serious problem by then.

Peter's six weeks got over on 19 March and he walked out a free man on 20 March 2020. On 22 March, the government announced a nationwide lockdown. And I was left to spend the lockdown in prison.

30

❧❦❧

During the Covid pandemic, the whole world was one big jail. One week of lockdown turned to one month and then to many months. Mulaqats were stopped and the prison was sealed. The jail authorities were staying inside the prison. The upstairs barrack in Circle 2 was used as the lodging quarters for the female jailers and guards. Food supplies would come in, but sometimes they would run short. This went on till July, but later in the year Covid cases again started rising.

Once relaxations began, the weekly phone call system started for families to contact inmates as per an order that was passed in the Bombay High Court. Initially, we were allowed a single ten-minute call a week. But in a month or two, it had been made into twenty minutes per week, to be divided into two calls. Even though Vidhie was in Hong Kong, I could speak to her. The mulaqats were shut until August but I stayed in touch with my lawyers daily. Vidhie returned to India in August.

The post office shut down so the money orders stopped for everyone. Bank transfers started. We couldn't meet our lawyers or our families. Our cases were at a complete standstill.

Once I applied for bail in the sessions court, I knew sooner or later that I'd be out as a higher court would eventually grant me bail. I felt my time in prison was nearing its end, call it an epiphany of sorts. Or maybe I deduced it from the fact that so much evidence had come on record—from forensics to other evidence—to back it. I knew then that not only would I get bail, I would win the case as well. My headspace got better when I realized that there's enough to get me acquitted. Because the lockdown allowed me time like everyone else in the world, I started reading the messages which were retrieved from Rahul's phone. I realized there was a larger conspiracy to my arrest. I had the nagging feeling that Peter had planned my arrest.

During this period, the prisoners were kept safe in Byculla Jail. By August 2020, judges started to attend court again briefly. I pleaded for bail based on the messages, and reasoned that if Sheena and Rahul had exchanged messages in October, many months after her alleged date of death, the details of the case built against me stood dismissed. The sessions judge captured all the points of the case and passed an order on 5 August 2020. The bail was rejected—it is almost customary to have a bail filed on a murder charge to be rejected in a sessions court. And so, I moved the Bombay High Court.

In February 2021, mulaqats resumed, only to be stopped after a month after the onset of the second wave of infections. Phone calls replaced the mulaqats once again. During the second wave, Vidhie and Nid went off to Uttarakhand to spend some time. She seemed more settled. She was going to finish her degree. Financially, I was supporting her as much as possible too.

In October 2020, I asked Gunjan to file for a bail application based on merit. It was only admitted in court in February 2021. The second wave of COVID-19 was bad in India. I caught COVID-19 when I went to Kasturba Hospital to get my vaccination. A day after returning, I was running a high fever. There was another female prisoner who was taken to JJ Hospital because she had a fever too. She tested positive for Covid and moved to another hospital, where she died. Many inmates during this time started showing symptoms in prison. The authorities started testing everyone and over eighty people tested positive. I was vaccinated but I still contracted the virus.

The eighty inmates were moved to a jumbo centre at a government school that was created outside the prison. I was very nervous. The last time I stepped out was on 6 March 2020. The next time I stepped out was for the vaccination. Even though I was in a separate cell, I still got it.

When I was hospitalized, Gunjan moved court to request that a month be given for me to recuperate. A CBI officer called and informed Vidhie about my health.

By the time the matter went to the high court judge, I had tested negative. So the temporary bail was denied to me. After returning to the cell, I waited for my next court date.

Vidhie sent my lawyers Gunjan and Edith a copy of the manuscript of her book. Like I said before, the title itself screamed at me—*Devil's Daughter*. My lawyers had an issue with the title to begin with. There were multiple inaccuracies in the facts stated in the book which contradicted the case's details. My lawyers wanted me to object to the book because they saw it as a strategy to stop my bail. It was essentially a 'bash me up' book. I discussed it with Edith and thought about it after I read it. It broke me to see that my daughter had written a lopsided story that was favourable to her father and against me.

I took a long time to decide what I wanted to do. But I eventually decided to let her go with it. Peter and his family had a massive influence on her and I wanted that to be out in the public domain. Peter was always the good cop and I was always the strict mom to a teenager. After my arrest, she was fed with a lot of lies about me. And she believed those narratives as a young girl. Some of them made it to the book which she was compelled to write. The realization for Vidhie was slow and painful, just like it was for me.

Vidhie was very surprised that I didn't change anything. I did flag off some parts saying that it was not true but she was too besotted by Peter to change some of the inaccuracies that she had been made to believe and had written in her book. In the end, I congratulated her on its publication day.

31

waited for my bail petition to get heard but nothing was moving.
I got restless. Every time I had a call with Gunjan, I brought it up
with her. In July 2021, I heard of Sana Raees Khan, earlier a junior
lawyer in Pasbola's team, who had started her own practice recently.
She had secured bail for another accused in a high-profile murder case.
I had met her briefly in 2017 when she was still working in Pasbola's
chamber. I reached out to her to handle my bail. She was young but
very sharp. And so, I called up Gunjan to pass the documents to
Sana and write to the court to inform them that I am changing my
lawyer. My trial was on hold at that point. I knew my decision did
not sit well with Gunjan, but when I spoke to Sana, I knew I was
making the right choice. My trial court was vacant. Justice P.D. Naik
was to preside in the Bombay High Court where my bail matter was
going to be heard. But when my matter finally came up for hearing,
Justice Sambre, who had given bail to Peter, presided. Sana suggested
that we wait because he wouldn't grant us bail but I was willing to
take that chance. I knew I would get bail in the Supreme Court.

Sana argued my bail application in Bombay High Court on 15
November 2021. Justice Sambre suggested that we withdraw the
bail because the trial was on and he was not inclined to grant bail on
merit. He did not accept her written submission. He said he would
consider it if we submitted a medical bail. Sana knew my decision
even before she came to meet me the next day.

I refused to withdraw my bail application on merit. My grounds were solid. My co-accused was out, over 190 witnesses were left; I wouldn't have absconded in any way because I had my roots in society. My passport was in the court's possession.

When we went to the Supreme Court, we brought on board Advocate Mukul Rohatgi to fight the bail application. We filed a petition in December 2021. On 1 February 2022, the matter was admitted.

We stated in the Special Leave Petition the elaborate facts of the case:

We have made detailed submissions before the Hon'ble Supreme Court of India in an application for permission to bring additional documents on record, in the Special Leave Petition (SLP) filed by us. The same has been disposed of. My lawyer, Ms. Sana Raees Khan, has in an interview in 2022, also explained the submissions made by us in this application in brief[14.]

As mentioned by her, the body alleged by Prosecution to be (Sheena Bora) found in Penn, Raigad on May 23, 2012 remains unidentified till date.

Additionally, the prosecution had claimed that the body/ skeleton (allegedly Sheena Bora's but identity not known till date) found in Penn on May 23, 2012 by Penn Police Station was exhumed by Khar Police Station three years three months later on August 28, 2015 (3 days after the arrest of the Applicant on August 25, 2015 by Khar Police Station). However, during the course of the trial the Prosecution has not been able to corroborate this claim.

Moreover, the skull of the skeleton alleged by Prosecution as Sheena Bora's discovered by Penn Police Station is not the same skull by Khar Police Station, as the 2012 skull was cut open during autopsy whereas the 2015 skull produced by Prosecution is an intact skull. The soil where the body was allegedly buried in 2012 does not match the soil where the body was allegedly exhumed by the Khar P.S. in 2015. No DNA profiling was done to establish the identity of the body discovered in 2012 May alleged by Prosecution as Sheena Bora's body. The Left Femur Bone and Maxillary Teeth of the 2015 Body did not yield any interpretable data for DNA Profiling. As regards to the DNA reports of the Right Femur and the Cervical Vertebrae of 2015 exhumed body, the Prosecution's DNA expert has confirmed in his deposition that he has altered the data at several places in both the electropherogram to match my blood sample.

SMS records retrieved from Rahul Mukerjea's mobile phone seized by the CBI show that intimate messages were exchanged between Sheena and Rahul in the month of September, five months after the alleged murder. This evidence therefore suggests that Sheena was alive after such date of the alleged murder.

Shyamvar Rai, who became an approver in this case, was allegedly arrested by Khar Police Station on August 25, 2015 i.e. 2 days prior to my arrest for possession of a 7.65 bore pistol and magazines. A F.I.R. was registered against him for possession of illegal arms under the ARMS Act. It is pertinent to state here that before the Metropolitan Magistrate Court, Bandra where the ARMS Act case is pending, Shyamvar Rai did not admit the charge and pleaded "Not Guilty". However, before the trial court, he has confessed to the same.

All in all, I filed the SLP because I knew that enough evidence had come on record and that now was the time to strike down all the lies.

After March, I knew I would be out that year. I asked Edith to get my cars serviced and home renovated. I was no longer returning to the apartment I was arrested in. The erstwhile lounging pad was converted into a studio apartment for me to live in.

Vidhie came to meet me and said, 'Papa said your bail will get rejected!'

I told her it could but I didn't want to regret not taking this risk. I wouldn't know unless and until I try to get bail. If I didn't get it, I would believe that staying in prison for a bit longer is my destiny. I had the emotional strength to fight for justice by then.

But just like it is common in our justice system, '*tarikh pe tarikh* (date upon date)', my date kept moving. On 20 May, the Supreme Court would shut for summer break till 11 July. I was prepared for the matter to get listed after the break. But the date didn't move. Sana and I kept getting nervous as the date approached. On the night of 16 May, my matter got listed. It was Justice Nagashwar Rao's second last day before retirement. On 17 May, Sana flew to Delhi. A three-member judge bench were to hear my bail application at the Supreme Court.

This was a win or lose situation. At 11 a.m., on 18 May 2022, Mukul Rohatgi and Sana Raees Khan went to the courtroom designated for my hearing. As Sana described it to me later, 'Honourable Justice Rao heard both sides, looked to his right and left, and in ten minutes bail was granted to me.'

I didn't expect a judgment that day. So in jail, I had lunch and was napping for a bit. I had assumed they would give me bail after the vacation.

Sometime in the afternoon, I was woken up by the Circle jailer, 'It's your time to be set free …'

The entire prison was cheering for me. Everyone was so happy, watching the news and hooting for me. In prison, I realized women have the least amount of bad will for each other. They would dance joyously for others. They are genuinely happy when something good happens to another person, which you don't see outside. In the outside world, more often than not, when something good happens to you, people put up the farce of happiness for you. It happened to me. When bad times fell on me, people rushed out to settle old scores, soothe their grouses and tear me apart. But the real idea of what female camaraderie stands for, what sisterhood truly is and how women stand by each other in a most glorious show of strength, I experienced in prison.

EPILOGUE

❧

The alleged happenings of 24 April 2012 have been written about a lot for years. And the takeaway of it was only one—a blanket judgement about the kind of mother I am. The most horrific one, of course.

While I have managed to gather the strength to be absolutely unperturbed by what's said about me, I have frequently reflected upon what my equation with my children has been, especially Sheena.

We didn't have a conventional parent–child relationship. I discovered what Sheena was like only when she was fifteen years of age. Right from the start, we bonded like friends. Sheena considered my mother as her parent because she grew up with my parents; she saw me more as a sibling.

We looked really similar, too, and we even liked similar food. People talk a whole deal about blood ties, and that was the bond between Sheena and me. We were raised so differently, but our commonalities were not lost on those who knew us. For most of her growing up years, I wasn't around her. But, strangely enough, her mannerisms were so much like mine. The way she talked, her expressions. She was ambitious, like me. Mekhail, on the other hand, wanted all the good things in life but he was always greedy.

Sheena was passionate about life. She wanted to shine wherever she went. She wanted to top her class. Her focus only shifted when she met Rahul. This behaviour is natural for puppy love; but that's when my maternal instinct kicked in for her. I felt she needed to get herself back in order and in doing so, I lost that bond we had so painstakingly created.

I am usually very affectionate as a person but I have a wall around myself. Once someone gets past that wall, I can give myself completely to them. It's a trait in me and in Sheena as well. I think she made a mistake with Rahul. She gave herself so completely that she lost her own sense of self. I can't say this about Mekhail because he and I haven't spent as much quality time with each other over the years. But Vidhie isn't like that. She knows how to retain a bit of herself. She won't mould herself according to someone else's personality or needs.

I understand this about Sheena, because I am the same. Sheena and I are very giving, and sometimes a bit too giving for our own good.

When Sheena moved to Bombay, she finally got to know me. Up until then, she probably nurtured the hurt of being abandoned within her. But for all the time we spent together, Sheena never brought it up with me even once. Of course, up till 2012, Sheena had no idea why I really left Guwahati. She was told since her childhood that I picked up my bags and simply left. While she found out the answer to her innumerable whys many years later, she felt my warmth right from the time she met me.

To her credit, Sheena and I both invested in creating a bond. I brought her to Bombay and wanted to build a relationship with her. And she came, despite having the option of going anywhere else. Mekhail chose to be in Bangalore and then moved to Delhi. He wanted to be unattached. I knew I couldn't impose myself on either of them. The first instinct was to hold them and never let them go. But I wish making-up-for-lost-time worked like that. Giving each other space and time was required and I had hoped that would get us through.

Sheena and I bonded primarily over rom-coms, vacations and food. We had a ritual—watching sappy movies together and crying. On one of my birthdays, we sat on the bed and watched *Veer–Zaara*. Peter was away travelling and we decided to make it a movie marathon night. An hour into the film, she suddenly turned around to find me holding her hand and crying. I was weeping inconsolably. She gave me a puzzled look and then burst out laughing. 'You are such a softie!' she said.

Sheena and I truly enjoyed spending time together. There is an age gap of sixteen years between us, which is less than the gap between Peter and me. Over the years, our bond intensified. We shared everything—from food to jewellery to clothes. We were the same size and that worked out well for her. Everytime she had a date, she'd raid my wardrobe. She had a running joke, 'It's your fault that I am not well-endowed.' That's what our bond was like. There were no pretensions, no garbs. When we were around each other, we were lost in our happy little world. But that was unfortunately short-lived. I didn't know the challenges of being a parent to a twenty-one-year-old. The minute I stopped playing the cool parent and became the strict one, things changed.

A lot was said about my rage in the months after my arrest. Vidhie's book too cites a whole page about how I would be angry a lot. Over my years of marriage, I admit, Peter and I have had our share of fights (like any other couple). He was in touch with his ex-wife without my knowledge, which led to a few blow ups. At twenty-four, Vidhie understands me better. She gets why some conversations with Peter got exasperating. I have had days when he drove me up the wall. Vidhie, as a grown up now, has had her fair share of similar run-ins with him.

But I never expressed my rage to Sheena. She was my kid who could do no wrong. I treated her like an adult and respected her decisions. I was strict but I also trusted her to handle her life and conflicts with maturity and tenacity. After all, she was like me! So when she decided to not stay in touch, I respected her space. I knew badgering her would get us nowhere. Just like the first time, the effort to reconcile had to come from her end. And then, 2015 happened.

Tonight, as I write this, from the window next to my bed, I see the Sea Link glisten against the night sky. I am yet to process the last seven years of my life. But slipping into daily life helped me get myself back in order. I have, over the months, busied myself with writing this book, enrolled for yoga, kickboxing, salsa lessons, renovating the house and catching up on everything that I had missed while I was gone. Friends often drop by to take me out for movies and sumptuous meals. Vidhie calls me from our home in Spain, where she is living now. Just today she sent me pictures of our newly done-up living room—pristine white against the blue sea view visible from our balcony.

I am almost healed, nearly at peace.

Vidhie has healed me from the burden of all the pain I was carrying, the hurt from my expectations of those I loved.

A few months after I returned home from Byculla Jail, Vidhie moved an application before a special CBI court seeking permission to stay with me in Mumbai after she returned to India. Vidhie mentioned in her plea that she was deprived of her mother's companionship as a minor when I was arrested in 2015 and the separation had affected her 'emotional well-being'. She wanted to be able to freely communicate and live with her mother as and when she wished to. And just a few weeks ago, her name was dropped from the witness list. She can now live with me and my heart yearns to hold her.

And still, the more everything changes, the more they stay the same.

But I do not worry about it anymore.

I am by no measure an easy mother. But I know that I have always been a loving mother. I am the mother who is tough on her kids. They could have the world if they worked hard and did well at school. I am ambitious and want the world for my children. I wanted them to grow up and reach for the stars.

Today as I sit back, I am reminded about all the times I was told that I had failed as a mother.

My biggest failure was my inability to protect Vidhie from everything she was put through. I should have been around to handhold her. It did make her a strong girl but she didn't need to be robbed of her innocence so early on in life. I know Vidhie and I have an entire lifetime to make up for the lost years. There will be several beach vacations and ample mother–daughter time that will help us heal from our broken dreams and failed expectations of each other. We will be good.

Mekhail and I might never get back to where we were. Till just a few months before I went to prison, I was the one he'd text or email, 'Love you, Mom'. And then, under pressure, he crumbled. He propelled a false narrative about me that was becoming popular then. He was left to fend for himself with no one to shield him. So he did what he had to for survival.

The world says, mothers are all-forgiving, all-loving, sacrificial entities. Sure, I am a little bit of that. But I don't believe Mekhail and I will get over the things that were said. His guilt and my hurt might never go away. I suppose we'd both have to live with this unfulfilled equation for as long as we are alive.

And what about Sheena? The child of mine I allegedly throttled with my own hands. Sheena and I have the same soul. We carried the same pain, with a smile big enough to hide all of it underneath the shine. She was bright and warm, loving and kind. She had inherited my strength of spirit.

I am now at peace after Sheena was spotted at the Guwahati airport by my friend—Saveena. Being an advocate herself, her quick thinking got us the footage of Sheena from the airport. Saveena and Sheena used to be thick as thieves. They made movie and dinner plans without me. They did sleepovers together. Saveena was dead sure that she had seen Sheena.

Something changed in me after this information came to the fore. The person I am accused of killing is out and about, while I was rotting in jail. Why hasn't she come out openly? I don't know. I am sure there are reasons and pressures holding her back. But this is the second time I have been told Sheena is alive. When I was in prison, an inmate at Byculla Jail too claimed to have seen Sheena in Kashmir. She was a 'female government official'. I, through my lawyer Sana, urged the CBI to probe this. It went nowhere. But when Saveena saw her, recently, we knew we had to look for her.

A special CBI court in Mumbai asked the Airports Authority of India (AAI) to secure the CCTV footage of Guwahati airport and find out the identity of the girl who allegedly looked like Sheena Bora. Special CBI judge S.P. Naik Nimbalkar asked, 'What is the harm?' He directed the AAI to hand over footage of 5 January, between 5.30 a.m. and 6 a.m. near the boarding gate of Guwahati airport. This gave ground to what I was feeling all along—Sheena is alive and out there.

Now, if history remembers this case, they will also remember that I spent six years and eight months of my life in prison serving a term for a crime that never happened.

Just as I finish typing this out, my phone buzzes. One of my lawyers has sent me a quote that reads, 'Karma is the hero without a cape!' I smile, knowing that someone somewhere is spinning the karmic wheel that will correct the wrongs done over the last seven years.

And, through it all, I am grateful that the universe has ensured that I remain UNBROKEN …

ACKNOWLEDGEMENTS

Reflecting on the journey of writing my memoir, I can't help but feel a surge of gratitude for the eclectic mix of individuals who have played pivotal roles in shaping my story. From lawyers to fitness trainers, friends, and everyone in between, these remarkable people have left an indelible mark on my life. Their dedication, support and profound impact on my life deserve heartfelt acknowledgment and recognition.

This book is for my daughter, Vidhie. You give me roots and wings, let me soar and, yet, keep me tied to hope by having faith in my innocence. Our journey together has been a testament to the unbreakable bond between a mother and her child. Although we were separated when you were just a child, destiny has now brought us together as two women who share a profound understanding of each other's experiences. Through the years apart, you have grown into a remarkable woman and, in doing so, have gained a unique perspective that allows you to comprehend my journey from a legal and a woman's standpoint. This has deepened our connection, bringing a profound sense of empathy, shared strength, and wisdom to our relationship. As we stand side by side now, I am in awe of the woman you have become. Your compassion, resilience and ability to empathize has forged an unbreakable bond that transcends the years we spent apart. This book is a tribute to the extraordinary path we have travelled together. It is a celebration of the profound understanding we now share, born out of the experiences that shaped us both.

To the legal eagles who swooped in to fight for justice and guide me through the treacherous legal labyrinth, you were the superheroes in my legal saga. Mukul Rohatgi, Mahesh Jethmalani, Sudeep Pasbola, Edith Dey, Ranjeet Sangle, Gunjan Mangla and Sana Raees Khan—each of you tirelessly fought for justice and guided me through the intricate web of the legal system. Your expertise, belief in my cause and tireless efforts have granted me a renewed sense of faith in the legal system. Thank you for championing my rights and giving voice to my story.

Now, on to the prison staff who work tirelessly behind the scenes. Your compassion, professionalism and commitment to rehabilitation have not gone unnoticed. Through your support and guidance, you have helped me find the strength to face my past, transform my present and embrace a brighter future. Your dedication to creating a safe and nurturing environment within the confines of the prison walls has touched my life in immeasurable ways.

To the doctors and healthcare professionals who have supported me on my journey towards physical and emotional well-being. Dr Wiqar Sheikh, a big shout out to you for standing up for me and for ensuring that I lived to fight my battle.

Prison medical officers, Dr Khan and Dr Nivedita; the doctors, nurses and healthcare staff at JJ Hospital who took care of me at a time when I had no family around me. Your expertise, compassion and dedication to my health have been vital in helping me heal, grow and rebuild my life.

I am indebted to every prisoner I encountered during my confinement. In the shared struggle, I found solace, understanding and a sense of belonging. Each of you have left a mark on my journey, reminding me of the strength and resilience that lies within us all. I thank you for your courage, for the lessons learnt, and for the moments of connection that have forever shaped my perspective towards life. Amidst a band of misfits bound together by shared misfortunes, I found an unlikely fellowship, finding camaraderie in the most unexpected of places.

To my loyal friends: Ramesh Pancholi, Sivarital Ringdal, Saveena Bedi Sachar, Edith Dey, late Trichy Radhakrishna, Yusuf Ayaz, Amit Parekh, Nidhesh Tulsiyani, Rikin Mehta, Vijay Anand, Pablo Iturmendi, Miguel Angel Nueves—in the darkest moments of my life, you shone like beacons of light, banishing the shadows of doubt and despair. You listened to my tales of woe and celebrated my triumphs with unbridled joy. Together, we wove a tapestry of friendship so vibrant and enduring. Your loyalty and magical presence in my life is priceless. The Shahs—Chintan, Parul Aunty and Arvind Uncle—you are family to me. My love to Arjun and Kabir, for enriching my life with your warmth and affection.

Dr Sandip Soparrkar, you've been an excellent dance mentor and made me believe that I too can dance. It is delightful to now have you girls—Smilie Suri, Avan Mehta and Rhea Ginwalla—helping me branch out into different forms of dance.

I extend my heartfelt appreciation to the fitness trainers, Abbas Morbiwala and Satyendra Mandal, who have guided me on a path of physical and mental transformation. Your expertise, motivation and support have empowered me to reclaim my health, strengthen my body and nurture my mind. Through your guidance, I have discovered the transformative power of physical fitness and its profound impact on personal growth. You have been beacons of inspiration and have helped me unleash my full potential. Rasheeda Morbiwala, I must mention you for the delicious food that you cook and send to me at times; your food is something I look forward to after your son Abbas puts me through the rigorous workouts.

Gunjan Mangla, I have not forgotten the support and affection that I received from you in my tough times, particularly in the initial days of incarceration when I was weak physically and bruised emotionally.

Sana Khan, you have not only gone that extra mile as a lawyer to restore my freedom but have become a dear friend. I love watching sappy Bollywood movies with you while sipping on popcorn milk shakes and eating truffle cheese fries and pizza.

To the Khanna and Kapur family, I extend my sincere respect for the love and acceptance you gave me. From the moment I entered your lives, you embraced me as one of your own. In your home, I discovered a sanctuary of laughter, shared meals and heartfelt conversations that made me feel cherished. Your genuine care and open hearts created a safe space where I could be my truest self. Through the years, we created beautiful memories together. Our family ties transcend the boundaries of marriage. In times of joy, you celebrated alongside me with infectious enthusiasm. During moments of struggle, your comforting gestures became pillars of strength, reminding me that I was never alone.

The building staff and neighbours at Marlow—your acts of kindness, going above and beyond by sending me meals, and displaying genuine grace even when it was not expected—your warmth reiterates my faith that thoughtfulness and humanity exists within our community.

My profound gratitude to the teachers and professors who have not only imparted knowledge but also taught me how to fight the good fight. Your guidance has equipped me with the courage to stand up for justice and pursue truth through every adversity.

My colleagues—the bonds we forged were unbreakable, woven with laughter, late-night brainstorming sessions and support. In INX and IMD Global, our collective brilliance shone. Each colleague brought a unique perspective, pushing boundaries and challenging the status quo. The synergy we created was electrifying, propelling us to surpass expectations and achieve remarkable feats. I appreciate our spirited debates that sparked creativity and moments of triumph that brought us closer. Through victories and setbacks, we lifted each other up. Our shared experiences forged lifelong memories that will forever resonate in my heart.

To my publicist, Ebrahim Contractor, and the supportive team at Pearl Media.

Aditya Kapoor and Zishaan A. Latif, you have captured my soul in the cover image.

Mohar Basu, our collaboration was a joy. You were the yin to my yang. Together, we embarked on a thrilling adventure, blending our thoughts into a seamless narrative. We weathered self-doubt, celebrated the triumphs of creative breakthroughs and ultimately crafted a memoir that is a true reflection of my vision.

And what can I say about Bushra Ahmed, my editor! Your keen eye and masterful touch turned my words into a strong narrative. Your ability to discern the heart of my story, to polish its rough edges and to breathe life into each chapter is truly wonderful. You have been patient, wise and have believed in the power of my words.

And everyone else at HarperCollins India—Ananth Padmanabhan, Poulomi Chatterjee, Amit Malhotra, Shabnam Srivastava, Paloma Dutta, Ashima Obhan, Seerat Bhutani and the team who have worked behind the scenes.

I finally acknowledge my dear readers for joining my journey of rising. I'll quote Shannen Heartz here about my path ahead: 'And just as the Phoenix rose from the ashes, she too will rise. Returning from the flames, clothed in nothing but her strength, more beautiful than ever before.'

NOTES

•◆•

1. 'Jail officials say Indrani did not overdose on prescribed medicines', *The Times of India*, 20 April 2018; http://timesofindia.indiatimes.com/ articleshow/63837995.cms?utm_source=contentofinterest&utm_ medium=text&utm_campaign=cppsthttps://timesofindia. indiatimes.com/city/mumbai/jail-officials-say-indrani-did-not-overdose-on-prescribed-medicines/articleshow/63837995.cms

2. https://www.youtube.com/watch?v=Lvltj1PmFfc

3. 'Rs 900 cr allegedly siphoned from INX to Sheena Bora's account that was being run by Indrani: CBI', First Post, 27 November 2015; https://www.firstpost.com/india/rs-900-cr-allegedly-siphoned-from-inx-to-sheena-boras-account-that-was-being-run-by-indrani-cbi-2523432.html

4. 'Ex-colleague Ravina Raj Kohli on Indrani's rise and fall', India Today, 28 August 2015; https://www.indiatoday.in/india/video/ex-colleague-ravina-raj-kohli-tells-rise-and-fall-of-indrani-432154-2015-08-27

5. 'Inside the Mind of a Woman', Mumbai Mirror, 5 May 2018; https:// mumbaimirror.indiatimes.com/opinion/columnists/shobhaa-de/ inside-the-mind-of-a-woman/articleshow/64035101.cms

6. 'From the small-town Indrani Bora of Guwahati to the reinvented Indrani Khanna of Kolkata to the glamorous Mrs Peter Mukerjea in Mumbai and now the prime suspect in her daughter's murder', *India Today*, 14 September 2015; https://www.indiatoday.in/ magazine/cover-story/story/20150914-life-loves-and-lies-of-indrani-820396-2015-09-03

7. 'Indrani wanted power, had delusions of grandeur: Vir Sanghvi', *Hindustan Times*, 3 September 2015; https://www.hindustantimes.

com/india/indrani-wanted-power-had-delusions-of-grandeur-vir-sanghvi/story-iYHehNgIqTGIsi3uRi5ugP.html

8. On Twitter; https://twitter.com/chintskap/status/ 63655400 2289848320?ref_src=twsrc%5Etfw%7Ctwcamp%5Etweet embed%7Ctwterm%5E63655400 2289848320%7C twgr%5E828b8f906fcdfe6c86adadbbee9fff52319ef424%7 Ctwcon%5Es1_&ref_url=https%3A%2F%2F www.hindustantimes.com%2Fbollywood%2Findrani -mukerjea-was-a-real-weirdo-says-rishi-kapoor%2Fstory-SEb3XTj0BkufhhWfnw9NnJ.html

9. 'Sheena Bora murder case: Why Alpha men are putty in the hands of Alpha women', Firstpost, 28 August 2015; https://www.firstpost. com/living/sheena-bora-murder-case-why-alpha-men-are-putty-in-the-hands-of-alpha-women-2411838.html

10. 'Peter may not have known what was on with wife', *The Times of India*, 27 August 2015; https://timesofindia.indiatimes.com/city/ mumbai/peter-may-not-have-known-what-was-on-with-wife/ articleshow/48687994.cms

11. 'Indrani threatened suicide to get joint ownership of flat: Peter Mukerjea', *The Indian Express*, 1 December 2015; https://indianexpress. com/article/india/india-news-india/indrani-threatened-suicide-to-get-joint-ownership-of-flat-peter-mukerjea/

12. '"Like Romeo & Juliet", Peter's touching letter to Indrani on her birthday', *Deccan Chronicle*, 4 May 2016; https://www. deccanchronicle.com/nation/in-other-news/040516/like-romeo-and-juliet-peter-mukerjea-s-touching-to-indrani-on-her-birthday. html

13. 'Revealed: Sheena Bora's emails before and "after death"', *The Times of India*, 24 November 2015; https://timesofindia.indiatimes. com/india/revealed-sheena-boras-emails-before-and-after-death/ articleshow/49909859.cms

14. Indrani Mukerjea, former TV Channel Owner, accused of killing her daughter, in her first interview, YouTube

ABOUT THE AUTHOR

Indrani Mukerjea is an accomplished Indian-born British media baron. From founding INX Services Private Limited in Kolkata to co-founding and leading INX Media in Mumbai, Indrani's entrepreneurial spirit and exceptional achievements propelled her to great heights.

As the regional director for the Asia Pacific region at IMD International Search Group, she garnered recognition for her expertise and leadership abilities. *The Wall Street Journal* acknowledged her remarkable contributions by including her in their prestigious list of '50 Women to Watch'.

Mukerjea has also embraced philanthropy and is actively engaged in improving the lives of prison inmates in undertrial prisons. She has become a beacon of hope for prison inmates, working tirelessly to provide them with easy access to legal aid and teaching them their rights. Her commitment to promoting fairness, justice and rehabilitation within the prison system is unwavering, as she strives to break down social and legal barriers faced by incarcerated individuals. She can be found at @indranimukerjea on Instagram.

30 Years *of*

 HarperCollins *Publishers* India

At HarperCollins, we believe in telling the best stories and finding the widest possible readership for our books in every format possible. We started publishing 30 years ago; a great deal has changed since then, but what has remained constant is the passion with which our authors write their books, the love with which readers receive them, and the sheer joy and excitement that we as publishers feel in being a part of the publishing process.

Over the years, we've had the pleasure of publishing some of the finest writing from the subcontinent and around the world, and some of the biggest bestsellers in India's publishing history. Our books and authors have won a phenomenal range of awards, and we ourselves have been named Publisher of the Year the greatest number of times. But nothing has meant more to us than the fact that millions of people have read the books we published, and somewhere, a book of ours might have made a difference.

As we step into our fourth decade, we go back to that one word – a word which has been a driving force for us all these years.

Read.

Harper
Collins

th

HARPER
PERENNIAL

HARPER
BUSINESS

HARPER
BLACK

हार्पर
हिन्दी

HarperCollins
Children'sBooks

HARPER
DESIGN

HARPER
VANTAGE

Harper
Sport